D1563272

Interpreting the Death
of Edward VI

Interpreting the Death of Edward VI

The Life and Mysterious Demise of the Last Tudor King

Kyra Krammer

PEN & SWORD
HISTORY

First published in Great Britain in 2022 by
Pen & Sword History
An imprint of
Pen & Sword Books Ltd
Yorkshire – Philadelphia

ISBN 978 1 39909 208 1

Typeset by Mac Style
Printed and bound in the UK by CPI Group (UK) Ltd,
Croydon, CR0 4YY.

MIX
Paper from
responsible sources
FSC
www.fsc.org   FSC® C013604

Pen & Sword Books Limited incorporates the imprints of Atlas,
Archaeology, Aviation, Discovery, Family History, Fiction, History,
Maritime, Military, Military Classics, Politics, Select, Transport,
True Crime, Air World, Frontline Publishing, Leo Cooper, Remember
When, Seaforth Publishing, The Praetorian Press, Wharncliffe
Local History, Wharncliffe Transport, Wharncliffe True Crime
and White Owl.

For a complete list of Pen & Sword titles please contact

PEN & SWORD BOOKS LIMITED
47 Church Street, Barnsley, South Yorkshire, S70 2AS, England
E-mail: enquiries@pen-and-sword.co.uk
Website: www.pen-and-sword.co.uk

Or

PEN AND SWORD BOOKS
1950 Lawrence Rd, Havertown, PA 19083, USA
E-mail: Uspen-and-sword@casematepublishers.com
Website: www.penandswordbooks.com

This book is dedicated to my beloved aunt, Alana Begley Parks, with admiration for her deep faith and quiet courage.

Contents

Foreword
The Mysterious Deaths of the Tudor Heirs   viii

Chapter 1	Brought to Childbed of a Prince	1
Chapter 2	A Nursery for the Whole Realm's Most Precious Jewel	14
Chapter 3	A Household Fit for a Prince	25
Chapter 4	An Imp Worthy of Such a Father	35
Chapter 5	Manoeuvring to Manipulate a Future King	48
Chapter 6	The Boy King is Crowned	61
Chapter 7	A King in a Golden Cage	74
Chapter 8	An Uncle's Fall from the King's Favour	83
Chapter 9	Somerset Loses Control of the King	95
Chapter 10	Edward is Becoming a King in Truth	108
Chapter 11	Edward's Reign Begins	123
Chapter 12	Religious Reform and Troublesome Relatives	139
Chapter 13	The King's Health Begins to Fail	149
Chapter 14	Edward's Attempt to Secure the Succession of Lady Jane Grey	155
Chapter 15	What Killed the Tudor Boys?	168
Chapter 16	The Aftermath of Edward's Death	181
Notes		185
Bibliography		191

Foreword

The Mysterious Deaths of the Tudor Heirs

King Edward VI is often overlooked because his short reign fell between the much more dynamic tenures of his father, King Henry VIII, and the regimes of his elder half-sisters, Queen Mary I and Queen Elizabeth I. Additionally, since Edward was merely nine years old when he gained the throne and only fifteen when he died, there is also an assumption that he would have had very little influence over his own rule. In reality, the precocious boy was taking charge of his own statecraft by the tender age of thirteen, and his brief command of his kingdom had a profound effect on England and Wales. In the little time he was allotted by fate to use his powers as monarch he showed himself to be as fiscally canny as his grandfather, Henry VII, and as politically far-sighted as his sibling, Queen Elizabeth I, whose impressive rule now completely overshadows his own. Sadly, his rule also revealed Edward to be as dogmatic and religiously intractable as his other half-sister, who is saddled by the unfortunate nickname of 'Bloody Mary'. If he had lived, the last Tudor king would have had as much impact – both good and bad – on the course of English history as men who began his famous dynasty and the women who ended it after him.

But he did not live. Moreover, his death was relatively sudden and unexpected. The narrative in popular history books often assumes that because he passed away so young that he had always been unhealthy. This is inaccurate. Edward had been blessed with a robust constitution in childhood, surviving many of the ailments that underlay the horrific child mortality rates in early modern Europe. It was only a few months before his untimely demise that the king's health began to fail. His ultimate cause of death is still being debated by historians, but what is seldom discussed is the fact his fate was shared by two other teenagers in his famous family – his uncle Arthur Tudor and his half-brother Henry Fitzroy.

By the time Edward was born, the preceding generations of the Tudor dynasty had lost all but one of its male heirs. King Henry VIII would be the only Tudor prince to ever survive to adulthood. His older brother, Arthur, had died at age fifteen. His sons by his first queen, Katherina of Aragon, had all died shortly after their birth or were stillborn. His illegitimate son, Henry Fitzroy, had died in his mid-teens. His second queen, Anne Boleyn, had 'miscarried of her savior' when she lost a supposedly male fetus in 1536. Jane Seymour's son was Henry's last hope for his lineage, but in spite of all the precautions taken by the royal physicians, King Edward also died before his sixteenth birthday. While the Tudor genes live on in the current monarch of Great Britain, they have been passed down through the children of Henry VIII's sister, Margaret, rather than the king himself.

Why did the Tudor kings have such a hard time keeping their sons alive? All children of that time were acutely vulnerable, with more than 40% of children dying before their tenth birthday.[1] As is still the case, boys were more vulnerable than girls, succumbing to accidents and illnesses more often than their female counterparts. Nevertheless, the Tudor lack of surviving princes stands out as a statistical oddity. Henry VIII had at least five acknowledged sons; surely one of them should have lived long enough to marry and reproduce?

The fetal losses of Henry's wives can potentially be explained by Kell alloimmunisation, wherein his possible Kell blood type would have caused his reproductive partners to experience an unusually high rate of late-term miscarriage.[2] However, the king's theoretical blood type would have had no negative effect on his children who were carried successfully to term. His eldest daughter, Mary, lived past her fortieth birthday. His second daughter, Elizabeth, was almost seventy when she passed away. Why, then, did his sons die? The death of his first son, Henry, Duke of Cornwall, at less than two months old is most easily explained; he was very likely the victim of one of the myriad illnesses that gave that era such a terrifyingly high infant mortality rate. In contrast, the deaths of Henry Fitzroy and Edward VI are much harder to account for. Once a child reached the age of ten, the odds were good he would reach adulthood. So why did Fitzroy and Edward die in their mid-teens? Did it have any connection with Arthur Tudor's similar demise?

Although there is scant historical information regarding the circumstances of the early deaths of Prince Arthur and Fitzroy, or the medical interventions they received, there is a comprehensive chronicle of

Edward VI's childhood health and rapid decline. It was while researching the life of the last Tudor king – particularly the records of his sudden descent into his final illness – that I saw a possible explanation of why he, his half-brother, and his uncle all passed away in their mid-teens. I hope you find the details of Edward's brief life and reign as fascinating as I did, and that my theory to explain why the Tudor dynasty lasted only three generations gives you plenty of food for thought.

Chapter One

Brought to Childbed of a Prince

King Henry VIII was nearly forty-six years old when he married his third queen, Jane Seymour, in May 1536. By Tudor reckoning old age began at forty, and the king was thought to be almost out of time to father more children. He wanted a legitimate male heir more than any other earthly thing, so when his wife suspected she was pregnant in the early months of 1537, Henry and his whole court crossed their fingers and prayed that her menses had stopped because of a fetus, rather than an illness. The royal prayers appeared to have been answered when Jane felt a quickening in her womb that spring. On 27 May 1537, one week after their first anniversary, the queen's pregnancy was announced. Peals of gratitude rang out from the church bells across Henry's realm, and the *Te Deum* was sung by the choir of St Paul's Cathedral to give thanks to God for the blessing of royal fecundity.

The king hoped, of course, that the baby growing in the queen's belly was a boy, but he wasn't alone in wishing for a prince rather than a princess. Almost everyone in the kingdom would have petitioned the Almighty that the infant be born with a penis. The importance of Jane's pregnancy to the entire nation, and the need for a male to inherit the crown, is hard to overstate and almost beyond modern comprehension. We know, with the benefit of historical hindsight, that England would do just fine under the rule of Queen Elizabeth I, but the suggestion that Anne Boleyn's bastardised daughter could reign more ably than a legitimate brother would have been laughed to scorn by the Tudors. For Jane's contemporaries, the outcome of her pregnancy was, quite literally, a potential matter of life and death. The economic and political stability of Britain could be determined by the baby's gender. A lack of a legitimate male heir could lead to another period of anarchy, as had happened when there was an attempt to enthrone Empress Matilda as Queen of England in the twelfth century. Without a clear successor to the throne, the king's eventual death could lead to a bloody civil war between contesting heirs, as it had just a generation before in the Wars of the Roses. The birth of a princess, therefore, carried with it the threat of battles and collateral civilian deaths, as well as economic devastation when trade and commerce were disrupted. The biological sex of the queen's child could therefore be the difference between periodic hunger or outright starvation for the poor, especially in urban centres like London.

Jane, herself, must have been particularly anxious not to disappoint the king and his kingdom. Aside from the larger socio-political ramifications, she would have almost certainly wondered what would happen to her if she failed to give Henry the son he wanted on the first try. If she produced an unwanted daughter, would she be given another chance to provide a male heir, or would she suffer the same unhappy fate as Henry's first two queens? Would she be cast aside, as Queen Katharina of Aragon had been, or worse – beheaded like Queen Anne Boleyn?

While there was nothing anyone could do to ensure the birth of a prince, the royal physicians could at least take steps to protect the health of the queen and her fetus. Lacking modern medical equipment and theory, they would have tried to keep Jane's humours – the four liquids believed to regulate the human body and determine a person's health – as balanced as possible. Following the teachings of influential medical texts, such as Bernard de Gordon's *Lilium Medicinae*, Jane's doctors would have seen her diet as the best way to achieve the ideal humoral equilibrium for a healthy mother and child. They would have therefore closely monitored what the queen ate and drank. The intake of foods considered bitter or salty would have been heavily restricted, in case it brought on premature labour by cooling the queen's humours too much. Jane would have been allowed to drink only dilute white wine with her meals, or possets of warmed milk in the evenings, since the common beverages of ale, small-beer, and strong wines were believed to engender 'grosse' humours that would be harmful to her pregnancy. She would have been provided meals thought to make 'good blood' and to gently warm her humours, such as roasted poultry or lamb served with sweet or fragrant sauces.[1]

Happily for her doctors, Jane developed a passion for eating quails during her pregnancy. To appease the gravid queen's craving the king wrote to Arthur Plantagenet, Viscount Lisle, who was the Lord Deputy of Calais, and commanded him to send the court some quails from the English territory in France. Henry informed Lisle that the birds should even be imported from Flanders if necessary.[2] This was not simply a case of Henry being a doting husband; there was a contemporary belief that if a pregnant woman wasn't given the foods she yearned for then her unfulfilled desires might unbalance her humours and cause her to miscarry. The king's determination to find quails was as much about protecting his unborn theoretical son as it was from concern for his wife. Fortunately, Lisle was able to send a few dozen fat quails for the royal kitchens without delay. This not only satisfied Jane's cravings, but it also secured a place in the royal court for one of his stepdaughters as a lady-in-waiting for the queen.

Jane's physicians would have also instructed her to go for daily walks, since gentle exercise had been considered essential for a pregnant woman's health for aeons. Medieval physicians knew that a pregnant woman could develop lethal blood clots in her legs if she was sedentary, even if they thought the thrombosis was caused by the blockage of the mythical humours. The queen would have most likely confined these walks to the environs of carefully curated castle gardens, to guarantee that she wouldn't see anything unpleasant during her perambulations. Not only was it feared Jane would miscarry if she saw something grotesque or upsetting, but it was also firmly believed that whatever an expectant mother saw, whether good or bad, affected fetal development. Doctors and midwives warned that 'pregnant women should not look at ugly beasts ... in case they should bring children into the world who resemble these'.[3] Women were also encouraged to look at beautiful objects or people to ensure they had beautiful babies. It was even recommended that if a gravid woman couldn't surround herself with loveliness, she should at least strive to *think* of pretty things as often as she could.

Both benign birthmarks and harmful congenital abnormalities were believed to be the result of something the mother had seen while pregnant, particularly if she had been startled. Therefore, people marred by leprosy, or even badly scarred by an accident, would have been kept from the queen's sight in case the baby was born with similar disfigurations. Jane would have also been prevented from seeing anyone with a club foot or a cleft palate, lest her unborn baby be 'marked' by these conditions as well. Even some of the pets popular at court would also have been kept away from the queen, since until the twentieth century it was commonly thought that infant microcephaly was the result of the mother looking at a monkey too often or for too long.

Every effort would have been made to keep the pregnant queen away from unpleasant odours as well. Doctors not only thought that scent affected the humours, they believed that foul-smelling 'vapours' transmitted diseases. The only way to protect Jane and her pregnancy from dangerous stinks was to constantly surround her with pleasant aromatics. Thus, the queen would have been provided with a prophylactic potpourri of dried flowers, herbs, and spices for the pomander she carried on her gown. Her clothes and bed linens would have also been stored with fragrant sachets, and they would have been sprinkled with perfume before she used them. As a final measure of pungent protection, she would have been anointed with aromatic oils and unguents. If the queen encountered a fetid smell in spite of these precautions, her ladies would burn frankincense so she could inhale its smoke to neutralise her exposure to anything noisome.[4] She would have also been encouraged to inhale the scent of roses, violets, lilies, white and red sandalwood, musk, and camphor at every opportunity, since those fragrances in particular were thought to ward off summer contagions.

During the queen's pregnancy, the king would have made sure to visit her frequently, and not simply to check on her welfare. Although pregnant women were advised to avoid sexual intercourse for the first four months of their suspected gestation, as well as during the sixth month and the eighth month, 'for fear of shaking the child and bringing down her courses', it was also thought that a woman should have as much sex as possible with the father of her baby during the seventh and ninth month of pregnancy. Copious sex would allow the father to 'fashion' the fetus in his image and 'get his influence on it'.[5] Henry would have wanted to make sure that his child was imbued with as much of his royal Tudor essence as possible. It was often noted how much his youngest daughter, Elizabeth, resembled him, and the king would have surely wanted his presumed son and heir to be similarly blessed.

In late September, Jane went to Hampton Court to begin her confinement, the customary period when any woman who could afford to do so would retreat into the privacy of a single room to await the start of labour. The queen's birthing room was arranged according to the Ordinances of Royal Birth, which had been set in place by the king's grandmother, Margaret Beaufort, long before. Some of the ordinances, such as the orders that the walls of the birthing room should be covered in tapestries and cloth hangings, 'except one window, which must be hanged so as [the gravid queen] may have light when it pleaseth her',[6] seem draconian to the modern eye, but the king's grandmother was merely following the best medical advice of the times. Physicians believed that drafts of cold air could easily upset a pregnant woman's humours, thus endangering the health of mother and child, and so the input of fresh air was to be carefully controlled. Margaret Beaufort herself had been no older than fifteen (and maybe as young as thirteen) when she gave birth to her only child, the future King Henry VII. She had barely survived the ordeal, and it seems to have made her determined that the royal women of the Tudor court would be given the best possible care during their deliveries.

Once ensconced in a well-heated and dimly lit birthing chamber, the coddled queen would have nothing to do but rest, grow larger, and hope for a son. The kingdom was eager for Jane to give birth, but everyone – including the king – had to twiddle their thumbs and await the whims of Mother Nature. Babies are notoriously born on their own schedule, with no concern for anyone's expectations or convenience.

On 9 October 1537, the queen went into labour. At last, the long months of anticipation were almost over. However, as happens with many first births, it would be a long travail before Jane finally delivered. Protracted labours were worrisome. They could easily be fatal to the baby or the mother during this time of limited medical technology. As the hours of Jane's labour stretched into days, there was little anyone could do but petition God for the queen's safety and a healthy baby. On the 11th there was a 'general procession in London, with all the orders of friars, priests, and clerkes going all in capes, the mayor and aldermen, with all the crafts of the city, following their liveries, which was done to pray for the queen that was then in labour of child'.[7] The petitioners then could do nothing but continue to wait anxiously as Jane's labour entered the third day.

Happily for the court, country, and king (and doubtlessly as a great relief to Jane herself), the queen was delivered of a proverbial bouncing baby boy in the dawn hours of Friday, 12 October.

The rejoicing was immense. Messengers were sent rushing 'to all estates and cities of the realm' bearing great gifts and glad tidings of the king's new son.[8] Jane had come through the long labour without undue complications and appeared to be in no danger, so there was no worry or mourning for the queen to mar the celebrations for the newborn prince.[9] The baby himself appeared to be healthy and strong. He had even propitiously been born on the feast of St Wilfrid, the eve of St Edward's Day, which was taken as a sign of God's favour for England and the Tudor king. Churches in London sang the *Te Deum*, and there was a formal procession to St Paul Cathedral to give thanks for the arrival of the king's son. Bonfires were lit in the streets and revelled around, and 'fruits and wine' were distributed generously by royal command so the king's subjects could have 'goodly banqueting'. The Tower of London set off a two thousand gun salute. Across the realm church bells rang all through the day and into the night, forming a continuous tintinnabulation to express the nation's happiness that there was a male heir to the throne at last.

Meanwhile, the infant who was inspiring all this brouhaha had been washed with warm wine, slathered with perfumed oil or grease to protect his skin, swaddled, and whisked away from his mother to be placed immediately in the care of his wet-nurses and nursemaids. The newly-built nursery in Hampton Court had been thoroughly scrubbed down on Henry's orders, and the tiny prince was taken there post-haste by his caregivers and royal guards. There is no record, as there was with Anne Boleyn regarding her daughter Elizabeth, that Jane asked to be allowed to nurse the baby herself. This does not mean, of course, that the queen loved her son less than Anne had loved her baby; it is just as likely that Jane did not want to ask for something she already knew she would be denied. Jane would have been well aware of the protocol of royal births and historical evidence suggests she was not the kind of person to raise much of a fuss to challenge the status quo. With few exceptions, what we know of Jane suggests she was easy-going and conciliatory.

Jane, though doubtlessly exhausted from the physical efforts of such a drawn-out delivery, couldn't use the baby's absence as an excuse to rest. She had one more very important chore to perform before she could sleep. By tradition, it was the queen's job to formally announce the birth to the king. There is still a record of her letter to Henry, and it bursts with the elation and pride she was clearly feeling:

Right trusty and well beloved, we greet you well, and for as much as by the inestimable goodness and grace of Almighty God, we be delivered and brought in childbed of a prince, conceived in most lawful matrimony between my the king's majesty and us, doubting not but that for the love and affection which you bear unto us and to the commonwealth of this realm, the knowledge thereof should be joyous and glad tidings unto you, we have thought good to certify you of the same. To the intent you might not only render unto God condign thanks and prayers for so great a benefit but also continually pray for the long continuance and preservation of the same here in this life to the honour of God, joy and pleasure of my lord the king and us, and the universal wealth, quiet and tranquility of this whole realm.

Edward was baptised in the royal chapel at Hampton Court three days after his birth. The protocol for a royal christening was followed to the letter, just as Margaret Beaufort had dictated it should be decades before, with no expense spared for the ceremony. Elaborate precautions were also taken to safeguard the baby's health during the ceremony. An eight-sided screen was erected around the silver-gilt baptismal font, and was hung with tapestries and cloth of gold to keep any drafts away from the newborn during the christening. Henry was taking no chances that his precious son might be taken ill due to chilly air touching the infant's wet head after the holy water had been applied.

The baptism procession into the chapel consisted of several gentlemen of high rank walking two-by-two and carrying unlit torches. Behind these gentlemen came the dean of the king's chapel, accompanied by his fellow chapel ministers and the children's choir. More gentleman, knights, esquires, ministers of state, important chaplains, abbots, bishops, councillors, lords, and ambassadors – also walking two abreast and carrying unlit torches – followed the dean and choir. Two of the baby's godfathers, Thomas Howard, 3rd Duke of Norfolk, and Thomas Cranmer, Archbishop of Canterbury, entered the chapel next. They were in turn followed by Robert Radcliffe, Earl of Sussex, and the king's maternal cousin, Henry Pole, Lord Montague, whom both carried covered basins of water, as well as Henry Bourchier, Earl of Essex, who carried a saltcellar of gold to be gifted to the church in the baby's name.

Amazingly, Thomas Boleyn, Earl of Wiltshire, was also in the procession, carrying a baptism candle and a towel to dry the prince's head. This almost seems as though Henry VIII was being deliberately cruel by forcing the earl to attend the christening. After all, this was a ceremony in honour of a prince that would have saved Anne Boleyn's life, but had been birthed instead by the woman who had supplanted her and benefited from her death. The king had judicially murdered Wiltshire's son, but now the earl was being made to celebrate the fact that Henry now had a son of his own. Nevertheless, the king may not have been trying to hurt Thomas Boleyn by including him. For one thing, it is not certain Henry had sufficient empathy at this time in his life to understand the pain Wiltshire might be feeling. The king seems to have been egotistical enough to assume that because he was delighted, everyone else felt the same way. The king wasn't mourning Anne or George Boleyn, and thus no one else could be mourning them either. Or perhaps Thomas Boleyn participated in the christening because he was the monster he's often portrayed as in fiction, who had thought of his children only in terms of what they could bring him. What is more likely, however, is that Wiltshire's sixteenth-century mindset toward God's will and the Divine Rights of a king rendered him compliant to his monarch's wishes in a way a modern person would find hard to truly understand. If Henry, the man God chose to rule England, had killed Wiltshire's children, then QED it was God's will that they should die. To question the king's actions was to question God's plans, which was almost unthinkable. Wiltshire may have believed himself to be adhering to the doctrine of Christian resignation by his continued service to Henry. Correspondingly, the king may have considered himself to be rewarding Wiltshire for that Christian resignation by including him in the baptism, since it was a singular honour to have a part to play in the christening of a king's heir.

Lady Elizabeth, the king's four-year-old daughter, was similarly honoured with a prominent role in her half-brother's christening. Although she had been bastardised by her father, she was still his acknowledged daughter and had therefore been given the high office of bearing Prince Edward's baptismal chrism. This was a great privilege, but the heavyweight of the chrism cloth necessitated that Queen Jane's brother, Edward Seymour, had to carry the little girl and her burden in his arms down the aisle to the font.[10]

Finally, the star of the show entered the chapel. Prince Edward was transported toward the baptismal font on a pillow by Gertrude Courtenay, who was assisted by her husband, Henry Courtenay, Marquess of Exeter, and the baby's third godfather, Charles Brandon, Duke of Suffolk. Six gentlemen of the privy chamber walked alongside the tiny prince's entourage, supporting a canopy above him. The white christening gown was so long that its train had to be carried by the Earl of Arundel and William Howard, the son of the Duke of Norfolk. A nurse and a midwife also walked near the baby, in case there was royal spit-up or some other emergency to deal with. Following the canopy was Lady Mary, Edward's oldest half-sister by the king's first queen, Katharina of Aragon. As with Lady Elizabeth, Lady Mary had been declared illegitimate by her father, but she was nonetheless given the honour of being the baby's godmother. Mary's train was carried by her loyal friend and supporter, Lady Kingston, who had been one of the women to escort Mary's hated stepmother, Anne Boleyn, to her beheading. A further mass of ladies, positioned by rank and all bearing unlit tapers of virgin wax, completed the procession.

Edward was taken carefully into the secluded space formed by the octagonal screen around the baptism font. The area had been warmed by a fire pan of hot coals 'with good perfume',[11] to provide a maximum safeguard for the heir's health. A select handful of the participants crowded into the enclosure with the baby and the Archbishop of Canterbury. They included the infant's godparents, as well as Sussex and Montague with the basins of water and Wiltshire with the towel. There, in the semi-private surroundings of sumptuous cloth hangings, Archbishop Cranmer baptised and named the newborn prince. When the rite was complete, trumpets rang out, all the torches were lit, and the Garter King-of-Arms cried out, 'God of His Almighty and infinite grace give and grand good life and long to the right high, right excellent and noble Prince, Prince Edward, Duke of Cornwall and Earl of Chester, most dear and most entirely beloved son to our most dread and gracious Lord, King Henry VIII'.[12]

All the attendees were then given hypocras, a traditional drink of sweetened and spiced hot wine, to toast the baby's health. Ladies Mary and Elizabeth were additionally given wafers, the thin sugary biscuits that were only supposed to be eaten by those of the highest rank. Wine and bread were also sent out to the crowd of well-wishers who milled around the chapel doors. Christening presents, including gold cups, silver bowls, and gilt flagons, were presented as ostentatiously as possible by the godparents and a few other nobles who had sufficient social standing to gift the prince publicly.

It's strange to think of the fate that awaited many of those who drank and made merry together that night. A little over a year later the king would execute his cousins, Henry Courtenay and Henry Pole, on trumped-up charges of treason, done to make sure they would not threaten the succession of the baby boy they had just seen christened. Thomas Cromwell wouldn't outlive them by much, falling prey to Henry's temper in the summer of 1540. The Duke of Norfolk would be also accused of fictitious treason in December 1546, but Henry's death a few weeks later meant he would avoid the headsman's axe in favour of being imprisoned for the six and half years of the prince's reign. Edward Seymour, after promoting himself to the Duke of Somerset, would rule in his nephew's name for a few years, and would kill his own brother before eventually being executed himself in January 1552. It was Archbishop Thomas Cramer, however, who perhaps faced the most gruesome destiny. He would be burned alive at the stake by his fellow godparent, the future Queen Mary I, in the spring of 1556.

Luckily, there were no fortune-tellers among the revellers, so no one was told of their impending doom as they drank their spicy sweetened wine and made cheerful small talk in the chapel.

By custom, neither of the baby's parents had attended the christening. Instead, they sat in state in the queen's apartments, where they were congratulated by the attendees and well-wishers both before and after the ceremony. Jane, who was still in good health at this time, was richly and warmly bundled in fur and velvet as she received the steady stream of visitors into her rooms. There would have undoubtedly been many people wanting to butter her up with their compliments. She had birthed the king a son, and her place by Henry's side was secure. Jane and her Seymour relations could now be thought of as perpetually favoured by the king, and having a pathway to power and position in the Tudor court.

With a fanfare of trumpets, the christening party brought Prince Edward to his parents, where he was formally blessed in the name of God, the Virgin Mary, and St George. The king was almost certainly swelling with pride and happiness. Edward was everything Henry had been hoping for, 'a child worthy of such a parent'.[13] Not only did the baby boy promise the continuation of the Tudor dynasty, his birth vindicated Henry's manhood. It was the prevalent belief at the time that only strong 'seed' from manly men could make a son, while lesser seed created girls and that inadequate men with weak seed produced no children at all. Edward's birth was proof to the world that Henry was man enough to produce male heirs. Furthermore, it was believed conception could only happen if the woman had achieved an orgasm during coitus, so all babies were evidence of a man's sexual prowess as well as the power of his sperm. Since both the strength of a man's seed and his skills as a lover were seen as reflections of his innate virility, a man with no sons was a man whose masculinity could be called into question. The newborn male heir was, therefore, a testimony of Henry's fitness as a man, and thus his worthiness to be monarch.

For a week, all seemed perfect in the royal household. Jane rested and recuperated in her apartments, where she was waited on hand and foot by her ladies. She was attended there frequently by half a dozen medical men, including Henry's personal doctor, William Butts. Butts was one of the founders of the Royal College of Physicians and was lauded for his healing skills throughout England, so the king was indisputably trying to provide his wife with the best care available. Her doctors would have made sure she ate foods that warmed her humours, including rice cooked in milk and sweetened with sugar, which was believed to be particularly good for women recovering from childbirth.[14] Jane was a queen, however, and what she asked for she would get. Her ladies would therefore bring her 'such things as her fantasy'[15] desired to eat. Unfortunately, this meant that many people blamed her indulgent ladies-in-waiting for Jane's unexpected and untimely death eleven days after Edward's birth.

It is obvious that disturbed humours caused by eating treats did not kill the queen, but the actual cause of her death is still a topic of debate. She has been assumed to have died of childbed fever, but her symptoms came on suddenly, unlike the lingering agony of postpartum infection. On 23 October the convalescing queen experienced 'an naturall laxe',[16] and began bleeding heavily. A severe haemorrhage occurring so long after the actual birth was probably a result of a piece of the placenta being retained in her womb.[17] If that is true, then Jane ironically died because her husband's attempts to provide the best possible medical care had left her in the hands of male doctors, rather than the less-respected midwives. Midwives, who were highly knowledgeable in obstetrical matters, would have known to check the queen's afterbirth to make sure it was whole. Once they had realised that a part of the placenta remained inside the queen, there were life-saving steps they could take to remove it. Midwives would have known how to apply fundal pressure or uterine massage to help the womb contract and expel the remaining afterbirth. Midwives would have also been aware that allowing Jane to breastfeed her baby would encourage uterine contractions as well. If desperate, they could have even reached inside the uterus through the still-dilated cervix to try to coax out the last shreds of the placenta. This would have increased the risk of childbed fever, but they would have risked it because some women survived postpartum infection, whereas the inevitable haemorrhage caused by leaving the placenta in place was always fatal.

Unlike the midwives, the royal physicians wouldn't have known to check the afterbirth and wouldn't have known what to do if they *had* spotted the problem. Doctors of this time period seldom touched a patient, leaving surgery for the lower-ranking chirurgeons and birth to midwives. Physicians were trained in humoral theory and the advanced mathematics needed for astrology, so they could have drawn up Jane's natal chart, examined her urine, and speculated on her levels of black bile, but they knew nothing of how to prevent postpartum haemorrhage. When she began bleeding, all that the doctors around her bed could do was summon her confessor to perform last rites and then wait by her bedside as she exsanguinated.

Henry VIII was said to have been devastated by the death of his third queen. He wrote to King Francis I of France that 'Divine Providence has mingled my joy with the bitterness of the death of her who brought me this happiness', and was, according to Thomas Cromwell, 'little disposed to marry again'.[18] But was the king really brokenhearted by Jane's passing, or was he perhaps enthusiastically embracing the romantic ideal of a knight mourning his lost love after the fact? He certainly didn't appear to be overly concerned when first informed of his wife's illness. On the day of the queen's death, John Russell, 1st Earl of Bedford, had written to Cromwell to inform him that, 'the king intended to remove to Asher, and, because the Queen was very sick this night and today, he tarried, but he will be there tomorrow'. Henry then told Russell that he would go hunting the next day even if his wife 'amend not' because 'he could not find in his heart to tarry'.

Although Henry's reluctance to remain near the queen could possibly be chalked up to his well-known dislike of illness and his borderline hypochondria, his determination to go to Asher even if his wife sickened further does not support the idea that he had a great emotional attachment to Jane. His purported indifference to another marriage after her death is as likely to indicate that the fussy king wanted to make sure he picked the right wife as it is to indicate lasting grief. In fact, marriage seems to have been on his mind shortly after his queen's funeral. Within weeks of Jane's death, Cromwell was contacting England's ambassadors to suss out potential brides for Henry. Less than six months after the queen's demise the king had already sent Hans Holbein to paint a portrait of a potential bride, the Duchess Christina of Milan.

Chapter Two

A Nursery for the Whole Realm's Most Precious Jewel

While the king looked for someone to replace Edward's mother, the infant prince continued to thrive and 'sucketh like a child of his puissance.'[1] A new nursery had been constructed on the north range of Hampton Court, at enormous expense, and was laid out as a smaller imitation of his father's apartments. The baby's rooms could only be reached by ascending a processional staircase and entering through a watching chamber, so named because it was where Edward's plethora of guards kept watch. Beyond the watching chamber lay the presence chamber, where the grandiose cradle of state stood. Whenever someone was granted permission by the king to see the prince, the baby would be placed in the cradle of state and the lucky visitor would be allowed to creep close enough to see the Tudor heir.

In general, people tended to like what they saw in the king's new son. His extremely pale skin and auburn hair would have certainly appealed to the beauty standards of his time. The king's chancellor, Thomas Audley, gushed in a letter to Thomas Cromwell that he had never seen 'so goodly a child' or one with 'so good and loving countenance, and so earnest an eye as it were a sage judgment towards every person'. While this praise could be attributed to Audley's desire to please the king, others with no reason to flatter the baby also reported he was quite the cutie. The ambassadors to Spain, Eustace Chaupuys and Don Diego de Mendoza, got to see Edward in February 1538, and they reported that the little prince 'in reality is one of the prettiest children of his age that could be seen any where'.[2] Unlike Audley, the ambassadors had no reason to make a false claim of the child's handsomeness to their boss, so the prince probably would have been legitimately seen as adorable by those privileged enough to take a peek at him.

Most of Edward's time was spent in the smaller room past the presence chamber, known as his privy chamber. There he was cared for and coddled by various nursery-maids and wet-nurses under the supervision of Lady Margaret Bryan, the nursery governess. Lady Bryan had been in charge of the nurseries for all of Henry VIII's children, including his illegitimate son, Henry Fitzroy, and the king trusted her implicitly. The nursery had a small bedroom tucked behind the privy chamber, known as the rocking chamber, where the infant prince slept in a serviceable cradle. No less than four women were employed specifically to rock the baby's cradle and watch over him during the night.

Ever concerned about the safety of his son, the king put two loyal military men in the most important positions of Edward's household. Sir William Sidney, a cousin of Charles Brandon, Duke of Suffolk, was made the prince's chamberlain. His family had supported Henry VII's coup against Richard III, and Sidney had commanded the right flank of England's army in its victory against the Scots in the Battle of Flodden. The baby's steward, Sir John Cornwallis, had fought at Henry's side during the English campaign into France in 1513,[3] and was another man-at-arms the king felt he could trust unreservedly to guard his heir.

It might seem to be ridiculous for the king to be so paranoid about an attack on his son, but there was reasoning behind his worries. Pope Paul III was blatantly trying to cajole the Holy Roman Empire and/or France to invade England and restore Catholicism, the 'true' form of Christianity, as England's state religion. Henry was particularly anxious to know what Emperor Charles V, arguably the most powerful man in Europe, was planning. The emperor had actually sacked Rome in 1536 and taken the pope hostage, and England would have been seen as a lesser challenge. Moreover, the emperor was the maternal cousin of Henry's eldest daughter, Mary. Imperial forces could depose Henry and put Mary on the throne, and she could wed the emperor's as-yet-unmarried son, King Philip III of Spain. Mary's husband would actually rule the realm through her, thus effectively rendering England a vassal state. Even if Mary was only given the role of regent until her baby brother came of age, imperial agents could have easily arranged for Edward to die in an 'accident' or from a purported illness without his sister being any the wiser. Although it seems that the emperor never seriously considered an invasion (mainly because England wasn't a big enough fish to be worth the imperial expenditure to catch it), it was enough of a possibility to keep the king on edge.

It wasn't just foreign enemies that Henry feared. There were devout Catholics in his own kingdom who prayed daily that Edward would die so that Mary would come to the throne instead. Some of them did more than pray. In January 1538, a wax figure, seemingly a model of the infant prince, was found stuck through with pins and buried in a London churchyard.[4] Soon afterwards yet another wax poppet, one more obviously representing the infant heir, was found at Oxford with a knife thrust into it.[5] For the Tudors, such a magical attack was as serious and threatening as a physical attempt to murder the prince.

Additionally, there were negative prophecies being spread about Edward that Henry found distressing. A fruit-seller named John Ryan confessed to being told by a 'prophesyer' in the king's own service about a prediction by Merlin that although 'Edward should succeed Henry and wear the crown of England … that there should be more murder and traitors in his time than in his father's; and that the same prophesyer said to him, "O thou child that murdered thy mother in her womb, thou shalt have so much treason wrought in thy time more than ever thy father had, and yet shalt thou prosper and go forth".' Ryan had also been told by two other men that there 'should never be king of England crowned after the present King'.[6] If people believed these prophecies, it might lead to future accusations that the boy crowned after Henry's death wasn't really Prince Edward, allowing an alternative heir to make a play for the throne.

Henry had his son – whom he dubbed the 'whole realm's most precious jewel' – guarded against illness as well as theoretical assassins. The king had lost his first legitimate son in 1511, when the infant was only a few weeks old, and he was taking no chances with the health of this prince. Edward was given his own personal doctor, George Owen, who was ordered to constantly monitor the baby's health. The king ordered the nursery's floors, walls, and even the ceilings be swabbed down with soap and hot water several times a day. Although there was no concept of germ theory yet, people had noticed for millennia that a dairy had to be kept scrupulously clean if you wanted to keep milk from spoiling, and it had therefore long been assumed that dirt spread disease and illness. Serving boys, pages, and dogs were also not allowed to enter the nursery, because they 'without any respect go to and fro and be not wary of the dangers of infection and do often times resort into suspect places'. Anyone feeling even the first faint signs of ill-health was instructed to isolate themselves from the prince's household immediately, and no member of the prince's household was allowed to visit London during the summer months when sweating sickness and other epidemics were most common. A separate kitchen, washhouse, and outhouse were all built for the nursery's use, so that there was less risk of cross-contamination. As final precautions, the nursery's food was taste-tested for poison, and the prince's clothing had to be washed and worn by another child at least once to show that there were no poisons secreted in the garments.

Edward was kept in lavish comfort, as well as protective seclusion. When Lady Bryan wrote to Cromwell in June 1538 to let him know that the baby 'was in good health and merry' with 'four teeth, three full out and the fourth appearing', she also warned him that the nursery was 'but very bare for such a time', and did not meet the king's expectations for his heir.[7] She despaired that the 'best coat my lord Prince has is tinsel' and that the baby had 'never a good jewel to set in his cap', then passive-aggressively promised to 'order all for my Lord's honour the best I can'. After receiving the letter, Cromwell hastened to put an additional £5000 at the disposal of the nursery's chamberlain. This meant that roughly £1.5 million in modern money was given over to make sure an eight-month-old baby had furniture and apparel worthy of a future king.[8]

Lady Mary came to see her baby brother frequently, starting when he was only a few weeks old. Her household was at Richmond Palace, an easy distance from Hampton Court, and she visited several times in the spring of 1538, often riding one of the palfreys that had belonged to Jane Seymour.[9] Edward's eldest half-sister seems to have loved him very much, in spite of the fact that his birth theoretically removed her from any possibility of ruling England after her father's death. The prince appears to have reciprocated this love as he grew older, provided that the letters he wrote to her were a sincere reflection of his feelings. If so, the later contention between the very Protestant King Edward VI and the still very Catholic Lady Mary must have been emotionally scarring for both of them. As Mary cooed over the adorable baby in his cot, she could not have known that he would one day bring both himself and his beloved sister to tears over their immutable religious differences.[10] For now, at least, the infant prince had no religious opinions to vex his godmother, allowing her to enjoy an uncomplicated affection for her sibling.

The king was a much less frequent visitor to the prince's nursery. Hands-on contact between parent and child was not the royal custom. Neither Henry nor his elder brother, Arthur, had spent any significant amount of time with their own father before they were old enough to be instructed in statecraft, and the king clearly had no intention of breaking that tradition. He wouldn't come to see his son until May 1538, when after 'dallying with him in his arms a long space' he displayed himself holding the baby at a window 'to the sight and great comfort of all the people'.[11]

The prince was expected to remove to various royal residences in the same way as the adult members of his family, albeit with less frequency. He and the members of his household left Hampton Court soon after the king's visit so the baby could spend the summer at Havering Palace, an estate in Essex a bit south of the royal woodlands of Epping Forest. The palace had been one of the many given to Jane Seymour as part of her jointure when she married Henry VIII, and was believed to have very healthy air in warm weather. Royal nurseries had also been established in several places, including Richmond Palace, Hundon Manor, and Elsyng Palace.

The king's chancellor, Thomas Audeley, came to check on the prince in the autumn of 1538, and was happy to report back to Cromwell that the baby 'waxeth firm and stiff' and would probably be taking his first steps already if his nurses would let him try it. The chancellor agreed with this caution on the part of the nurses, telling the lord privy seal that, 'They do yet best, considering his Grace is yet tender, that he should not strain himself, as his own courage would serve him, till he come above a year of age'.[12]

Edward turned one that October, which was a definite reason to celebrate in the sixteenth century, when as many as a quarter of all babies died before their first birthday.[13] Before the advent of antibiotics and the understanding of how to treat dehydration in an infant, scores of babies were lost to pneumonia and diarrhoea; illnesses that still kill all too many children in developing countries in modern times.[14] Infectious diseases that are now prevented (or have been eradicated) with vaccines, such as measles, mumps, pertussis, rubella, neonatal tetanus, diphtheria, rotavirus, smallpox, and some forms of meningitis, were the causes of death for multitudes of Tudor infants. Often the symptoms of these diseases were misconstrued as side-effects of teething, because they occurred around the same time as most babies began cutting their teeth. Therefore, teething itself was considered a cause of death in babies well into the twentieth century.[15] The prince would have undoubtedly been given polished coral to gnaw on, either as a necklace or on the end of a rattle, since it was thought that coral could protect an infant's health while the teeth were emerging.[16]

Once he was past the difficult first twelve months of life, the prince was weaned off breast milk and officially transitioned to a dry nurse. The nursery chamberlain, Sir Sidney, recommended his sister-in-law, Sibyl (Sibbel) Penne, for the position. He vouched for 'the good ability of my wife's sister', praising her for her 'wisdom, honest demeanor, and faithfulness', and promising that she was in 'every way an apt woman' to be given such a 'great charge'.[17] Thomas Cromwell took Sidney at his word, and hired Sibyl Penne. She would prove to be good value for the king's penny. From the time the prince 'left sucking' and 'so long as he remained in woman's government', she was always with him.[18] She even 'continually lay in bed with him' at night to keep him warm, and no doubt to chase away any imaginary boogeymen that might be hiding in the shadows of his chamber. In effect, she was more of a foster mother than a nurse to the little boy, and they naturally developed a close relationship. She took such good care of her charge that for 'consideration of her services in the nurture and education of Prince Edward', she was eventually granted a wealth of estates with enough income that her husband could aspire to knighthood.

As a belated first birthday gift, the king increased the security of Edward's future crown by slaughtering several of the boy's Plantagenet relatives. On 4 November the king's agents arrested Henry Pole, Baron Montagu, and Henry Courtenay, Marquess of Exeter, on the spurious charge of plotting treason against the monarch. No one had seen this coming. Both men were still being treated as the king's favourites until just before their arrest. Henry Courtenay was the king's first cousin via Princess Catherine of York, and had 'been brought up of a child with his grace in his chamber'[19] like a younger brother. Henry Pole was the king's second cousin, but as the grandson of George Plantagenet, 1st Duke of Clarence, he was arguably a much closer claimant to the throne than any Tudor. It's obvious that the motive behind their incarceration was their royal blood, since their prepubescent sons were also thrown into the Tower of London in spite of the fact that they were too young to have been part of plotting a coup.

Thomas Cromwell knew the men had 'little offended' except for being related too closely to their king, but it was his job to find the so-called evidence of their guilt needed to justify their execution. As ever, Cromwell fulfilled his duties. Both Pole and Courtenay were convicted of treason in December, and were beheaded for their genetic crimes in January 1539. Although it was indisputable that their sons could not have been part of a cabal to usurp the crown, the boys were nonetheless remanded to the Tower indefinitely. Pole's son disappeared from the historical record soon afterwards, and he presumably died in prison.[20] Courtenay's eleven-year-old son, Edward, was held in the Tower until 1553, when Queen Mary I took the throne and finally freed him from his long and unjust incarceration.

For good measure, the king also arrested Henry Pole's mother, Margaret, the elderly Countess of Salisbury. Margaret Pole had always been loyal to the king, and was even the godmother of his eldest daughter, but she was chucked into the Tower nonetheless. Her offence is apparently that her father was George Plantagenet, a younger brother of King Edward IV, and that she had given birth to sons. Henry VIII would gruesomely behead her in May of 1542, despite the fact it was clear that the sixty-seven-year-old widowed countess would be producing no more potential rivals to the Tudor dynasty.

The king didn't baulk at killing other people's sons, but his pride in his own healthy, growing heir was unbounded. Wise courtiers had soon learned to fawn over the toddler prince as well as their monarch. Richard Morison gave Henry a very flattering portrait of Edward as a New Year's Day present in 1539, and gilded the lily by including a few sentences of the most brazen blandishments underneath the picture:

Little one, emulate thy father and be the heir of his virtue; the word contains nothing greater. Heaven and earth could scarcely produce a son whose glory would surpass that of a father. Do thou but equal the deeds of thy parent and men can ask no more. Shouldst thou surpass him, thou has outstript all, nor shall any surpass thee in ages to come.[21]

While the modern reader can only chuckle at the over-the-top schmaltz of the inscription, it delighted Henry as much as the painting did. Members of the court rushed to praise the portrait and echo Morison's sentiments. They also made sure to shower the prince, who was too young to appreciate it yet, with expensive New Year's gifts to match his father's. Thomas Audley, Thomas Cranmer, Thomas Howard, Henry Howard, Charles Brandon, Thomas Cromwell, and John de Vere all gave him a porticue, a Portuguese gold coin worth around £3.5 or £4.[22] The seven porticues he received would have been equal to at least £24.5, which was much as a squire usually made in a year. Henry Bourchier, Earl of Essex, thoughtfully gave the prince 'a bell of gold with a whistle',[23] a noisy plaything which the toddler probably appreciated more than gold coins. A whistle with a coral knob on it was often given to a baby to ward off illness during teething, so Essex may have given the toddler a gift that aimed to promote his health as well as his amusement. The royal heir was also given multiple cups and bowls of decorated silver and gilt, each carefully weighed and valued accordingly, by other worthies of the court. The king then topped them all by giving his son a whopping 209oz of gold and silver-gilt tableware. The prince's sisters, however, gave him more personal gifts, to represent their love for him as well as his importance. Mary gave the baby a coat of crimson satin with tinsel sleeves, heavily decorated with gold embroidery and pearls, which had probably been personally sewn for him by his sister and her ladies in waiting. The five-year-old Lady Elizabeth gave him a less ostentatious, but even more personal, present of 'a shirt of cambric of her own working'.[24]

Edward's nursery was moved to Hunsdon Manor that spring, where he continued to flourish in the gentle Hertfordshire countryside. Lady Bryan was able to report to Cromwell that the 'lord Prince is in good health and merry'. She also added that she wished that 'the King and your Lordship had seen him last night. The minstrels played, and his Grace danced and played so wantonly that he could not stand still, and was as full of pretty toys as ever I saw a child in my life'.[25] It was clear from her letter that Lady Bryan was fond of her cheerful charge for his own sake, as well as for his importance to the realm.

The little prince must have been very engaging, because even Steven Gardiner, the rather fusty Bishop of Winchester, seemed fond of him.

Gardiner, who wanted England to return to the Catholic fold, was especially pleased with the prince when Henry Bouchier reported that Edward had taken an instant dislike to the Protestant ambassadors from Cleves. Sibyl Penne had tried to pass off the prince's distress as a natural fear of the Germanic representative's bushy beards, but the toddler had been happy to play with the similarly bearded Henry Bouchier. The ambassadors finally gave up their attempts to hold the prince and left. Bouchier, who was as Catholic at heart as Gardiner, had been deeply gratified by the rebuff the Protestants had received. He joyfully crowed that it was clear the prince knew that Bouchier was 'thy father's true man and thine, and these others be false knaves!'[26]

Children need playmates as well as caretakers, and Edward's chamberlain provided the little boy with his first companion in the form of Sidney's own ten-year-old son, Henry, sometime in 1539. Although Henry Sidney was eight years older than the heir to the throne, he was still considered young enough to be a fitting friend for the toddler prince. Henry seems to have formed a genuine attachment to Edward, whom he would later describe as 'my most dear master, prince, and sovereign'.[27] As the prince grew, other boys would have also joined him for both learning and frivolity. Among them were the sons of the Duke of Suffolk, Charles and Henry Brandon, as well as Barnaby Fitzpatrick, the heir of Baron Upper Ossory. The prince would remain very good friends with the Brandons, even after he had become king, but it was Barnaby who seems to have become his closest confidant.

Edward doesn't appear often in the historical record for the next few years, mainly because he was in good health and doing well. There was, in short, nothing of great importance to report to Cromwell or the king. There is evidence of ambassadors applying to see the prince (probably to report an accurate state of his health to their masters), but there's almost no follow-up confirmation that they saw him or what they thought if they did. The next significant life event for Edward wouldn't occur until the autumn of 1541, when the French ambassador, Charles de Marillac, reported that the little boy was 'handsome, well-fed and remarkably tall for his age' shortly before the prince's fourth birthday in early October.[28] Alas, soon after the ambassador's visit disaster struck the royal nursery. By Halloween, the young prince was suffering from a form of malaria known as quartan fever.

Quartan fever (so named because the fever came in roughly four-day intervals) was incredibly dangerous, especially for young children. Even now, with medicine available to treat it, malaria still causes the death of more than a quarter of a million children under the age of five each year. A desperate Henry summoned physicians from across his realm to come to his son's aid, but they could do nothing to effectively help him. The recommended medical cure for malaria in the Tudor era was a decoction of snails boiled in sweetened milk with candied eryngo root and chopped earthworms added to it, which was to be drunk twice a day.[29] Needless to say, this wasn't able to reduce the prince's fever. What the royal physicians needed was chloroquine, but that would not be available to them (in the form of the bark of the cinchona tree) for almost another century.

For ten days the prince's doctors feared he was on the brink of death, which he might truly have been. Ironically, they worried that the little boy's chubby physique was detrimental to his survival. One of them told the French ambassador that 'the prince seemed to him so gross (fat) and unhealthy that he could not believe, judging from what he could see now, that [Edward] would live long'.[30] The physician could not have been more wrong. Children who are underweight or malnourished are much more likely to perish from malaria than their plumper peers.[31] The pudgy prince was therefore able to recover from the quartan fever in a few weeks. His elder sister, Mary, purportedly contracted the same disease as an adult, but it took the thin and delicate princess much longer to recover.[32]

While the prince was convalescing, the doctors continued to insist that he be fed only soups and broths. This made the otherwise cheerful little boy fratchety and difficult to manage. Dr William Butts, who had been personally sent by the king, certainly seemed to find the recuperating lad a bit of a challenge. Butts wrote a letter to his fellow physician, Dr John Cambre, reporting that while he was glad 'the prince's grace … took yesterday broths; conveniently keeping and well digesting the same' and was strong enough to 'exercise himself on foot in his accustomed pastimes'. It meant that it would now be even harder to 'dissuade him from taking meats'.[33] The prince was so adamant about eating solids again that Butts finally gave in, and was relieved to see that his patient had 'no disposition to vomit' after the meal. Nevertheless, the royal heir was far from pleased with the doctor who had thwarted his appetite for so long. Butts wrote that Edward 'prayed me to go away and has called me a fool'. Ruefully, the doctor contended that if he had to 'tarry till [the prince] call me a knave', then he would say 'let now your servant depart in peace' and leave the child to his nurses, son of the king or not.

Edward quickly regained his health after his brush with malaria. A portrait of the prince painted by Hans Holbein in 1542 depicts a little boy with an extremely fair complexion and very similar facial features to Henry VIII, as well as the strawberry-blonde hair of his father's youth. Although the prince would grow to resemble his grandfather, Henry VII, more than his father as he aged, for the present, there was no denying that he had been sired by the king.

This evidence of paternity, as much as the boy's robustness, was what the king would have wanted visitors to see. When Conn O'Neill, the former King of Tír Eógain (pronounced in English as 'Tyrone'), came to submit himself to the king in Greenwich after a failed Irish rebellion, he was especially invited to go to the royal nursery and 'do his duties' to Prince Edward.[34] Henry had already secured his defeated foe by every means possible. He had taken O'Neill's son, Phelim Caoch, as a hostage for the deposed chieftain's compliance, as well as bribing O'Neill by creating him the Earl of Tyrone and appointing him a privy councillor in Ireland. Nonetheless, the king wanted to drive home the message that challenging England's rule in Ireland was futile. Pope Paul III may have called upon the Catholic chieftain to fight against Henry, but the Irish defeat was seen as evidence that the Almighty was on Henry's side, while the king's sturdy heir showed that God had provided another Tudor lion to roar if there were any further challenges from the Emerald Isle.

Chapter Three

A Household Fit for a Prince

E dward's last year in the nursery was an eventful one, if not for him personally then at least in terms of his putative betrothal. In December 1542, King James V of Scotland died and his six-day-old daughter inherited the throne. The infant Mary, Queen of Scots, was now one of the most well-dowered royals in the world. Henry was determined that she marry his son and unite England and Scotland under one crown. Prince Edward would be engaged to Mary by the following Christmas, or the king would know the reason why! The king accordingly formed a deputation of his chancellor, the Duke of Norfolk, and a handful of bishops to 'to treat and conclude with plenipotentiaries of Mary queen of Scotland for espousals *per verba de futuro* or a marriage *per verba de presenti* between Prince Edward and the said Queen'.[1] Henry, ever one to overreach, also demanded that the infant queen be brought up in England, on his terms, and that he be allowed to rule Scotland in her place until she came of age to marry his son.

The Scots were not best pleased.

Nevertheless, the queen's regent, James Hamilton, Earl of Arran, couldn't just turn down the English crown's proposal. He was in a terrible pickle. On one hand, his Protestant allies in Scotland would throw a fit if he sanctioned the marriage, especially on Henry VIII's unreasonable terms. It would also give his Catholic political adversaries the perfect weapon to depose him and install Cardinal David Beaton as the new regent. On the other hand, England had just kicked six colours of poo out of the Scottish forces at the Battle of Solway Moss, and Arran needed to make peace with their southern neighbour as soon as possible. Ergo, the Scots regent decided to handle the matter as diplomatically as possible. In other words, he would agree to the engagement but keep looking for a way to prevent the match in the future.

Arran signed the Treaties of Greenwich in the summer of 1543, which secured peace with England and betrothed the Queen of Scots to Prince

Edward. The treaties did come with some significant amendments to Henry's first round of demands, however. Under the new terms of the engagement, the queen would remain in Scotland until she was ten, but with the stipulation that 'for her better education and care, the King may send, at his expense, an English nobleman or gentleman, with his wife or other lady or ladies and their attendants, not exceeding 20 in all, to reside with her'.[2] Arran would also continue to manage in her place as governor of Scotland until she got married, rather than allowing Henry to rule the country through her. Additionally, she would be free to return to her homeland if Prince Edward should predecease her without having sired any children, preventing any attempts to marry her off to another English noble without consent of the Scottish Parliament. Most importantly, England had to agree that 'Scotland shall continue to be called the kingdom of Scotland and retain its ancient laws and liberties'.

There was still enough anti-English feeling among the Scots that many of the lords were openly contemptuous of the treaties and threatened to reject them, much to Henry's displeasure. The queen's mother, Marie of Guise, tried to smooth down his ruffled royal feathers as best she could. She met with the king's ambassador, Ralph Sadler, in early August and 'laboured to excuse' those who were publicly against the match. She assured the ambassador of 'her zeal to accomplish all things which might be to [Henry's] good contentation, and specially to the perfection of the marriage betwixt my lord prince's grace and her daughter'.[3] As part of her charm offensive toward the ambassador, Marie of Guise allowed him to see the infant monarch. Sadler was suitably impressed, telling the king that she was, 'a right fair and goodly child, as any that I have seen, for her age'.[4] While he was admiring the baby, Marie of Guise declared once more that 'nothing could be more honourable' than a marriage between her daughter and Prince Edward, and that the union was something she 'desired ... with all her heart'. Then she made Sadler promise to tell the king how happy she was about the engagement, and sent the ambassador on his way.

Why did the queen's mother go to such lengths to demonstrate her approval of the upcoming nuptials? Probably because she knew Henry would suspect otherwise. Marie of Guise was French from the top of her head to the tips of her toes, and wasn't disposed to like the English even at the best of times. She had considerably less reason to like them now, since they had recently killed her husband. Furthermore, she was a devoted Catholic, and would have considered Henry's reformation to be rank heresy. Religion was one of the reasons she had turned him down when he had asked to marry her in December 1537, choosing instead to strengthen the Auld Alliance between France and Scotland by marrying King James V. However, regardless of any personal dislike she may have felt, for the moment she had to pacify Henry and insist that she was delighted that her daughter was going to marry his son.

It is possible that Edward would have actually wed Mary, Queen of Scots, in spite of the difficulties with the Catholic faction in Scotland, if his father hadn't gone on to botch things so badly during the interim. The ink on the Treaty of Greenwich had barely dried when Henry's navy seized five Scots merchant ships and impounded their cargoes of fish.[5] Since the king had just signed an agreement not to do that sort of thing in exchange for marrying his son to their queen, the Scots were understandably vexed. In response to their protests, Henry argued that he had every right to grab the ships, because they had intended to sell their fish to the French and he was planning to start a war with France soon. The Scots were unpersuaded by the king's justifications, and remained irked by his assault on their economy. Arran warned Henry, through ambassador Sadler, that if 'the ships should be staid by your majesty, now that the peace is concluded and ratified … it would mean the whole realm would exclaim against' the earl and the treaty, which most people were already unhappy about.[6] Safe in the south of England, the king was unimpressed by the notion of unhappy Scots. Sadler, however, would soon have to flee Edinburgh to escape the irate locals.

The smart thing for the king to have done was to play nice and give the ships back, as the lesson of Aesop's fable about the sun and the wind should have taught him. He should have been especially careful not to provoke the Scots at this juncture, because the Earl of Arran was showing every sign that he might forge an alliance with the Catholics and Cardinal Beaton to fight the English. The factionalism in Scotland that prevented them from forming a united front against him was Henry's best shot at getting his hands on their queen. Returning the Scottish ships and their cargos of fish was indisputably less expensive to England than losing a chance to enfold Scotland under a Tudor crown, or the cost of another war. Alas, Henry's later reign was not overburdened with examples of his wisdom. Instead of trying to win over the Scots, he threatened them. He sent a nasty official letter to Edinburgh to let them know he was miffed that Sadler had been threatened, and that they should 'beware and eschew that outrage … for fear of the revenge of our sword to extend to that town and commonality'.[7]

This letter had the amazing effect of enraging almost every living soul in Scotland at once. Sadler had to tactfully explain to the king that the common people were 'much offended' by the king's letter, due to its 'sharpness'. The ambassador suggested that it would be 'much the better, if they might have their ships restored', and tried to get Henry to see that his actions would 'work the whole realm (being already almost wholly inclined thereto) to the devotion and cast of France', which would further undermine his plans an Anglo-Scots alliance.[8] The king not only ignored Sadler's advice, he made matters worse by letting his northern lords start raiding Scotland again.

Unsurprisingly, the Scots demanded that the ambassador tell them why, with the peace treaty still fresh, 'did proceed the raids, incursions, burnings, and spoils, daily made in Scotland by Englishmen'.[9] As he had been instructed by the king, Sadler told them that the trouble along the border was *their* fault, because they hadn't done *exactly* what Henry had wanted them to do. There can be no doubt that the Scots were unsatisfied by this explanation. They informed Sadler, in diplomatic terms, that Henry could kiss the marriage between the Queen of Scots and his heir goodbye if he didn't return the ships and make restitution for the border raids by the English.

Rather than just returning the ships and paying off the lords he needed as his allies, Henry foolishly doubled down on his contemptuous refusal to comply with Scotland's requests. He appears to have been of the opinion that he had done more than enough for the Scots when he made peace with them and released the prisoners from the Battle of Solway Moss. Miffed, he began to prepare for war, obviously planning to take the infant queen by force if not by treaty. The Scots, with solid reasons to 'greatly suspect' that the king was intent on invading their country, likewise began to get ready for a fight.[10]

Even if he had been kept informed about the drama unfolding around his engagement in the autumn of 1543, Prince Edward would have probably been much more interested in the fact he was being promoted to a big boy household after his sixth birthday. The little boy's nursery had been luxurious, but it would be considered humble compared to the opulence the king would now provide for his son.

For starters, the walls of his apartments were hung with woven tapestries from Flanders depicting scenes from classical mythology and the Bible. These brightly coloured textiles were usually more than 45 metres squared, and they were almost unimaginably expensive. A single modest tapestry could be worth more than 9kg of silver, which was nearly as much as an average Tudor would make from a decade of labouring. Most of the tapestries in Edward's household had been pilfered from Cardinal Wolsey after his downfall, and had been further enriched with silk and gilt metallic thread to denote the high status of their former owner. Thus, the prince would have been literally surrounded by what is the modern equivalent of millions of pounds worth of woven art in almost every room.

The furnishings provided for the king's son would have been equally ostentatious. The prince's new adult-sized bed would have been a masterwork of embellished wood. It would have been canopied, then draped with embroidered velvet, damask, sarsenet, or brocade hangings to keep away any possible drafts. The first layer of bedding on its slats would have been pricey woollen mattresses, which would have then been topped with a featherbed or two, each one crammed full of more than fifty pounds of goose or duck down. These featherbeds, or feather ticks, were so expensive that they were handed down as family heirlooms even in wealthy families, but the prince would have never slept on anything else. Lying prone was considered potentially dangerous for a person's health and suitable only for the very young or infirm, so Edward's servants would have then laid a kind of long, firmly packed pillow, called a bolster, at the head of his bed to support his back as he slept in a semi-upright position. Other kinds of pillows, however, would have probably been left off his bed, because they were considered needful only for women or the very ill. His bolster and mattresses would have been covered by sheets of Rennes linen, woven in Brittany and imported into England at great expense. In the rest of Northern Europe, people who could afford it would sleep under another feather tick, using it as a kind of duvet, but the English preferred coverlets. The prince's coverings would have been made of silks, velvets, and cloth of gold, some of which would have been trimmed, or even lined, with fur. These coverlets would have also sported a profusion of intricate embroidery, and probably would have been quilted as well.

Edward's tableware would have likewise been fit for royalty. The tablecloth and napkins, known collectively as the napery, would have been Rennes linen trimmed with even more expensive fabrics. His communal dishes, serving spoons, and platters would have been made of finely worked gold, or at least silver gilt, and would have been further embellished whenever possible with enamel, ivory, mother of pearl, crystal, or even gemstones. The middle and lower classes were still eating their dinner on a flat piece of stale bread known as a trencher, but the wealthiest Tudors had begun to use plates by this time, and Edward's would have been as grand as the servingware. He would have drunk from one of his several solid gold cups, or perhaps used a goblet of colourful Venetian glass that had cost a small fortune to import. Small vessels made of precious metals, enamelled ceramic, or rock crystal would have been scattered around the table, all filled with sauces to compliment his meal. Soup would have been served in covered bowls of gold or silver-gilt, and would have been drunk from the container without using a spoon. Finger bowls and small jugs called 'layers' would have been set out between courses so that the diners could wash their hands, and naturally, these items would have been as exquisite as the rest of his tableware.

Edward's household would have also been supplied with a bath for the prince. It is still a common misconception that people didn't bathe in the Middle Ages, but even the lowest peasant would have made regular use of communal bathhouses. English elites would have certainly bathed often and, when possible, extravagantly. From the time of King Edward I, royal bathing chambers had been supplied with water from cisterns and had taps for both hot and cold water.[11] The prince would have probably had to 'make do' with bathing in his chamber at most residences, but it would have still been a luxurious experience. The bath itself would be a waterproof wooden tub, sometimes coated in thin copper plating, that looked a bit like a large rain barrel. It would have been comfortably lined with soft fabric and bottomed with a large sponge cushion for the bather to sit on, and a cloth tent would have been erected over it to keep out cold air.

Before the reign of the Tudor monarchs, bathwater was kept tepid to preserve the bather's humility before Christ. However, King Henry

VIII liked his bathwater hot and sprinkled with pleasant-smelling herbs, and he would have undoubtedly insisted on the same luxury for his son. Once in the water, the prince's attendants would have washed him with small sponges and white Castile soap, which was made with olive oil and imported from Spain at outrageous expense. There would have been a separate basin of warmed, spiced water especially for rinsing his hair after it was shampooed.[12] Since pleasant smells were thought to help prevent disease, his bath would have been scented with the strongest (and costliest) aromatics available, such as cinnamon, liquorice, cumin, nutmeg, rosemary, lavender, and cloves. Once he was done bathing, the prince would have been rinsed a final time with warm rosewater, and then dried with perfumed towels.

Edward received new clothes from his father as well, designed to reinforce his status as the royal heir. His shirts were fashioned from Rennes linen or finest fustian, and heavily embroidered at the cuffs and collar. His hosiery was made of twilled silk, rather than wool. The garments tailored for him used only the most expensive materials dyed with the deepest colours, and were trimmed with gilt thread embroidery, tassels, furbelows, and furs. Even his matching codpieces would have been made of stuffed velvet and brocade. His buttons were made of gold or gilded silver, often with jewels set in them. There were so many diamonds, pearls, sapphires, emeralds, rubies, and semiprecious stones sewn onto his clothes that a French visitor to the English court would claim that rooms were filled with sparkling light whenever Edward entered them.[13] His hats and caps were likewise decorated with metallic embroidery and gems, as well as the feathery plumes of exotic birds. The icing on the sartorial cake, however, was the knife he usually wore on a rope of pearls around his waist. Called a ballock dagger (due to the bulging lobes on the hilt), the weapon was a symbol of the prince's manhood and ability to protect himself. The handle of the blade was made of gilded wood embedded with a large green stone, thought to have been a cabochon emerald, and the dagger's sheath was practically encrusted with precious and semiprecious stones.

The prince did not take his opulent surroundings and attire for granted. From an early age, he was taught to be grateful to the king for the munificence he received. He, therefore, wrote letters expressing his 'exceeding thanks' that Henry treated him 'so kindly, like a most loving father', by gifting him with 'great and costly gifts, as chains, rings, jewelled buttons, neck-chains, and breast-pins, and necklaces, garments, and many other things'.[14] The prince explained that he valued the gifts because they were evidence of the king's 'fatherly affection towards me; for, if you did not love me, you would not give me these fine gifts of jewelry'. He told the king that he understood that the gifts were to ensure that he 'might feel as great love towards you, as you have towards me'. As a child who had lived without regular visits from the king, he was clearly willing to accept the clink of coins as a proxy for parental care. Nonetheless, one cannot help but suspect that the prince would have given a great many of his jewels in exchange for a hug from an affectionate father.

In spite of the splendour surrounding him, there was at least one thing that the young boy would have viewed as a downside regarding his new household – there would be no more women to cuddle him. Lady Bryan and his adoring nurse, Sybil Penne, were given annuities and released from service, and the prince was put almost entirely into the hands of male attendants and instructors.

There were also some significant rearrangements of his household offices. William Sidney was reassigned to the role of steward, replacing the elderly John Cornwallis, and Sir Richard Page was appointed as Edward's new chamberlain. Page had served as vice-chamberlain in the household of the king's illegitimate son, Henry Fitzroy, and had been knighted for his services. He had also been one of the men accused of committing adultery with Queen Anne Boleyn in 1536. Luckily for Page, the king believed his claims of innocence and had welcomed him back to court the following year, reinstating him as a gentleman of the privy chamber. The prince was also given an almoner and principal tutor, Richard Cox, who was a lauded instructor at St John's College in Cambridge. Cox was a Protestant-leaning theologian who had backed the reformation since its earliest days, rising to serve the king as a personal chaplain. Moreover, he had supported the annulment of the king's marriage to Anne of Cleves, and had probably been given his plum position in the heir's establishment as a reward for his loyalty.

Edward's coterie of friends and fellow students likewise grew as his household expanded. Along with Charles Brandon's sons, Philip Sidney, and Barnaby Fitzpatrick, those believed to have been the prince's company were the sons of John Dudley, Viscount Lisle, and Henry Hastings, heir to the Earldom of Huntingdon. Lord FitzWarin, eldest son of the Earl of Bath, was another of those lucky enough to attend lessons with the king's heir, as was Lord Maltravers, the only son of the Earl of Arundel. Thomas Butler, the Earl of Ormond's heir, was sent from Ireland to live in the prince's household for the purpose of learning 'English manners', but also to prove that his father was loyal to the Tudor crown. Although Butler got along well enough with Edward, he would form a much closer friendship with the prince's sister, Lady Elizabeth, which turned out to be really handy once she came to the throne. Such was the honour of attending the prince that the Earl of Shrewsbury even arranged to put his eldest son, George Talbot, into Edward's household despite the fact that the boy was well into his late teens and probably had little in common with the other children. The Earl of Derby was 'one of the great peers whose wealth made them independent of court favour',[15] but even he was anxious to get his son, Henry Stanley, into the prince's company. Only a few men of a rank lower than an earl were able to contrive placing their sons as companions of the king's heir, but among them was the king's treasurer, William Paulet, and the king's secretary, William Paget. The prince would also later be joined by his younger maternal cousins, Edward and Henry Seymour, as soon as they were old enough to leave their own nursery.

Although the prince was to make some lifelong and dear friends from among the boys who lived with him, they were not always a good influence. According to one of the ambassadors from Cleves, the young heir to the throne was 'once induced to adopt the use of such thundering oaths as he was told were appropriate to his sovereign dignity', and when asked why he had suddenly started cursing like an injured mariner he had 'ingenuously confessed that one of his playfellows had given him instructions in the right-royal accomplishment'.[16] His tutors then gave the guilty friend a whipping in front of the prince, and pointed out to Edward that he deserved the same punishment. This seems to have taken care of the prince's naughtiness, while simultaneously putting a damper on the ill-conceived shenanigans of the other boys around their future sovereign.

There was also at least one girl among Edward's friends. When the prince's household was at Ashridge, a beautiful royal estate in Hertfordshire, William Sidney arranged for his granddaughter, Jane Dormer, to come for a visit. Jane, who was a very pretty girl and only a few months younger than the prince, became one of his favourite companions almost instantly. He let his attendants know that he 'desired her company, taking particular pleasure in her conversation', and she was frequently sent over to Ashridge to spend time with him 'either in reading, playing, or dancing, and such like pastimes, answerable to their spirits and innocency of years'.[17] The prince might have even had a childhood crush on Jane. She would later recount how during one of the card games he had teased her by telling her, 'your king is gone, I shall [have to] be good enough for you'.[18]

Now that he was out of the nursery, the prince was considered old enough to attend court events with the king, and therefore spent Christmas of 1543 with his father and sisters at Elsyng Palace. It was a very momentous December, but it is unclear how much Edward would have understood about the political turmoil around him. The king had just received the news that the Scottish Parliament had renounced the Treaty of Greenwich, less than six months after ratifying it, which gave Henry the excuse he needed to invade the country, starting the war that would later be known as the 'Rough Wooing'. Since the king was certain that 'there would be no fear of invasion from Scotland' into England during his lifetime,[19] he erroneously thought he had enough money, time, and forces for other conflicts as well. Nonsensically, he allied himself to his long-standing diplomatic antagonist, Emperor Charles V, against the French. Apparently, the king could forgive the emperor for years of rivalry more easily than he could forgive France for being so full of French people. Henry was also determined to go into battle himself, even though that would leave his government to deal with the realm's internal Catholic/Protestant friction without the head of state.

Happily for Edward, none of this mess was his problem yet. The six-year-old boy was undoubtedly much more interested in being with his family for the holidays, and seeing his new stepmother, Kateryn Parr, again than he was in matters of foreign diplomacy – or lack thereof.

Chapter Four

An Imp Worthy of Such a Father

After Henry had beheaded his fifth queen, Kathryn Howard, one of the court ladies is said to have wondered aloud, 'How many wives *will* he have?'[1] Well, the answer would turn out to be six. The king married Kateryn Parr 'without ceremony' in the Queen's Privy Chamber of Hampton Court on 12 July 1543. It was the king's sixth wedding, but his bride was no stranger to taking her vows either. Her marriage to Henry would be her third, with no children resulting from either of her prior unions. No one seems to have understood why, of all the women he could strongarm into marriage, he had picked a seemingly infertile widow. His choice of Kateryn Parr certainly seems to have been a mystery to the king's fourth wife, Anne of Cleves, whom he had divorced in 1540. The Imperial ambassador, Eustace Chapuys, reported that he had 'heard in a good quarter' that Anna had 'taken great grief and despair at the King's espousal of this last wife, who is not nearly so beautiful as she, besides that there is no hope of issue, seeing that she had none with her two former husbands'.[2] There was probably a good reason for the king's choice, nevertheless. It is suspected that the king had become impotent, and a wife who was assumed barren was the perfect patsy for the lack of additional heirs in the royal nursery. Regardless of the reasons Henry chose Kateryn for his last queen, it would turn out to be a good decision on his part, especially for his children.

Although the king's daughters were present at his final wedding and the small celebration breakfast afterwards, his nursery-aged son had still been considered too young to attend. The first time the prince met his new stepmother was most likely that autumn, shortly after his new household had been established at Ashridge Estate. The royal newlyweds had almost immediately gone on a summer progress/honeymoon to escape the contagions of London, and did not return to the city for several months. It was only at the end of the summer the king and queen had gone to spend a few months at Ampthill Castle, only nineteen miles from

Ashridge Estate, and it appears that the king and his new wife visited Prince Edward and his sister Elizabeth there.[3]

The prince would have surely been impressed by his new stepmother. Not only was Kateryn an attractive woman – lightly built with chestnut hair, dark grey eyes, and a lovely face – she was also charming and intelligent. She was good at the things ladies were supposed to be good at, like dancing and hunting, but had a better appreciation of art and more talent in music than most people. The queen was also extremely fashionable, using the high-quality clothing and jewels the king gave her to make herself an ornament in his court. Best of all, from the perspective of her stepchildren, she was exceedingly kind and devoted to promoting the emotional bonds between them and their father.

The gentle Kateryn Parr would become a very influential figure in the life of the prince. She had already helped talk her new husband into restoring his daughters to the line of succession, which would give the prince a new political reality regarding his bastardised sisters in the future. For the present, however, the most important thing about the queen was that she provided the prince with a new surrogate mother to take the place of his beloved nurse, Sybil Penne, now that he was in a male-dominated household. Her high rank and close familial relationship to him also meant that she could be a trusted confidant in a way few other adults could be.

It is unsurprising, then, that Edward soon became a frequent correspondent with the queen. His earliest known missive to the queen began by calling her his 'most honourable and entirely beloved mother', and thanked her for her 'most loving and tender letters, which do give me much comfort and encouragement'.[4] His letters would continue to refer to the queen in terms of endearments, giving her 'hearty thanks for [her] loving kindness' and assuring her that his numerous messages to her were to 'testify [of his] respect and affection'.[5] The prince's letters to Kateryn not only show that they had a warm relationship; they suggest that she was emotionally more of a parent to him than his own father. Edward's relationship with the king was always burdened by the need for respectful formality. He could never simply be Henry's *child*. However, the prince could just be a little boy with his stepmother. It was her praise and advice he sought, and to her that he turned to for comfort.

While Edward was adjusting to his expanded household and bonding with his new stepmother, his father was busy destroying his chances of ever exchanging wedding vows with Mary, Queen of Scots. In the early months of 1544, the king authorised more English raids into Scotland, where they 'daily' did 'great hurt' in order to impress upon the Scots that Henry would 'not be hindered from following the enterprise' of a marriage between his son and their monarch.[6] That spring, Henry sent his forces into Scotland under the command of the prince's uncle, Edward Seymour, Earl of Hertford. The king was hoping to bring his disagreement with the northern nation to a swift conclusion by kidnapping his desired future daughter-in-law from her cradle and bringing the tiny queen back to his court. Barring that, he was counting on scorched-earth campaign tactics to bully Scotland into giving in quickly. He told Hertford to sack the Scottish capital, and gave him orders not to come to terms with the city or show it mercy if it surrendered. In the first week of May, the English troops entered Edinburgh 'by fine force and there slew a great number of Scots'. Once within the city, Hertford decided the best way to follow out the king's orders was 'utterly to ruinate and destroy the said town with fire'. Hertford set Edinburgh ablaze, and the conflagration 'continued that day and two days after burning'. Having destroyed almost all of the capital, the English troops moved on to Leith, where they 'set fire to every house, and burnt it to the ground'. Hertford's forces then headed back to England 'through all the main country of Scotland, burning and destroying every pile, fortress and village that was in their walk'.[7]

The English who lived in the north were also encouraged to continue their incursions into Scotland. Some of the most successful of these raiders were William Eure and his sons, Ralph and Henry. For his assurance of aiding in the war against the Scots, William Eure was made 1st Baron Eure by letters patent and his eldest son was given the offices of Warden of the East, West and Middle Marches. After helping with the destruction of Edinburgh and Leith, Lord William and his son Ralph led an attack on Jedburgh, which was one of the principal towns of Scotland at the time. They reported that 'the town was assaulted and won' and 'was all burnt', as was Jedburgh Abbey, but lamented that the 'Scots had fled out carrying the goods of the town and abbey with them', leaving insufficient spoils for the English raiders.[8] After burning the town and abbey, Baron Eure and his men turned back toward England, 'thinking to burn villages on the way' as Hertford had done. However, the Eures were forced to deal with a Scottish retaliatory raid into Northumberland, which 'spoilt so many horses' that there could be no further assaults on Scotland 'for a month or six weeks'. Nevertheless, before the summer was over the Eures were able to attack and burn 'the tower of Callyncrag, the castle of Sesforth, Otterburn, Cowboge, Marbottel church and many other like', including Coldingham and 'a place called Synlawes, where divers bastel houses (fortified farmhouses) were destroyed'.[9]

The attacks on Scotland would accomplish very little in terms of Henry's ultimate goals. Not only did Queen Mary remain safe at Stirling Castle, but the prevailing Scots attitude also became one of firm resolution against a martial alliance with England. Many of the Scots seem to have decided that they would rather have their wee monarch wed Satan himself than an English prince, and were willing to fight to the last man to prevent an Anglo-Scottish match.

Nevertheless, Henry seemed convinced that the Scottish war was going well, so he continued his plans to go fight in France. It wasn't just that the king was still craving the glory on the battlefield that had eluded him in his youth. He appears to have had a particular axe to grind regarding the French king, Francis I, ever since the rival monarch had beaten him at wrestling during their meeting at the Field of the Cloth of Gold in the summer of 1520. Although Henry was busy with war planning, his new queen reminded him that perhaps he should see his children again before he left the country for an indefinite period. Thus, Edward and his sisters were all summoned by their father to Whitehall in July 1544 for a farewell dinner with the king he sailed away to France. This would be the last Edward would see of Henry for several months, but the young prince would nevertheless get to experience more parental attention during the king's absence than he had ever received before, thanks to the efforts of Queen Kateryn.

Henry had left his queen in charge of the country, but although she was up to her eyebrows in work as regent she still found time for her stepchildren. She invited them to join her at Hampton Court in August, much to their happiness.[10] Edward's household installed themselves in the Prince's Lodgings, which encompassed the entire north side of Chapel Court and his former nursery area. His apartments were conveniently connected to the royal apartments by a long gallery, making it easy for him to see the queen whenever she had the time. Lady Mary, who had come to Hampton Court via the royal barge with her stepmother, had apartments that were less grand than her brother's to match her still-bastardised status. Lady Elizabeth was the last of Henry's children to arrive and was given relatively small accommodations compared to her siblings, but it should be noted that the queen was being exceptionally kind simply to include the king's youngest daughter in the family gathering. There was no political benefit, and even some increase in political vulnerability, to be had by the queen's graciousness to the unwanted child of the disgraced Anne Boleyn. It was this type of benevolence on Kateryn's part that inspired Edward to refer to her as a 'noble queen and most illustrious mother'.[11] Edward and his sisters would remain in the queen's company until the autumn, following along with her tour through the woodlands of Surrey as the court avoided the contagious environs of summertime London.

The queen also brought the king's children with her to Leeds Castle in Kent to welcome Henry home from France on 3 October. The king sent his son and daughters away again to their own residences rather quickly, however. Although he should have been riding high on the wave of his temporary triumph in the defeat and capture of the French city of Boulogne, the wind had been knocked out of the king's sails when the emperor had made peace with France without Henry's consent or knowledge. Between the erosion of his gains in France, the Scottish retaliatory incursions along the border, continuing plagues, and inflation of food prices in England, the king was too busy to have any time to devote to his offspring. He was even too distracted to invest Edward as the Prince of Wales, or induct him into the Order of the Garter. Henry didn't even seem to want letters from his children. He was satisfied to know they were writing to the queen, and that she would update him if there was an emergency. He also failed to summon his children to him that Christmas. They had to send their gifts to their father and the queen that year from their isolated households.

Suddenly deprived of his sisters and the parental affections of his stepmother, it is no wonder that the seven-year-old prince now went through a truculent phase with his tutor. Notwithstanding his obvious intelligence, the prince became difficult to teach. His attitude appears to have been that he would learn what he wanted, when he wanted, and his main tutor, Richard Cox, would just have to lump it. The prince also appears to have been sure that his tutor would not dare punish him for his misconduct. What he didn't realise yet was that Cox took his duties very seriously, and considered Edward more as his student than as the heir to the throne. Cox was eventually provoked into using his morris pike (the thick rod used in morris dancing) to wallop the prince so hard that the boy 'wist not what to do'. This crude method of discipline seems to have worked, since afterwards, Edward began to apply himself to his studies in good earnest.[12] Soon Cox was able to report that the prince had become 'a vessel most apt to receive all goodness and learning, whitty, sharp, and pleasant'.[13] The fair-minded prince appears to have borne no ill-will toward Cox for punishing him so harshly, later referring to his teacher 'my dearest almoner' and 'my most loving and kind preceptor'.[14]

As Prince Edward got closer to being able to read Cato's *Moral Precepts* in the original Latin, he was getting farther away from a union with Scotland. Sir Ralph Eure had continued to lead raids into Scotland, and as is the nature of such things, his men had participated in a multitude of atrocities. One of the most famous of these horrors is the occasion when he, assisted by Sir Brian Layton, attacked Brumehous Tower in January 1545. Appallingly, the English burned the Tower down with an elderly lady, her servants, and several small children trapped inside.[15] This disgusting barbarity had the quite foreseeable side effect of getting the Earl of Arran, Mary of Guise, and Archibald Douglas, 6th Earl of Angus, to put aside their political differences and team up against the English invaders. In late February, troops led by Eure and Layton were coming back from yet another raid into Scotland when they saw what they assumed was a small Scottish force on top of Peniel Heugh hill on Ancrum moor and charged at the meagre band of resistors. At this point, the rest of the Scots fighters came boiling up from where they lay in wait on the opposite side of the hill and hit the English forces like a ton of bricks. The seven hundred or so Scots who were 'assured men' fighting for Henry VIII also took this opportunity to turn against the English. The Battle of Ancrum Moor was a decisive victory for Scotland, with eighteen hundred Englishmen killed or taken prisoner. Furthermore, both Ralph Eure and Brian Layton died in action, depriving England of two skilled military commanders. This Scottish triumph prevented any further major incursions by the English for almost two years, giving the border a badly needed respite from the Rough Wooing.

Not only was it not looking good for Prince Edward's putative marriage to the Queen of Scots, odds were rapidly shrinking that he would one day inherit larger tracts of land in France. The dukes of Suffolk and Norfolk had abandoned Boulogne, leaving it vulnerable to recapture by the French, which angered the king to no end. Henry did not just fear that France would take back Boulogne, either. He also feared that they would invade England itself in retaliation for the assault on their country. Accordingly, the king began fortifying the bejeezus out of the southern coast.

Unlike most of Henry's other ideas in the last years of his reign, this one would actually turn out to have some merit. Two of the new fortifications the king ordered to be built were Southsea and Sandown castles. Southsea Castle was erected on the southern end of Portsea Island, a small bit of land that faces into the Solent, a strait between England and the Isle of Wight. Portsea is very near the naval shipyard at Portsmouth, and Southsea Castle was built with the idea of defending the docks from a French assault. Sandown Castle was built on the southeast coast of the Isle of Wight, on the opposite side of the island from the Solent. Its position was more suited to fend off French attacks before they could reach the straight, or to defend the island in case of a land invasion. Both of these castles, although still only half-finished, proved to be useful in the summer of 1545, when the French did indeed come sailing into the Solent with pummelling and plunder on their mind.

This was no paltry little foray into English waters by the French. More than two hundred ships transporting thirty thousand French fighters were led by Admiral Claude d'Annebault into the straight, where they were greeted with rather ineffectual long-range cannon fire from the English ships and the two great guns at Southsea Castle on 18 July. That night, the king brazenly dined on the flagship *Great Harry* as it was docked at Portsmouth harbour, seemingly convinced the French would not dare attack at night or fire at the ship with a king aboard. The next day 'the whole navy of the Englishmen made out, and purposed to set on the Frenchmen'[16] in what would be called the Battle of the Solent. In spite of a French advantage in numbers, Admiral John Dudley was able to use his superior knowledge of the tides in the strait to win the day. Henry watched the entire engagement from the uncompleted battlements of

Southsea Castle, and would have been very pleased with the result of the battle if it hadn't cost him one of his best carracks, the *Mary Rose*.

The loss of the *Mary Rose* doesn't appear to have been the result of enemy fire. Instead, the ship was by 'much folly drowned ... for she was laden with [too] much ordinance, and the ports left open, which were very low ... so that when the ship should turn the water entered, and suddenly she sank'.[17] Although the sinking of the carrack was a great loss for the Tudor navy, it would turn out to be a great boon to maritime archaeology. The *Mary Rose* settled on the bottom of the Solent in such a way as to deposit silt and a firmer layer of clay over it, which kept it relatively stable and preserved nearly half the structure. In the late 1970s, marine archaeologists began excavating and raising the ship, eventually recovering more than twenty thousand artefacts and the remains of more than a hundred crew members. Henry VIII may have lost the equivalent of millions of pounds when his carrack sank, but the historical information gleaned from the *Mary Rose* has been priceless.

The French didn't retreat far after their marginal defeat on the 19th. They merely sailed around to the other side of the Isle of Wight. After taking a day or so to recuperate, they invaded the island, hoping to use it as a base for further assaults on mainland England. The French landing forces, which numbered around two thousand men, split into multiple groups as part of their incursion strategy. Some of the troops came ashore at Whitecliff Bay to attack the unfinished Sandown Castle and the houses around it, some beached near the hamlets of Benbriged and St. Helens, and the largest part landed at Monk's Bay to go after the village of Bonchurch. The French were planning to march inland and regroup after pacifying the locals, but the locals in question refused to be pacified. The islanders had formed several militias armed with pikes and Welsh longbows, and were ready to defend themselves. Moreover, they had probably been reinforced by soldiers arriving from the mainland earlier. Notwithstanding that the invaders were able to burn down at least one village and cause a ghastly amount of casualties, the French 'were to their great loss and pain, driven again to their galleys' by the English defenders.[18]

After his defeat on the island, Admiral d'Annebault gathered his remaining fighters and led his fleet away from the Hampshire coast. He tried to assault England one more time, landing a force of more than a thousand men in East Sussex and attacking the town of Seaford. Again, the locals and their Welsh longbows fought the invaders off. The admiral finally limped away back to France, having gained almost nothing and lost much.

King Henry VIII had managed to oversee a defeat of the French on English soil and was holding onto the captured city of Boulogne, but his deteriorating health wasn't letting him enjoy these victories. The ulcers in the king's legs were inflamed and putrid once more, and his general state of unfitness was such that the Bishop of Winchester, Stephen Gardiner, confided to friends that he feared that Henry might die before Prince Edward 'may come to man's estate', circumstances that would be 'more ruin to our realm than any war could engender'.[19] Considering that it was treason to even 'envisage' the king's death, let alone speak of it, Gardiner must have been frightened indeed to risk addressing it. By that yuletide, the imperial ambassador claimed that the king was 'so unwell that, considering his age and corpulence, fears are entertained that he will be unable to survive further attacks such as he recently suffered'.[20] Furthermore, the king's ill health meant that he didn't want to spend Christmas with his children, not even his prized son. He had even sent the queen away to Greenwich, in spite of it being unheard of 'for them to be thus separated during the festivities'.[21]

Henry decided he missed Kateryn by early January 1546 and sent for her to join him, but it really wasn't doing her any favours. The king, 'by reason of his sore leg, the anguish whereof began more and more to increase' had become difficult to be pleased.[22] Not even his gentle-natured wife could keep his temper sweet. By late February 1546, the court was hearing rumours that Henry might be in the market for a new queen.

This was music to the ears of the court's conservative pro-Catholic faction. Kateryn's Reformist sympathies were becoming obvious, and she had been seen 'oftimes wishing, exhorting, and persuading the King, that as he had, to the glory of God, and his eternal fame, begun a good and godly work in banishing that monstrous idol of Rome, so he would thoroughly perfect and finish the same, cleansing and purging his church of England clean from the dregs thereof.'[23] One of the staunchest of the pro-Catholics in Henry's court was Stephen Gardiner, who hated Protestantism in part because it gave 'women courage and liberty to talk at their pleasure' about religious matters.[24] In March, when Henry complained to him about Kateryn outsmarting him in a debate, the wily Bishop of Winchester leapt at the chance to bring down the queen. With a suitable application of flattery, Gardiner was able to persuade Henry that he should have the queen arrested and questioned about her potential heresies.

Knowing how easily the king could change his mind, the Bishop quickly made plans with Henry's chancellor, Thomas Wriothesley, to arrest Kateryn and send her to the Tower. Gardiner, however, was unable to hide his plans from the Reformists and the queen's friends at court. In some way, possibly by a royal physician named Dr Thomas Wendy, Kateryn was warned of the plot against her.[25] She wisely reacted to the news with hysterics so loud they were audible even in the king's apartments. Hearing her cries, Henry sent Dr Wendy to check on her. The physician solemnly reported back to Henry that Kateryn was nearly at death's door from distress. Astounded, the king came to her rooms to find out what had her in such tizzy. She told him that her unbearable grief stemmed from her fears she had made him unhappy lately. Her contrition pleased Henry enough to give her a few encouraging words before heading back to his own chambers.

Thinking quickly, Kateryn grabbed some of her ladies-in-waiting and immediately sought an audience with her husband. The king was still in a snit, and asked her opinion on a religious topic to see if she would dare disagree with him again. The queen shrewdly begged him not to ask her about such things, since she was 'a poor silly woman, so much inferior in all respects of nature', and based all her opinions of Henry's wisdom as the 'Supreme Head and Governor here on earth, next under God'.[26] Sulkily, the king responded, 'Not so, by St. Mary, you are become a doctor, Kate, to instruct us, as we take it, and not to be instructed or directed by us'.[27] The queen humbly assured Henry that she argued with him in order to take his mind off his painful legs, and as a way of gaining more enlightenment from him. The king was satisfied with this response, and promised her that they were 'perfect friends' again.[28] Henry had forgiven Kateryn for her intelligence, and her head remained safely attached to her neck.

The brush with imprisonment would have made her more cautious in her suggestions, but the queen was nonetheless able to influence Henry about his son's education. The king, a lifelong scholar, had already determined that his son would be taught by the finest minds and Humanist intellectuals available, but it was Kateryn who facilitated the appointments of Protestant-leaning academics as the boy's teachers. When Richard Cox decided to return to Oxford in the spring of 1546, it was decided that while Cox would remain the official administrator of the prince's education Edward would need a new primary tutor to be with him in situ. Undoubtedly with the queen's encouragement, Henry chose John Cheke to head Edward's schoolroom. Cheke was the foremost Greek master in England, but he was also dangerously reformist in the opinion of the leaders of the powerful Catholics in Henry's court. Luckily for Cheke, he was also the friend and former student of the queen's almoner, George Day. It was almost certainly the queen's influence that convinced Henry to choose Cheke instead of a more conservative pedagogue to teach his son. The queen also worked behind the scenes to round out the prince's teaching staff with other Humanist reformers connected to Cheke, such as Sir Anthony Cooke and Roger Ascham. The lessons Edward received from his instructors would shape his worldview tremendously, and would make Catholic reunification anathema to him as a young king.

It must be said that Edward's education, on the whole, was excellent. He was taught what were considered the fundamentals of an educated gentleman at the time – Latin and Greek, rhetoric, Christian theology, and the works of classical authors – as well as mathematics, astronomy, history, geography, and music. An inventory of the royal palaces show that the prince's schoolroom would have been well-supplied with paper, quills, pen-knives, scales and weights, compasses, metal rulers, and astronomical instruments.[29] The prince also had several school books, which had enamelled gold covers set with gemstones and jewelled clasps to make them fit for royal use, and among them were Robert Recorde's *First Principles in Geometrie*, Juan Vives' philosophical work *Satellitium Animi* (The Soul's Escort), and *The Histories* by Herodotus.[30] There were also slate tables where Edward would have learned his ABCs from his writing master, Roger Ascham, followed by the more advanced techniques of calligraphy. His equipment additionally included his own writing desk, covered by black velvet embroidered 'E's to indicate the importance of the one using it, which he would have most likely used to compose his important correspondence. The prince had a personalised astronomical quadrant as well, designed by John Cheke and engraved by Thomas Geminus.[31] His teachers would have also made use of the large globe in the royal library for geography lessons, and to show the prince the countries with whom he would have to negotiate as king. Then the plethora of books about warfare and the model siege engines would have been used to teach him how to deal with those countries when negotiations broke down.

Additional staff were brought in for Edward in specialist subjects. John Leland, a famous 'antiquarius' who travelled throughout England and Wales to save the libraries of dissolved monasteries, was invited to visit the prince and tell him personally about the things the intrepid cataloguer had seen in his journeys across the kingdom. John Belmaine, a religious refugee married to Cheke's niece, was hired to instruct Edward in French, and it wasn't long before the clever prince could write his sister Elizabeth a letter in that language. Other, unnamed teachers must have been tasked to give him lessons in Spanish and Italian, since he would be able to converse with native speakers from Spain and Italy as a teen. Christopher Tye, the choral master of Ely Cathedral and a very famous composer in his day, appears to have taught the prince the basics of music theory and how to play the organ. Undoubtedly the learned men in the prince's household, such as his chaplain, Roger Tonge, also supplemented Edward's understanding of theology and the Henrician Reformation occurring around him.

One of the prince's most impressive visiting instructors was Philip van Wilder, who taught him how to play the lute. Van Wilder was a Franco-Flemish musician so highly regarded that he had been made a member of Henry VIII's privy chamber, and was considered the king's favourite performer. Edward was very aware of what an honour his father, who was considered a master lutenist in his own right, was bestowing on him. The prince wrote the king a letter to thank him for having 'deigned to send to me Philip your servant … that I may be more expert in striking the lute; herein your love appeareth to be very great'. However, the prince's thanks are followed by a rather heartbreaking wish that he be allowed to actually visit his much-absent father again, revealing that all the perks in Christendom are not actually substitutes for parental attention.

Edward proved to be an apt pupil in every subject, feeling that as the king's son it was his responsibility to study harder than any of the other boys in his household. In a letter he wrote to Cox in April of 1546, he claimed there was no need to praise him for his diligent studies because 'I have only done my duty'.[32] The prince moreover claimed that if he 'should be sluggish in my efforts' at learning, then even the 'ants should be better than I; for ants do toil'.[33] It is no wonder then that Cox should describe Edward as having 'such towardness in learning, godliness, gentleness, and all honest qualities' that 'all this realm out to think him and take him for a singular gift sent of God' and 'an imp worthy of such a father' who would 'content his father's expectations hereafter'.[34] The prince became such an able scholar that his godfather, Archbishop Cranmer, on 'beholding his towardness, his readiness in both tongues, in translating from Greek to Latin … would weep for joy' and declared that he would have never believed a boy so young could do so well 'except that he had seen it himself'.[35]

The prince was certainly an increasingly serious-minded child, prone to quoting Cicero and the Bible in his letters, but he wasn't always hunched over his studies. He was 'merry' and in good health and delighted in recreation, as well as education.[36] He had been taught various card games from an early age, and appears to have been good at them. He owned his own chess set, which he kept in an ebony box, so that he could play with his schoolmates whenever he chose. He had started riding almost as soon as he could walk, and was now being taught how to hunt with the other boys, in spite of the risks inherent in such a rough sport. He also seems to have liked falconry a great deal, since hawk's head caps and bells and hawking gloves were counted among his personal effects. The young prince almost certainly enjoyed the same pastimes as other boys in his social sphere, such as bowling, dancing, dice games, fencing, tennis, archery, and coursing for hares with greyhounds. Considering that he had had his own group of minstrels since infancy, it should be no surprise that he also relished music. His groom of the robes, Thomas Sternhold, noted that the prince 'doth delight in the holy songs' and would often 'command them to be sung'.[37] The prince wasn't satisfied to just learn to play the lute and the organ, but also used his own pocket-money to pay Sir John Ashley to give him lessons on the virginal too. Like his father, Edward would become a connoisseur of choral music, and would support schools of music that would have otherwise floundered when the Catholic Church lost most of its English holdings.

Chapter Five

Manoeuvring to Manipulate a Future King

Although the king did not summon his son to see him for months at a time, Henry was often on the prince's mind. At the beginning of June, Edward wrote to his 'most illustrious and noble father' to beg Henry's pardon both for the lack of frequent letters and the fact he dared to send any letter at all 'considering that your majesty is disturbed by the concerns of war'.[1] The prince confessed that he had 'some scruple' about disturbing his father, but 'reflecting that, as any labourer after his daily toil desires to refresh his spirit, so I hope ... that this letter will rather refresh than disturb your mind'. The letter was full of compliments to the king, but had no information about Edward himself. Perhaps the prince did not deem his activities or feelings to be worthy of describing to a monarch, even if that monarch was his father? The prince concluded the letter by asking for the king's blessings, and wishing Henry 'a happy issue to all your affairs', but there is clearly no expectation of either seeing his father or receiving a letter in return. Nonetheless, only a week later Edward wrote to Henry again, expressing his hopes to visit the king 'for I am anxious to be assured that you are safe and well'.[2]

The little boy's pleas to see his father were finally answered that August, but it was for the sake of royal showmanship rather than royal affection.

The French and English had agreed to peace in the Treaty of Ardres in June 1546, which basically pledged that each side would stop killing each other if France paid Henry two million crowns to give them Boulogne back. The king also guaranteed that he would stop his attacks on Scotland 'against whom England shall not move war without new occasion',[3] but it would turn out that Henry had his fingers crossed behind his back when he made that promise. In fact, Henry would turn out to have his fingers crossed about a lot of the treaty, but for the present peace was at hand. As part of the treaty, there was to be a return visit of French dignitaries to England in August to confirm the accords. This delegation was to be headed by the Lord High Admiral of France, Claude d'Annebaut, whom the English had recently tried to kill on the Solent, and would include the Bishop of Evreux, the earls of Nauteuile and Villiers, several lords, and at least two hundred other French gentlemen. Since the king couldn't get up the stairs anymore without a 'device' and footmen to help him, and had to be transported in a litter when travelling, he obviously couldn't be the one riding out to greet the diplomats when they arrived. A weak and sickly king was hardly a show of royal might. Ergo, it was decided that Prince Edward would be the representative of the crown to welcome the Frenchmen and escort them to the king at Hampton Court.

Being only eight years old, the prince was understabably nervous about this. What if he failed to impress them, and thus failed to be a worthy son of the king? Worse, he hadn't been taking French lessons all that long, and he wasn't sure how he'd be able to communicate in a proper manner. Edward was by this time fluent in Latin, and hoped to speak to the admiral in that language rather than French. Anxiously, he wrote to his stepmother to 'entreat your highness to let me know, whether the Lord High Admiral, who is coming from France, understands Latin well'.[4] Even if the admiral did speak Latin, the prince still wanted 'to learn further what I may say to him when I shall come to meet him' so that he could compose and practice a speech of welcome. This was his first official function, and he was determined to get it right.

Edward was wise to want to be able to impress the French. Not only would he be dealing with them when he was king himself, but their reports of him would be shared in almost every court in Europe. Moreover, he needed to be gracious enough to smooth over some of the shenanigans his father was pulling before the delegation even arrived in England. The king had not ceased fortifying Boulogne, as he had promised to do in the treaty, and it was vexing France. When the French crown called him out on it and demanded he destroy the fortifications, the king refused to do so, and 'replied that the fortifications will be for the benefit of the French as they will remain when the place is restored to them'.[5] Needless to say, King Francis I was a little sceptical that Henry was just trying to do him a favour. In retaliation, the French continued working on their own fortifications in Outreau, which in turn vexed England.[6] The peace was wobbly before both parties had even signed.

The French representatives sailed up the Thames in 'twelve fair galleys, well trimmed and decked',[7] and docked at the Tower Wharf in

London on 20 August, where they were brought with great ceremony to their lodgings at Fulham Palace. There they rested until the 22nd, then rode to meet Prince Edward at Hounslow \heath, where the prince, along with his uncle, the Earl of Hertford, the Archbishop of York, the Earl of Huntingdon, and 'diverse lords and gentleman in velvet coats on horseback, and also a thousand horse of yeoman all in new liveries'[8] were waiting for them. The prince, seated on a palfrey and wearing a crimson doublet liberally dotted with the extra jewels his father had recently sent him, welcomed Admiral d'Annebaut with a short speech 'and embraced him, in such a [humble] and honourable manner, that all the beholders greatly rejoiced and much marvelled at [Edward's] wit and audacity'.[9] The prince then led the French delegation to Hampton Court, where the chancellor and all the king's privy council welcomed them again.

The admiral and his fellow dignitaries were 'very richly banqueted'[10] and entertained by Henry and his nobles. The queen, as well as the king's former wife Anne of Cleves, were among those who helped the king to entertain the French with 'hunting, and rich masques every night ... with dancing in two new banqueting houses'.[11] The banqueting houses had been dressed to match the rest of Hampton Court, and so were the 'richly hanged' with tapestries on their temporary walls. Inside the banqueting halls were cupboards of gold plate 'set with rich stones and pearls, which shone' in the light of the gilt and silver candelabras. Even the torchbearers were adorned in cloth of gold in order to demonstrate the king's wealth to the French.[12]

This splendour also showcased the king's greatest treasure – his healthy son. The little boy danced and conversed and played the lute for the Frenchmen, parading his accomplishments, which were seen as a credit to his father's acumen as both monarch and parent. Edward's behaviour and charm had a very favourable effect on the French attendees. One of them would later tell the English ambassador to Flanders that he had been very pleased to meet the prince, 'whose praises he cannot speak of enough'.[13]

When the French left Hampton Court, the prince was dismissed from the king's presence as well. It was the last time he would ever see his father.

Edward and his household moved to Hatfield, where they were lodged in the old palace of the Bishops of Ely. From there, the prince wrote to the king to thank him for the 'very great kindness' shown to him when they were together at Hampton. Although the prince declared that while he could never 'do justice to and express the greatness of [Henry's] kindness', he would continue to 'strive and do what lies in me, to please your majesty'.[14] The prince also wrote to his sister Mary, who had remained with the queen. His eldest sibling had continued to send her little brother tokens of her love through the medium of gifts and letters, for which he gave her 'thanks from [his] heart', and promised that her 'inexpressible love' for him was 'very evident'.[15] He didn't have to write letters to his sister Elizabeth, because he saw her much more often than any other member of his family. Elizabeth's household was also in Hertfordshire, and they shared their tutors Ascham and Belmain in common.

Unbeknownst to Edward, his father was gravely ill. Courtiers were circling the dying king like vultures, hoping to pick estates and titles from his bones. The greatest prize of all would be to become the regent for the prince, through whom a man could gain almost monarchical control of England. The king had hoped to outsmart his greedy nobles by naming a large regency council for the prince, preventing anyone lord from gaining ascendancy. However, it had soon become clear that the court was choosing sides in anticipation of a power struggle between two main factions – the Seymours and the Howards.

The smart money was on the Seymours. Not only did their sister's memory still tug on the king's heartstrings, but the Earl of Hertford and Thomas Seymour had taken care to dote on the prince in an avuncular manner and win his affections. Hertford, in particular, had made sure to see his nephew often, as well as sending him regular letters and presents. Shortly before Henry's death, the prince had written Hertford to assure him that he was sure of his uncle's 'good-will' and 'that love of yours, which you have always borne me'.[16] Furthermore, Henry favoured them because he felt he could trust them, even if it was only trusting them to act in their own self-interest. Hertford and Thomas Seymour would have to take good care of the king's son, because they were virtually nobodies without their nephew.

In contrast, the Howards' genealogy made them a threat to Prince Edward. Not only was the Duke of Norfolk wealthy and in command of a private army, his son, the Earl of Surrey, was a direct male descendant of King Edward III through his maternal grandfather, the 3rd Duke of

Buckingham. Arguably, Surrey had more right to sit on the throne than any Tudor, including Henry VIII and his heir. Moreover, it was obvious that Surrey knew it. The earl had supposedly told a friend that it would be 'meetest' for the Howards to administer a regency government for the prince because the Seymours were just men of 'vile birth' who had been just lately 'made' by the king's favours.[17] This attitude infuriated the Seymours even more because the accusations were true. The Seymours' mother was related to the Plantagenets, but their father was merely a knight with a feudal barony, and while they had one brother-in-law who was king, they had another brother-in-law who was a blacksmith.[18] There was no admiration for social climbing in the Tudor era; your degree of distinction at birth was God's will and an attempt to rise higher usually got sneers rather than applause.

Unlike Surrey, the Seymours' parvenu status didn't blind Norfolk to their growing prominence. An opportunist to the core, the duke would hitch the Howard star to any wagon he could. He therefore brokered a marriage deal with the Seymours, and when the articles were hashed out he petitioned the crown to allow the weddings to take place.[19] The duke had offered his daughter, Mary Howard, Duchess of Richmond, as a wife for Thomas Seymour. Norfolk also proposed unions between some of Surrey's sons and Hertford's elder daughters. The Howards would be 'marrying down', but it would secure them an alliance with the future king's uncles. Surrey, however, blew a gasket when he found out what his father had planned.[20] In his mind, the advantages of the match could never make up for the degradation of a Howard marrying a son or granddaughter of a lowly rural sheriff.

As the king's health worsened, it became increasingly urgent for the Seymours to do something about the Howards if they were going to have a smooth takeover of the regency council. Since they couldn't intermarry their way into a truce, it seems as if Hertford and his brother decided to destroy their rivals for power. There is no way to be certain, but the circumstantial evidence that the Seymours arranged the judicial murder of the Earl of Surrey is compelling.

Sometime between Prince Edward's ninth birthday in October and the first day of December, the Seymours and the Protestant councillors moved against the Howards and the Catholic faction. They were aided by former Howard allies Chancellor Wriothesley and Richard Southwell, who had defected to the Seymour side when they saw that the king was favouring them. A statement was procured from a herald named Christopher Barker stating that Surrey had purposely used the insignia of Saint Edward the Confessor on his coat of arms.[21] This could be seen as tantamount to treason, inasmuch as it proclaimed that Surrey had a connection to the throne at least as strong as the king's. There is strong historical evidence, however, that Surrey was never expressly forbidden to bear Edward the Confessor's designs in his arms, and was therefore innocent of wilfully challenging the king.[22] For example, the king's own secretary, William Paget, had known of the earl having St Edward on his coat of arms, and although he told Surrey that he 'liked not the doing thereof' he did not forbid it or warn that it might be treasonous.[23] Moreover, the earl's accuser, Christopher Barker, was promoted to a Knight of the Bath as soon as the Seymours came to power after the king's death, and several other witnesses against Surrey who were likewise rewarded in a similar manner.[24]

On 2 December, armed with Barker's statement, Southwell informed the Privy Council that he had concerns about Surrey 'that touched his fidelity to the king'.[25] The earl was arrested and taken to the chancellor's house for interrogation. Meanwhile, the Howard family seat, Kenninghall, was searched for evidence against the duke and his son. Presumed evidence of treason was not hard to find. The walls of Kenninghall had recently been painted with heraldic badges featuring a broken pedestal with the letters H and R on either side of it. According to Surrey's accusers, the letters could only stand for Henricus Rex, and the heraldry was communicating a Howard plan to do away with Prince Edward and put their own family on the throne. Surrey protested this, of course. He insisted that the HR stood for Hereditas Restat (the inheritance remains), and that the broken pillar was an emblem of how the Howards had bowed before the Tudors. The Seymours and their allies scoffed at the earl's defence. They insisted the heraldic badges were, like the representations of King Edward the Confessor in Surrey's coat of arms, indubitably evidence of seditious plots.

On 12 December both Surrey and his father 'were sent to the Tower of London prisoners, the duke going by water, but the Earl of Surrey was led openly … through London' by the captain of the guard.[26] This was a bold move, since the earl's poetry had made him a very popular figure abroad and his arrest would spur international interest. A French ambassador,

Odet de Selve, wrote that there were two principal charges against the earl. The first was that 'he had the means of attempting [to capture] the castle of Hardelot, when he was at Boulogne, and neglected it',[27] and the other was that he was at least planning to seize power when the king died, even if he didn't plan on killing the prince. Many, de Selve concluded, 'hold that Surrey will suffer death'. The imperial ambassador, Francois van der Delft, was also quick to inform the Emperor of the scandal. According to van der Delft, Wriosthley himself sent a message 'saying that the cause of [the Howards] arrest was that they had planned by sinister means to obtain the government of the King, who was too old now to allow himself to be governed. Their intention was to usurp authority by means of the murder of all the members of the Council, and the control of the prince by them alone.'[28] The former imperial ambassador, Eustace Chapuys, had a more cynical take on things, pointing out that in regards to Protestantism in England 'there exists no counteracting influence amongst the secular nobility, except the Duke of Norfolk, who is against them and enjoys great power amongst the people of the north; this being, in my opinion the reason for his detention and that of his son, who also is considered a man of great courage.'[29]

Norfolk immediately sent a cringing, fawning letter to the king protesting his innocence and utter bewilderment as to why his enemies should be speaking such calumny against him. His son also sent a letter to the Privy Council, but even in his 'durance' it lacked the obsequious tone of his father's. Surrey lamented the fact his elderly father had been imprisoned, when he was clearly the real target. He also reminded them that he had just dealt with a false accusation of treason four years ago when Wriothesly, the Earl of Hertford, Bishop Gardiner, and Sir Anthony Brown 'had the examination of matters touching allegiance then laid to my charge, wherein God knoweth with what danger I escaped notwithstanding mine innocency'.[30] Now, it was strongly implied, they were obviously trying once more to destroy him with their lies. The only thing he had done wrong was 'to have conceived no small jealousy in your favour' from the king, and he was willing to apologise for that. He also demanded that his formal examination take place before the king, and if 'this request seem too bold, I trust his Majesty shall be content when I am heard'. However, the council, fearful that Surrey would talk his way out of trouble if he spoke to the king, made sure to give Henry the written testimony against the earl well ahead of the trial to convince him of Surrey's guilt in advance.

Anyone with a grudge against the Howards, or who wanted to curry favour with the Seymours, was eager to testify against Norfolk and Surrey. Jehan Torr accused them of colluding with the French, but most of the testimony was about Surrey's dislike of the 'new men' around the king, rather than any treason against the crown. Sir Edmund Knyvet reported that the earl had complained that the 'new erected men would by their wills leave no noble man on life'. Sir Gawen Carew said that Surrey had told him 'those men which are made by the King's Majesty of vile birth hath been the distraction (*sic*) of all the nobility of this realm', and if 'God should call the King's Majesty unto His mercy ... he thought no man so meet to have the governance of the Prince as my lord his father'.[31] Other testimony was pure hearsay. Edward Rogers had heard that the earl thought Norfolk should be regent, and had been told the earl had advised his sister, Mary Howard, the widow of the king's illegitimate son Henry Fitzroy, to sleep with the king in order to influence him in favour of her family. Gawen Carew also claimed that Mary Howard had told him the same thing, and she told her brother that she would 'cut her own throat [rather] than consent to such a villainy' as allowing her dead husband's father to bed her.[32] The worst deposition by far against Surrey was that of his sister, Mary Howard. Perhaps not realising that her brother would actually be executed for it, regardless of his high rank, she confirmed that the earl had indeed advised her to become the king's mistress.

The king was so caught up in the accusations against the Howards, and so miserable in his body, that for the second year in a row he didn't summon Prince Edward to his court for the Christmas festivities. Henry did remember to send his son a gift for New Year's Day, however, and in the little boy's carefully penned thank you note to his father there is no hint that the prince knew anything about the turmoil his potential regency was causing. Nor is there any sign that anyone had bothered to tell Edward that a regency was probably inevitable. Separated from the king and queen at his household in Hertfordshire, the prince had no idea that his father was at death's door.

Despite the fact that he was very close to shuffling off his mortal coil, King Henry VIII was nonetheless determined to make sure his son's future was as secure as possible. He had carefully gone through the accusations against Norfolk and Surrey, and appears to have been most angry about their theoretical plans for Edward's regency. Henry had already drawn up a document declaring that his son would have a council of sixteen men to help him, rather than being controlled by a singular regent. A regent, especially one with royal blood, such as the Earl of Surrey, might not be content simply with ruling as a de facto king during the prince's minority. A strong and popular regent might usurp Edward's throne with the help of a discrete poison. The king was also highly vexed that Surrey thought to control him via a mistress. By the evidence of his own handwriting, Henry thought that a man 'compassing with himself to govern the realm' by controlling a minor king, and a man who would 'advise his daughter or sister to become [the king's] harlot thinking thereby to … rule both father and son', was a man who had committed high treason.[33] The king now saw the earl as a threat to the Tudor dynasty, and Surrey was probably already a dead man walking by the time he came to trial on 13 January.

The earl's chances of acquittal were worsened further by his father's last-minute confession. Clearly hoping to save his own hide, Norfolk threw his son to the wolves. In his confession, Norfolk not only declared himself guilty of 'no less than high treason' by trying to thwart the king's plans for a regency, but also said he had 'concealed high treason in keeping secret the false acts of my son … in using the arms of St Edward the Confessor'.[34] By confessing to everything, true or not, he hoped Henry would 'have pity' on him and forgive him enough to either free him or at least spare him a traitor's agonizing death of being hung, drawn, and quartered. Norfolk could have confessed to his own crimes while claiming Surrey was innocent, and therefore sacrificed himself for his child, but the duke doesn't seem to have given even a microscopic poo about his son's life.

Surrey, however, would not go down without a fight. At his trial, he pleaded not guilty and then 'kept the commissioners from nine of the clock in the [morning] till five of the clock at night'[35] vigorously defending himself from the charges. The earl, with 'manly courage' told one accuser, Sir Richard Rich, that he was 'false, and to earn a piece of gold would condemn [his] own father'. Surrey also denied that he had tried to steal kingly prerogatives for his coat of arms, because the Howards had always had the right to use them. He pointed out that anyone could 'to the church in Norfolk and … see them there, for they have been ours for five hundred years'.[36] He was correct, but the earl was not only working uphill against the king's opinion; some of his most dedicated enemies were serving as his judge and jury. Nor did he make any friends when he declared that 'the kingdom has never been well since the king put mean creatures … into the government'.[37] It is therefore not surprising that Henry Howard, Earl of Surrey, was condemned to die.

On 19 January 1547, the earl was led out of his prison and onto the scaffold on Tower Hill. Usually, a condemned man or woman would at least admit that they were a sinner, and ask that people pray for the king, but Surrey didn't follow these rules. Instead, the earl demanded 'Of what have you found me guilty? Surely you will find no law that justifies you; but I know that the king wants to get rid of the noble blood around him, and to employ none but low people'.[38] Fighting to the last, one of England's greatest Renaissance poets was beheaded with an axe, his royal blood spilt on rough planks and quickly cooled in the frigid winter air.

Over time, more and more people would come to agree with Surrey's accusations, and to think that there had indeed been a conspiracy against him. In 1563, John Foxe would say in his *Book of Martyrs* that Edward Seymour brought 'God's scourge and rod' upon himself because he had 'distained his honour' by the judicial murder of the Earl of Surrey.[39] However, for the present there were few people willing to risk their lives by mourning for the earl, although his death was 'greatly lamented of many, for that he was a gentleman imbued with great learning and many excellent virtues'.[40] The Duke of Norfolk certainly didn't, being much more concerned with keeping his own head on his own neck. Perhaps the duke's worm-like grovelling had convinced the king that he posed no threat to Prince Edward, because Henry never signed the attainder against Norfolk. Instead, the attainder was verified by a 'dry stamp' that simply imprinted the king's signature with ink the day before Henry died, when he was too ill to understand everything that was being done in his name. The international outrage against Surrey's death seems to have made Edward Seymour and the council leery of signing off on the execution of a duke without an adult king to authorize it, so Norfolk would continue to avoid the headsman's axe. He was kept imprisoned in the Tower for the whole of Edward VI's reign, and was restored to political prominence when Queen Mary I took the throne.

Even with the Howards dead or neutralised, the Protestant faction, led by the Earl of Hertford, was careful to keep the king surrounded by like-minded reformers. Therefore, when the king, 'now languishing and lying in the extremes of death',[41] finalised his last will and testament he made some significant changes among the sixteen councillors who were to advise the prince until he came of age. Most notably, the pro-Catholic bishops of Winchester and Westminster, Stephan Gardiner and Thomas Thirlby, were given the heave-ho. Since others were serving as scribes for the king, there were even councillors who might have gotten on the list despite the king's objections. John Dudley claimed that Henry had decidedly refused to have Thomas Seymour as an executor of the king's will, yet shortly before Henry's death his secretary, William Paget, told everyone that Henry had changed his mind and the younger Seymour brother's name was added. In short, the new list of regency councillors 'read like a roll-call of those either supportive or compliant' to Hertford's agenda.[42] Nevertheless, it is clear from the terms of the will that the king wanted no one man to have more authority over the prince than any other. It was to be a true government of consensus, without a de facto monarch ruling in Edward's place.

The king also reaffirmed the Third Act of Succession in his will, with some strong conditions on his daughters' eligibility to inherit the kingdom. If they dared to marry without the permission of their brother, or the consent of the regency councillors, then they would be barred from the succession. This would, he hoped, prevent someone from trying to take Edward's throne by staging a coup after marrying Mary or Elizabeth. If both his daughters were disqualified from succession, then the crown would pass to the heirs of his nieces by his youngest sister – Lady Francis Brandon Grey and Lady Eleanor Brandon Clifford.

It was widely known that Henry was nearing the end, and there was some international thought that he could be coaxed back into the arms of the Catholic Church on his deathbed. But when asked if there was any chance the ailing King Henry might return to the fold, Eustace Chapuys, was blunt in his opinion that Edward Seymour and John Dudley 'have determined to drag the whole country into [the] damnable error' of Protestantism. Moreover, Queen Kateryn and several of her ladies, including Catherine Willoughby, Duchess of Suffolk, and the wives of Seymour and Dudley, were likewise 'infected by the sect' and were actively encouraging the king to continue to cling to his reformist views. Even if the Holy Roman Emperor himself asked Henry to convert back to Catholicism, it would just make the king more prone to embrace hearsay 'and harden him in his obstinacy, in order that he might show his absolute power and his independence of anyone'. Chapuys also warned, with some gift of foresight, that if the king died the English return to the Catholic Church would become even less likely, inasmuch as Seymour and Dudley 'would have the management of affairs, because, apart from the King's affection for them, and other reasons, there are no other nobles of a fit age and ability for the task'.[43]

The king remained in complete denial about his failing health until the bitter end. He seemed to think the worst of his illness was behind him, telling the imperial ambassador that he 'had suffered and passed through a great deal' before discussing other affairs of state.[44] Moreover, the king made plans to have more apple trees planted in his private garden in the spring, clearly believing he'd be there to see them bloom. He also wished to have his son formally invested as the Prince of Wales, but displayed no urgency to have the ceremony done in the near future. There were additional rumours that he was planning to hand out several advancements to fill the gaps left by the Howards. The imperial ambassador reported that Edward Seymour would be created a duke, and that Thomas Wriothseley, John Dudley, Anthony Browne, William Paget, and Thomas Seymour would all receive new titles as well. However, the king was in no hurry to arrange for the patents. He was acting, in short, as if he had plenty of time left on Earth and that he had only made his will from an abundance of caution.

In contrast, Edward Seymour was manifestly not in denial about Henry's approaching death. Not only was he acting to secure the king's last will and testament in his favour, but he also moved his nephew under guard from Hertfordshire to Elsyng Palace in Enfield, which was only about ten miles from the Tower and put the prince in easy reach of his uncle. If anyone was going to grab the boy-king and rule as regent, the Earl of Hertford was obviously determined that it should be him.

King Henry was still refusing to accept that he was mortal just a few hours before his death. His physicians, who could see plainly that the end was near, were afraid to tell the king their opinion in case he would lash out at them from his deathbed. Sir Anthony Denny, the king's groom of the stool, was the only one of the attendants brave enough to let Henry know 'what case he was in, to man's judgment not like to live'.[45] Denny then asked the king if he wanted a priest to hear his confession. Henry said that he would like Thomas Cranmer to be his confessor, but didn't think he needed the archbishop just yet. He told Denny that he would 'take a little sleep; and then as I feel myself, I will advise upon the matter'. Notwithstanding his disavowal of his imminent passing, when the king awoke an hour or two later even he could feel that the grim reaper had entered the room. He 'commanded that Dr Cranmer be sent for; but before he could come, the king was speechless, and almost senseless'. The archbishop asked the king if he could at least 'give some token with his eyes or hand, that he trusted the Lord'. Henry, though in extremis, was able to squeeze Cranmer's hand. Then, around three o'clock in the morning, the king 'yielded his spirit to almighty God, and departed this world'[46] on 28 January 1547.

Chapter Six

The Boy King is Crowned

With his father's death, the nine-year-old prince became King Edward VI. However, no one rushed to tell him that he was the new monarch. It seems that Edward Seymour and his cohort needed a few days to get up to some serious shenanigans regarding Henry's will first.

The most significant irregularity was the sudden appearance of the unfulfilled gifts clause in the will, which allowed the executors the freedom to give themselves 'all such grants and gifts' that they said Henry had *planned* to give them. According to the beneficiaries of this clause, the deceased king had been planning to give them a virtual cornucopia of titles, estates, and positions in the government. Edward Seymour became the Duke of Somerset and inducted himself into the Order of the Garter. Likewise, John Dudley moved up from Lord Admiral and Viscount Lisle to the Earl of Warwick, and was appointed as Great Chamberlain for the new king. The now-vacant spot of Lord Admiral was given to Thomas Seymour, who also got promoted to Baron of Sudeley. Thomas Wriothesley, the son of a mere officer at arms, became the Earl of Southampton. The queen's brother, William Parr, was elevated to the Marquess of Northampton. Sir Anthony Browne, who had coincidently been the keeper of the dry stamp used to sign official documents (like wills) for King Henry, was given the lucrative position of Keeper of Oatlands Palace, and his eldest son became a Knight of the Bath. William Willoughby, a cousin of Catherine Willoughby Brandon and an ardent Protestant supporter of Edward Seymour, became the 1st Baron Willoughby of Parham. William Paget, whose parents had barely been middle-class, was given a knighthood and made the comptroller of the king's household, as well becoming the chancellor of the Duchy of Lancaster. Just two years later, Paget would be given an additional promotion, and become 1st Baron Paget de Beaudesert. Richard Rich, who had no antecedents to speak of, became 1st Baron Rich of Leez.

Additional lands, peerages, and money were distributed with a generous hand to many others by the executors of Henry's will, and thus no complaints were raised.

Nonetheless, the unfulfilled gifts clause was extremely suspect. Henry's will was only signed with a dry stamp, making it impossible to know if the king had known what was in the final version of the document. The unfulfilled gifts clause was also supposedly added on the day before Henry's death, but it was written on a separate piece of parchment from the rest of the will and it would have been easy to surreptitiously combine with the other papers. Moreover, William Paget explained the late incorporation of the clause by saying that Henry remembered 'in his death bed that he had promised great things to divers men' and so 'willed in his treatment that whatsoever should in any wise appear to his council to be promised by him, the same should be performed'.[1] It would have certainly been convenient for his council if he had!

In spite of Henry's attempts to prevent a regent from using Edward to rule England, the newly titled Duke of Somerset also managed to get himself named Lord Protector of the Realm and Governor of the King's Person by the rest of the regency council. If the late king had already been interred, he would have surely been rolling in his grave, inasmuch as the last person to be the Protector of a minor king was Richard, Duke of Gloucester ... which ended with that duke being crowned King Richard III and young King Henry VI disappearing. For a man who liked to be in control as much as Henry VIII did, this disobedience by his councillors would have infuriated him. Luckily for Somerset, there was nothing the dead king could do about it.

Edward Seymour had undoubtedly gotten his role of Lord Protector in exchange for the lavish gifts the former king's will had mysteriously allowed him to provide, but he would have surely thought it was worth it to become king of England in all but name. However, a pseudo-monarch who gets his pseudo-crown by bribes leaves himself open to blackmail and manipulation. William Paget, angered by a policy he disagreed with, would later send the Lord Protector a letter demanding that Somerset remember 'what you promised me in the gallery at Westminster before the breath was out of the body of the king that dead is. Remember what you promised immediately after, devising with me concerning the place which you now occupy'.[2] Paget then told the duke that he would 'trust in the end to good purpose, howsoever things thwart now', which was just a thinly veiled way of saying 'do as I want or I'll tell everyone about how you got the protectorate and you'll lose it'. Somerset would learn that men who swear fealty to a king are not automatically loyal to a king's stand-in.

Rumours rapidly began to spread regarding the king's demise. Almost before Henry's body was cold the imperial ambassador, François Van der Delft, had 'learnt from a very confidential source that the King, whom may God receive in His Grace, had departed this life, although not the slightest signs of such a thing were to be seen at Court'.[3] According to van der Delft, the council was so determined to keep Henry's death a secret that 'even the usual ceremony of bearing in the royal dishes to the sound of trumpets was continued without interruption'. Another measure of how tightly the executors were trying to keep a lid on the information is that the roads were closed down, and anyone needing to send a letter had to obtain a passport to do so. The French ambassador, Odet de Selve, likewise heard that Henry was dead from the son of the Venetian secretary and 'five or six other quarters, although the thing is still kept so secret that no man dare mention it, and the exact time when the death occurred is not yet certain' and as a consequence 'all ships here have been arrested' but he didn't know 'whether this is for fear that the King's death may be divulged' or if it was in preparation for war.[4] Doubtlessly, there were other influential people, such as the queen and Lady Mary, who were hearing the scuttlebutt that the king was dead as well. Considering the number of servants needed to run a palace's kitchen and sweep its halls, the news was most likely leaking out into London as well. Nevertheless, the heir to the throne would be kept completely in the dark until his uncle saw fit to enlighten him.

On 31 January, Edward Seymour and his coterie finally began to tell the world of Henry VIII's death. Thomas Wriothesley informed the House of Commons that the old king had died. The mayor of London was likewise summoned to Westminster to be given the news, and was commanded to keep the peace until the new king was crowned. Afterwards, a group of heralds, accompanied by a trumpeter, proclaimed throughout the city that the former prince was now King Edward VI. No mention was made, however, of the fact that the boy king had a Lord Protector or of the elevations that had accompanied the unfulfilled gifts clause of the late king's will.

All that remained to do was to let Edward know that the throne had become his. Somerset and Anthony Browne rode to Elsyng Palace with a suitable contingent of yeoman guards to inform their young sovereign of the regime change. Supposedly, when Somerset came to tell his nephew of the late king's death Edward and Elizabeth were together.[5] They reacted to the news the way that almost any child would have responded to hearing about their father's sudden death: with 'great lamentation and weeping'.[6]

The little boy was not allowed time to deal with his grief, though. That same day he was taken to his royal apartments in the Tower of London. Not only was it customary for a monarch to await his coronation there, but the king would be safe from kidnappings or harm within the stout walls of the fortress. The Protestant counsellors were worried about a potential Catholic rebellion. Like the former king, they were concerned that the Holy Roman Empire or the Vatican would fund a putsch to put Mary on the throne, or at least install her as regent. If the oh-so-Catholic Mary became either queen or regent, the whole of England would be strong-armed back into the Mother Church, rather than being strong-armed out of it. Moreover, as regent, Mary would make sure that her little brother was raised to venerate Catholicism as much as she did. Reformist counsellors would lose power, and maybe their heads. Catholic sympathisers, both foreign and domestic, were well aware of these Protestant fears, and had corresponding fears of a Catholic purge. Ambassador van der Delft warned that Mary's potential role in the new king's life was not being discussed, and that many people were 'saying that the Duke of Norfolk has been secretly despatched in the Tower of London, which is easily believed'.[7] When Mary, Dowager Queen of Hungary, replied she cautioned him to remain vigilant, and told him she was refraining from sending 'any letters for our cousin the Princess Mary, as we do not know yet how she will be treated'. The nine-year-old king had clearly inherited a shedload of religious tension to go with his crown.

Edward entered London that afternoon with his uncle riding in front of him and Anthony Browne riding behind him. At the Tower, the king was greeted first by its constable, John Gage, and then by the great lords of his council who 'brought him to his chamber of presence, where they were sworn to his majesty'.[8] The little boy was then taken to his rooms, which were 'garnished with rich cloth of arras and clothes of estate as pertains unto such a royal king'.[9] There is nothing in the historical record to show that any of the adults in Edward's life took the time and effort to go to the royal apartments and console the king for the loss of his father. It can only be hoped that someone thought to comfort the heartbroken child, even if it was from their own self-interest.

The councillors remained in close enough proximity to the king, and thus their lodestone of power, with most of them taking rooms or suites in the Tower. There the councillors met every day 'for determination of many causes, as well about the internment of his grace's father as for the expectation of his highness's coronation'.[10] These were no easy tasks. To bury one king fittingly, and then to crown another king with equal pomp, required intense planning as well as massive outlays of cash. Multiple 'hearses', the massive temporary canopies of moulded and carved wax that stood over the deceased, had to be built and suitably embellished with cloth and gems in order to shelter Henry VIII's coffin and effigy. The hearse at Syon, where the royal corpse would rest for only one night, was described as nine 'stairs' in height, and the one at Windsor was claimed to be thirteen stairs high. The king's body also had to be surrounded in a continual vigil by his former chaplains and no less than thirty members of the Privy Chamber while it lay in state, but several of those same men were also needed for their duties on the new king's council. Moreover, there had to be an impressive procession around the king's body for his funeral on 15 February, yet an even more impressive procession around the new king for his coronation on the 20th. Some of the cloth and jewels used to decorate Henry's funeral could be used for Edward's crowning, but that meant that the repurposing had to be done rapidly. Added to all this, there was still the basic governing of the country to maintain, and the remnants of wars to be dealt with.

The kingdom as a whole also seemed to be confused as to how they should rejoice in Edward's rising sun while repining Henry's setting one. The people were officially ordered to don their 'mourning weeds' for the old king, yet they were also ordered to start preparing for the pageants and parties that would celebrate the new king's coronation. This caused a great deal of confusion, and not a little resentment among the always touchy Tudor nobility. When the Bishop of Winchester, Stephen Gardiner, found out that the Earl of Oxford was planning to show a play on the same day that he had planned to hold a solemn dirge and mass for the late king, he was mightily displeased. The bishop was already fratchety over being overlooked by the new government, and seemed to be determined to make the council acknowledge his importance. He wrote William Paget a sharp letter, complaining that 'what the lewd fellows should mean ... I cannot tell, nor can reform it', and demanding to know who would have 'most resort, they in game or I in earnest'.[11] Apparently the council saw the importance of being earnest, because on 8 February 'every parish church within the city of London and the suburbs of the same kept a solemn dirge ... with all the bells ringing',[12] as Gardiner had wanted.

Although he did not have to deal with the actual governing of the realm, King Edward was not left alone to mourn and adjust to his changed circumstances either. He had a plethora of ceremonial duties to perform in the weeks before his coronation. He had not even been in the Tower for twenty-four hours when the 'most part of the nobility of his realm, as well spiritual as temporal' came to see him and 'all the said lords, according to their degrees, proceed in order one after another, and there kneeling kissed his majesty's hand, saying every one of them God save your grace'.[13] Once everyone had acknowledged that Edward would be king, his uncle took advantage of the high emotions in the room and the royal presence to announce that the council had made him Lord Protector and Governor of the King's Person, to which all the lords in attendance agreed. Edward thanked them, and then with what was surely a prompting by Somerset to let them know they'd be rewarded for the complacence, the king told the lords, 'hereafter in all that you shall have to do with us for any suits or causes you shall be heartily welcome to us'.[14]

The young king had another day of accepting allegiance on 6 February, but this time it was from the cream of the London upper-middle-class. The mayor and aldermen 'rode in scarlett gowns' to the Tower, alongside 'the judges also riding thither in violett, and the sergeants at law with their scarlett hoods'.[15] There, the king came out to greet them 'in a robe of purple velvet and a hood of the same velvet', accompanied by his councillors and William Parr bearing the sword of state. The Lord Protector then formally knighted Edward, which the late king had never gotten around to doing. Once his own knighting was accomplished, the king knighted the mayor. After the knighting, the assembled judges were called 'before the king, who put forth his hand, and every [one] of them kissed it'. As a final act, the king knighted a judge named William Portman, and then 'departed to his private chamber again'.

As Edward performed his duties as showman and prepared for his coronation, he was probably unaware of the tensions that were already brewing among his council and the Duke of Somerset. The recently raised Lord Admiral, Thomas Seymour, had already told his elder brother that it wasn't fair that only one of the king's uncles should take so much upon himself. The admiral then demanded, in front of the larger council, that he be made Governor of the King's Person to counterbalance his brother's role as Lord Protector. Somerset simply stalked out of the room without replying. The next day, however, the Protector named the admiral to the Privy Council, which was clearly an attempt to placate his younger brother. This would not hold off Thomas Seymour for very long, though. Other members of the council would also quickly come to resent Somerset's ersatz kingship, which they had never authorised. In hindsight, it is obvious that the duke would have been much wiser to have shared his power more equitably from the start. Certainly, the imperial ambassador, being an intelligent man, could see which way the wind was blowing regarding the boy-king's councillors and Somerset. Before the old king had even been buried, van der Delft was reporting that it was 'quite likely that some jealousy or rivalry may arise between [Somerset] and [John Dudley], because, although they both belong to the same sect they are nevertheless widely different in character'. The ambassador explained that Dudley, 'being of high courage will not willingly submit to his colleague. He is, moreover, in higher favour both with the people and with the nobles than [Somerset], owing to his liberality and splendour. The Protector, on the other hand, is not so accomplished in this respect, and is indeed looked down upon by everybody as a dry, sour, opinionated man.'[16]

Despite all the hubbub surrounding him before his coronation, Edward took the time to write to both his stepmother and his sister Mary regarding the death of the late king. He sympathised with the queen and tried to give her comfort by reminding her that 'although nature prompts us to grieve and shed tears … scripture and wisdom prompt us to moderate those feelings lest we appear to have no hope at all of the resurrection of the dead' through their common belief in Christ. He also expressed no doubt that the former king had gone on to a better place, because 'whoever here leads a vitreous life, and governs the state aright, as my noble father has done, who ever prompted piety and banished all ignorance, has a most certain journey into heaven'.[17] His faith in Henry's goodness makes it manifestly obvious that Edward's education had been given only a sweetened version of his father's reign, and that he had no clue that truth might be otherwise. His letter to Mary was in a similar vein of mourning and religious devotion. He acknowledged that their 'natural affection' would spur them 'to lament our dearest father's death', but tells his sister that 'we ought not to mourn our father's death, since it is [God's] will, who worketh all things for good'.[18]

It is evident from reading his letters that Edward was an unusually contemplative and serious child, one who had not only been taught religious subjects, but actually thought about them. It is also plain that he believed it was his job to give consolation to his stepmother and sister, in spite of his youth and their adulthood, because his father's death made him both king and head of his family as well. His letters in childhood additionally reveal that he trusted that the adults in his life whom he loved also loved him in return, and that they had his best interests at heart. This innocent faith in his friends and relations would unfortunately not be able to survive into his teenage years, but at least he was given the solace of perceived security during the frightening and tumultuous years of his early kingship.

On 19 February the young king was the showpiece of a spectacular procession through London as he rode slowly toward Westminster, where he would be crowned the following morning. John Dudley rode at the king's right side, and Edward Seymour rode beside him on his left. By choosing the left side of his nephew rather than right, the Lord Protector was sending a message to his Tudor audience that while he may be the adult face of the boy's kingship, he considered himself a mere helpmate to his sovereign. This message would soon be exposed as disingenuous, but for the present, it was excellent theatre and reassuring to the other councillors. Six honoured knights bore the canopy of estate to cover the king, but Edward thoughtfully 'went a little before it in order that the people might better see him'.[19] Certainly there was a lot to see, at least in terms of sartorial splendour. The king was 'richly apparelled with a gown of cloth of silver, all over embroidered with damask gold, with a girdle of white velvet wrought with Venice silver, garnished with precious stones, as rubies and diamonds, with true-lover's knots of pearls'. A white velvet cap covered most of his russet hair, and the jaunty ostrich feather it sported would have cost as much, pound-for-pound, as the diamonds and pearls around it. Underneath his open-fronted gown, he wore a matching doublet of white velvet, likewise embroidered with silver thread and dotted liberally with gemstones and pearls. Even his riding gloves were made of expensive white velvet, which would have been shredded beyond salvage by the leather reins. The little boy must have gleamed like a royal jewel in the pale winter sunlight.

A jewel needs a proper setting, so the king's horse had been draped in a crimson satin in order to better contrast and display Edward's white clothing. Instead of the usual palfrey, he might have been riding a courser or destrier, which were impressively tall war horses fit for a newly-knighted monarch. That means that a good six feet of bright red satin would have been flowing down each side of the king's mount. Moreover, the horse's livery was embroidered with damask gold and pearls. There was no such thing as a cultivated pearl in the Tudor time period, so each pearl had been harvested in the wild. The pearls would have been as costly as rubies, yet they were threaded onto a glorified horse blanket. This was apex ostentation. None of the onlookers would have seen the signs of royal coffers nearly bankrupted by wars or the worries of having a boy-king on the throne. Instead, they would have seen pearls and gold thread on a horse, and would have hopefully assumed all was well in his majesty's realm.

Herald's would have announced the oncoming procession with trumpets, and the king would have rode constantly forward into the din of cheering crowds who roared, 'Sing up heart, sing up heart, sing no more down, but joy in King Edward that weareth the crown!'[20] Children dressed as allegories of Grace, Fortune, Charity, Nature, and Truth greeted him, as well as adults costumed as Edward the Confessor and Saint George. Almost every house along his route had been hung with tapestries or cloth of gold 'as richly as might be devised' by the homeowners. He was presented with gifts, including bags of gold coins. His councillors, lords, ladies, chaplains, churchmen, knights, and yeoman rode before and behind him, making him symbolically the centre of the realm and all earthly things. The hopes or ambitions of everyone around him, commoner and noble alike, would have fallen like rain onto the shoulders of the nine-year-old boy. How would a child feel in the midst of all that adulation and expectation, even a child as precocious and serious as Edward?

If the king felt overwhelmed by his circumstances, however, then he was careful not to show it.

The procession had to stop multiple times to see the pageants, choirs, plays, and tableaux arranged by the citizens and guilds of the city to welcome and entertain their sovereign. Although all the performances were elaborate, the king appears to have enjoyed one exhibition more than the others. He lingered for 'a good space of time' at St Paul's Cathedral to 'watch the performance of a rope-dancer, a native of Aragon, for whom a cable was stretched from the battlements of the steeple to a great anchor at the deanery gate'. Between watching the displays and negotiating a way through the crowds, it took the royal parade more than four hours to traverse the three miles from the Tower to the abbey. By that time the small king would have almost certainly been tired, and in need of warm food and a comfy bed. Nonetheless, at Westminster, he was required to greet a throng of ambassadors, all of whom were determined to pay their respects to the new monarch. It was after sunset before the king was taken by barge to the nearby royal residence of Whitehall, where he could spend the night in relative peace.

On the day of his coronation, the king was awakened at dawn to get ready. On top of his already elaborate clothes, he had to wear the Parliamentary robes he would be crowned in. These adult-length robes were made of crimson velvet trimmed with gold embroidery and ermine fur, and would have been heavy. The coronation robes Queen Elizabeth II wore in 1953 weighed almost twenty-five pounds, and they were made of a slightly lighter weave of velvet. The king was healthy, but looking at his portraits it is undeniable that he was a skinny little boy. It would have been hard for him to walk in his finery, even with his attendants to help him.

The king took the royal barge from Whitehall, arriving at the privy stairs of the Palace of Westminster at nine o'clock in the morning. Due to the weight of his robes, and the assemblage of dignitaries who no doubt wanted to have a quick word with him and wish him well, it took him more than an hour to walk to the abbey. Once there, it took another half hour to get everything in place for the king to make his royal entrance into his coronation.

Finally, all was ready. Edward entered Westminster Abbey with the barons of Cinque Ports carrying the poles of the golden canopy of estate above him. Francis Talbot, the 5th Earl of Shrewsbury and a tremendously powerful lord in the north of England, walked as a symbolic guard on his right side. Cuthbert Tunstal, the Bishop of Durham, walked on his left side. The train his robe was carried by three of his councillors: Thomas Seymour, William Parr, and John Dudley. He processed slowly to the front of the church, where a raised platform had been built to the coronation throne, called King Edward's Chair in honour of the last Anglo-Saxon monarch, St Edward the Confessor. The seat of the chair encased the Stone of the Scone, or Stone of Destiny. This large oblong of sandstone had been used for centuries during the crowning of the kings of Scotland. When King Edward I had stolen from the Scots in the late 13th century, he had hoped to make himself and his heir's symbolically King of Scots by using it during the English coronation.[21] The king's attendants helped him onto the dais and to take his place on the throne. The huge chair had to be prepared in advance with the padding of two cushions to keep it from swallowing the little boy whole when he sat down.

After the royal buttocks had sat on the throne for a moment or two, the king was 'placed in a lighter chair, garnished with cloth of tissue, in which he was carried by four gentleman ushers to the four sides of the mount or platform, in order to be shown to the assembled people'. The crowd was asked if they accepted him as their king, and they shouted back, 'Yea, yea, yea, God save King Edward!'

The king's godfather, Archbishop Cranmer, conducted the coronation ceremony. It had been pared down in case its 'tedious length should weary the king, being yet of tender age', but even then there was still a lot to do. First, the archbishop solemnly administered the coronation oath, so that Edward could promise to uphold the laws of the kingdom. Then Cranmer preached a sermon, assuring the king that if he made the effort then he could create a realm where 'God [was] truly worshiped, and idolatry destroyed, the tyranny of the bishops of Rome banished from your subjects, and images removed'.[22] Moreover, doing so would be the sign the new king was 'a second Josiah', the Biblical monarch who ascended the throne as a child and removed the false idols from the Kingdom of Judah, returning his people to the path of righteousness. Cranmer also told the king it was his duty to 'reward virtue, to revenge sin, to justify the innocent, to relieve the poor, to procure, to repress violence, and to execute justice through your realms'. The king must have been paying careful attention to the archbishop's words, because he would try to live up to those ideals.

When the archbishop finished his sermon, he anointed his godson's head with the holy oil conferring sovereignty, and then crowned him thrice. Cranmer first symbolically placed St Edward's crown on the king's head, followed by the imperial crown, and then finally with a specially prepared crown that was light enough not to burden the small boy's neck with its weight. Once crowned, Edward was given the Sovereign's Orb and Sceptre, which symbolised his Godly and secular powers. A set of spurs, reputed to belong to St Edward the Confessor and symbolising the ideals of chivalry, were also given to the king. However, they were taken back quickly by the archbishop since the king couldn't hold all three items in his small hands. The newly anointed and crowned monarch then had to hold the orb and sceptre and sit patiently while the nobility of England filed past one by one, allowing them all to kiss his left cheek. The golden sceptre was so heavy that Francis Talbot had to stand beside the little boy and help him keep it upright. Fortunately, they did not make the king hear every lord swear fealty individually, but instead allowed the nobles to kneel down en masse to indicate their agreement to be loyal to their sovereign.

A nine-year-old child was now Edward VI, King of England, France, and Ireland, Defender of the Faith, and the Supreme Head of the Church on earth, for better or for worse.

Nonetheless, the king's coronation was only half-finished. Now he must be feasted and feted by his court in the Great Hall at Westminster, which would involve multiple ritualistic events to signify Edward's sovereignty and the relative positions of his courtiers. Nor was the king allowed to simply sit and rest between his uncle Somerset and the archbishop after his busy morning. He had to give an active response in the toasts and pageants. For example, between the second and third course, a knight named Sir Edward Dymmocke 'came riding into the hall in clean while complete harness, richly gilded ... and cast his gauntlett to wage battle against all men'[23] who would dispute Edward's right to be king. No one accepted the knight's challenge, of course, so 'then the king drank to him and gave him a cup of gold' and everyone cheered. When the feast ended, the king's day was still not complete. He then had to knight several men, with all the trappings that such ceremonies entailed. All told, the coronation and celebrations afterwards took roughly seven hours to complete. It was late in the evening before the little boy was finally able to crawl into the royal bed and get some well-earned rest.

For the next two days, there were banquets, plays, and contests of chivalry held for the king's entertainment and honour. The young monarch watched the 'many noble feats done' on his behalf from one of Westminster Palace's galleries, surrounded by councillors and notables. This would turn out to be a portent of how the first few years of the king's reign would go. Edward would be kept marginalised from any kind of power and given over simply to education, religious instruction, and ceremonial duties. He would, in effect, be left to watch others perform governance on his behalf at a distance.

Chapter Seven

A King in a Golden Cage

Themes young king was shuffled off to continue his studies, dividing his time between his court at St James and his summer retreat at Hampton Court. Somerset was careful not to let his nephew go any further afield, fearing that someone else could steal the source of his power if he did not keep it close. The Lord Protector also began to secure his position as the shadow sovereign by ruthlessly removing anyone who thwarted his will or compromised his authority.

The first to go was the king's chancellor, Thomas Wriothesley. When he had given Somerset the protectorate in exchange for the promotion to Earl of Southampton, it is doubtful Wriothesley saw how far the duke was planning to extend his authority as Protector. After all, the chancellor was the one who carried the Great Seal, and Somerset would need him to agree to any policy or order if he wanted it to be legitimised. Thus, both Wriothesley and the council would have the ability to check Somerset if he got too big for his doublet. Moreover, the Protector would want to keep the many religious conservatives who still held high offices on his side, and the chancellor was their de facto head. Alas for Wriothesley, this underestimated how savage Somerset could be when it came to gaining primacy.

On 5 March, less than two weeks after the coronation, Wriothesley was blindsided by being put under house arrest and charged with bad-mouthing the Lord Protector 'to the prejudice of the King's estate and the hindrance of his Majesty's affairs'.[1] The duke also acted swiftly against anyone he suspected would support the chancellor. Ambassador van der Delft reported that the Protector had ordered 'the late King's old servitors formerly members of the Council, who are known to be opposed to any change in their ancient religion to withdraw to their homes',[2] which was essentially house arrest without having made charges against them. This move was especially bold considering that these men were not just little fish in the pro-Catholic pond. Among those ordered to remain in their homes was Sir Thomas Cheyne, the royal household's treasurer and Lord Warden of the Cinque Ports, who had just been carrying one of the poles holding the canopy over the king at his coronation. Sir John Gage, the constable of the Tower whom Somerset had elevated to Comptroller of the Household a few weeks before, was also locked down. According to van der Delft, there were likewise 'certain other gentlemen' ordered to remain in their London residences as well.

Having recently seen what had happened to the Earl of Surrey when he had crossed Somerset, Wriothesley decided breathing was better than a high position and handed over the Great Seal meekly, asking only that he be allowed to 'forgo his office with as little slander and bruit as might be'.[3] The Lord Protector then graciously allowed the former chancellor to slink away without further harm.

The office of Chancellor was now bestowed upon Richard Rich, 1st Baron Rich, who was (to be frank) one of the sleaziest opportunists in an era full of unapologetic opportunists. Rich appears to have had no moral compass, pandering ceaselessly to the powerful in the hope of being rewarded. Rich had happily persecuted Catholics and Protestants alike. He had helped arrange Thomas More's date with a headsman, and later had given Henry VIII the same help to judicially murder Thomas Cromwell. Rich had also assisted Thomas Wriothesley in torturing Anne Askew, a noted Evangelical reformer, with his own hands before she was burned at the stake. Rich would serve Somerset loyally … as long as there was something in it for him. The moment it became apparent that John Dudley's star was rising, Rich would turn on Somerset to curry favour with the ascendant Earl of Warwick.

King Edward was only kept abreast of these matters from the point of view of Lord Protector, who naturally informed the boy all his actions were done to keep his nephew safe. The king appears to have trusted Somerset absolutely, calling himself 'indebted … on many accounts, dearest uncle, for your very great kindness'.[4] Edward seems to have been completely unaware of how much of what the Lord Protector did was to feather his own nest.

The preadolescent king also trusted his younger uncle, Thomas Seymour, which was understandable by nonetheless a profound mistake. Seymour had been made Lord Admiral, but was deeply dissatisfied with his position compared to his elder brother's. The admiral was determined to make his fortune and gain power, and doesn't seem to have had many scruples about how he would do it. Initially, he put out feelers among the council to see if there was any support for allowing him to marry one of the king's sisters, but there was none. Rebuffed by his acquaintances, Thomas Seymour then went to ask his brother if he could wed Lady Mary. This went about as well as could be expected. According to ambassador van der Delft, the Lord Protector 'was displeased and reproved him, saying that neither of them was born to be King, nor to marry King's daughters ... besides which he knew the Lady Mary would never consent'.[5] The admiral, handsome and charming and well aware of it, 'replied that he merely asked for his brother's countenance, and he would look after the rest'.[6] This naturally caused Somerset to 'chid him again more sharply'.

Seymour then looked toward his back-up plan – the Dowager Queen Kateryn. She was only thirty-five, pretty, politically well-connected, and now in possession of fat jointure estates. He knew she had been enamoured of him before Henry VIII decided to marry her, and he knew she'd be easy to woo over once more. He promptly began to court Kateryn, and his confidence was rewarded when she married him in secret sometime in May. The only trouble was that Somerset, the council, and most of the court were going to be less than happy about the clandestine union, especially since it took place so soon after Henry VII's death. They would need some serious protection if they were to avoid suffering some serious consequences from their wedding. They would need the favour of the king.

Kateryn had continued to visit Edward as often as she could at St James Palace, and it was clear the little boy loved his stepmother. At the end of May he had written to the dowager queen, assuring her that 'if there be anything wherein I may do you a kindness, either in word or deed, I will do it willingly'. Moreover, Thomas Seymour had taken pains to win his nephew's affections through gifts and money. The admiral would laugh and shake his head about the 'beggarly' state the Protector had left the king in, and arranged to send the young sovereign lavish amounts of extra pocket money via John Fowler, who was one of the gentlemen of the privy chamber. This had pleased Edward, as it would have almost any boy his age. Thomas Grey, Marquess of Dorset, would later note that the king had told him somewhat bitterly that, 'My uncle of Somerset dealeth very hardly with me and keepeth me so straight that I cannot have money at my wil, but my Lord Admiral both sends me money and gives me money'.[7] Surely, they must have thought, the king would be on their side.

Being a man who knew well how to manipulate others, Thomas Seymour took the extra precaution of getting Edward to think that a marriage between his uncle and stepmother had been his idea. He had his cat's paw, Fowler, say to his sovereign, 'And it please your grace, I marvell at my lord admiral marieth not.' Fowler then asked the king whom he thought Seymour should wed. Thinking over the single women he knew, the king replied that the admiral should marry Anne of Cleves. Thinking about it a little longer, he decided his Protestant uncle should take his sister Mary to the altar, 'to turn her opinions' from Catholicism. Neither of these were the answers Seymour needed, so the next day he had Fowler ask Edward directly if he thought the admiral should wed the dowager queen. Edward, young as he was, nonetheless had the presence of mind to hesitate. His father had been dead less than half a year. It was unseemly for any woman, let alone one who had been queen, to remarry so soon. Never one to hesitate, Thomas Seymour came to see the king in person. The child was unable to withstand his beloved uncle's blandishments for long, and soon produced a letter that not only gave Kateryn permission to wed the admiral – it essentially requested her to do so. Better yet, the king promised that they 'need not fear any grief to come, or to suspect a lack of aid in need', and assuring them that his Protector would 'not be troublesome'. Even if Somerset had a hissy fit, Edward promised that he would be 'a sufficient succour' for the couple.[8]

Safeguarded by the king, the couple let the world know that they were married. Edward would record in his personal diary that his uncle Somerset had indeed been 'much offended' by the union. Although the couple could not be punished directly, thanks to the king's blessing on the match, the Lord Protector and his wife sought other ways to hurt the couple. Somerset refused to give the dowager queen the jewellery that Henry VIII had left to her in his will, keeping even her wedding ring and a personal cross of gold that she had been given by her mother. She was sorely provoked, but she told her new husband not to make trouble over it with his brother. They would just have to bear the insult as best they could. However, the Protector's next step, which was to lease out her dower lands without her consent, sparked even Kateryn's patience. She wrote that it was good that the duke was nowhere near her estate of Chelsea when she found out, 'for I suppose I would have bitten him'.

The Lord Protector should have spent more time in diplomatic strategising and less time hassling his sister-in-law, because he was making a dog's breakfast of England's foreign policy that summer. The peace with France, the same one that had been formalised only a year ago, was wobbling by the first week of June. The English were building a wall in Boulogne's harbour, which contravened the Treaty of Camp. Somerset's government insisted that they were not breaking the treaty; they were merely building a breakwater to make the harbour safer. The French were unconvinced. Of course, the French were also in defiance of the treaty. They had, 'with twenty galleys and certain ships, passed the narrow seas into Scotland', providing reinforcements to help the Scots in their resistance of England's Rough Wooing. Bolstered by their mutual aid, the Auld Alliance struck that July. Scots forces led by the Earl of Arran destroyed an English fort on the Scottish border at Langholm, while the French recaptured St Andrews Castle from English sympathisers. Shored up by the French allies, the Scots then hunkered down and waited for an invasion from the South.

Rather than responding to advice or critique by his fellow councillors after these setbacks, Somerset tightened his grip on the government. By mid-July, he had basically stopped pretending that he wasn't the de facto king of England. He didn't bother having the councillors sign off on his orders anymore, and was flat out ruling by fiat. He was even signing royal warrants and raising troops with a dry stamp of Edward's signature, without even making a pro forma show of getting the king's approval.[9] The council, which had never agreed to give the Lord Protector unlimited authority over the realm, were less than happy about his overreach. The duke may have grabbed power, but he was gaining enemies with every handful.

For the moment, however, the very powerful Earl of Warwick was still on Somerset's side. John Dudley had come down hard on Thomas Seymour for continuing to give his brother political grief. He 'used strong language to the Admiral', and reminded him 'that he had come to occupy such a high position through the favour of his brother'. Dudley harshly pointed out that Thomas Seymour had been made a member of the council 'against the late King's wish; who being on his deathbed, and hearing his name among those elected to the Council, cried out "No, no", though his breath was failing him.' Everything the admiral now had he had been given only because his brother favoured him. 'Be content, therefore,' Dudley told him 'with the honour done to you for your brother's sake, and with your office of Lord High Admiral which I gave up to you for the same motive.' The Earl of Warwick finished by pointing out that Somerset's 'virtues and loyalty towards the King and the kingdom make him the man fittest to administer the affairs of the country during the King's minority', and no one thought the same of Thomas Seymour. Ambassador van der Delft wrote that Dudley's 'words, and threats he used besides, had such good effect that the admiral went off at once and made up the quarrel with his brother'.[10]

It has long been fashionable for historians to see all of John Dudley's actions as part of a clever, long-term scheme to destroy Somerset and take power for himself, but that is reading backwards from the outcome. Nor does the outcome indicate that Warwick's animosity was there from the beginning. A divorcing couple who have come to hate each other may have loved each other with an equal passion on the day of their wedding. There is no real evidence that Dudley was anything other than a supporter of the duke in the first year of the protectorate. He had also been intensely loyal to Henry VIII, in spite of his father's execution when the late king came to the throne.[11] As a part of that loyalty, he would have been looking out for King Edward's best interest, as Somerset was appearing to do. Another of his motivations for standing by the Lord Protector was probably their shared religious beliefs. Although Somerset had supported the pro-Catholic position a decade earlier, he and his family had embraced Reformism once his nephew was born to replace Lady Mary as heir. He was also making sure that the king was being raised ultra-Protestant. Edward's religious education was overseen by Archbishop Cranmer, and there was 'preaching every day before the king, and the preachers seem to vie with each other as to who can abuse most strongly the old religion'. John Dudley and his family had embraced the Reformation early. His wife, Jane, was a member of the Protestant ladies around Kateryn Parr who had supported Anne Askew and other 'gospelers'. Religious belief, especially in these tumultuous times, could form strong bonds between political allies.

The Lord Protector certainly tried to force Protestantism on everyone in the kingdom. In August, he 'sent out through this realm of England certain Godly injunctions for reformation of the clergy, the true preaching and setting forth of God's word, and utter abolishing of idolatry, which were clean out down in every parish church'.[12] While this was celebrated by some of his fellow Reformers, other people were not exactly rejoicing. Catholics were appalled that the English had 'taken it into their heads to do away with all the images in the churches except the Crucifix and a few of the Virgin'.[13] It wasn't just the Catholics who disliked the changes, either. More moderate Protestants were unhappy that their worship had been altered so rapidly and vehemently. There were forms and rituals of Christianity which most people had learned since childhood to find spiritually fulfilling, and they mourned the loss of the older rites. Unlike other countries with Protestant populations, the reformation had not started with the demands of common and middle-class people. It had been brought down on them from the top by the late king. The populace had adjusted, for the most part, because most of the practices of their faith had remained the same. Now the government was melting their icons, painting the walls of their churches white, and tampering with the service itself. The early rumblings of religious revolt soon began to spread, particularly in the areas of England farthest away from London.

Somerset didn't seem to be doing anything right, and had stripped the king of any vestiges of royal authority, but nevertheless, his nephew was delighted by his efforts. In a letter dated at the end of August, King Edward praised him 'for striving that this kingdom be quiet and replenished with the true religion'.[14] He also expressed his gratitude toward his uncle for the preparations being made for renewed war with Scotland, which would 'restore to my state its own right and property, and are doing your best that the Scots may be our subjects'. Finally, the young king thanked the duke for practically stealing the crown off his head, saying that he was, 'obliged ... most especially, because, while I am in boyhood, you undertake all matters belonging to me'. It is self-evident that the king had almost as much faith in the Lord Protector as he had in the Lord God.

England now prepared 'a great and puissant army to pass by land into Scotland'[15] to secure Edward's intended bride by hook or by crook. It would be led by Somerset himself, aided by John Dudley as second in command. A naval force was also sent northward, including the flagship formerly known as the *Great Harry*, and a large fleet of 'tall ships [that] were well furnished with men and munitions for the war ... [and] many merchant's ships and other smaller vessels which secured the carriage of victuals'. Thomas Seymour, as Lord High Admiral, should have been in charge of the waterborne invasion. Somerset, however, had instead given command of the fleet to Edward Finnes, Lord Clinton, and Vice-Admiral Thomas Woodhouse. This looks as though the Lord Protector was simply being malicious. For all his other faults, Thomas Seymour had proven himself an able commander of ships in Henry VIII's last war against France, and there was no real reason he should not have been put in charge of the naval forces against Scotland.[16]

Thomas Seymour must have wanted to retaliate against his brother for the slight, because he used Somerset's absence to try to sweet-talk the king into favouring him over the Lord Protector. As soon as he could he visited the king to drip poison in his ear regarding their mutual relation. Edward recorded that the admiral, 'told me that mine uncle, being gone into Scotland, should not pass the peace without the loss of a great number of men or of himself, and that he did spend much money in [that] vein'.[17] He also advised the king that he was being 'too bashful' with Somerset, and that he was failing to speak up for himself, to which Edward tersely replied that he 'was well enough'. Seymour also asked the king to write something for him, and promised 'it was none ill'. The king was not quite ten years old yet, but he was nonetheless too savvy to do as his younger uncle asked. Instead, he dismissed the admiral and turned to someone he trusted more for advice. He talked to his tutor, John Cheke, about what Seymour had said. Cheke reminded the king that Somerset had asked him 'not to believe men that would slander him, till he came himself'. Edward decided that that was indeed the best course of action.

The admiral had made a tactical error. He was bold enough to be ambitious, but not smart enough to be clever about it. His scheming was too overt, and too clumsy, to fool a child as intelligent as his nephew.

King Edward VI has frequently been described by historians as cold, priggish, and unloving, but this characterisation of the king is perhaps too harsh. As a little boy, based on his letters and his attachment to his family and tutors, he seems loving enough. He unquestionably revelled in the warmth and affections of his stepmother, and showed his fondness for his sisters in both word and deed. He was, categorically, a proto-puritan regarding anything touching on religious matters, including 'foreign dances' that might contain hints of Catholicism, but he could have hardly been otherwise when you consider his carefully designed Reformist upbringing. It was only after his crowning that Edward grew suspicious and reserved, but he had good reasons for his behaviour. Like his grandfather, Henry VII, he had learned early and well that there were few people who could truly be trusted. He was also like his grandfather in that once his trust was broken, it could never be recovered. Worse, the little boy had discovered much too young that some of those who professed to love him were only using him to further their own goals. Is it really so strange that a child as intelligent as Edward would learn to emotionally distance himself from those he feared were trying to use him, even if they were connected by blood?

Chapter Eight

An Uncle's Fall from the King's Favour

T he king's faith in his younger uncle had been shaken, but his faith in his elder uncle remained solid. He sent the Lord Protector a letter of encouragement by a special messenger on 12 September to tell him that he hoped the Catholics of Scotland would be 'conquered and routed', and that 'the ringleaders of this tumult and mischief' would finally be 'out of the world'.[1] Moreover, he assured Somerset, there was 'no doubt we shall conquer; for we fight for the cause of God, [while] they for that of the Pope'. What the king did not know was that the English forces had already decimated the Scots at the Battle of Pinkie two days earlier.

It would have certainly seemed to the Protestants that God was on their side when they learned of the English triumph at Pinkie. When ambassador van der Delft heard 'great and glorious news' of England's victory, he sent a messenger immediately to Oatlands to congratulate the king and his council and to ask for the 'full particulars of the matter'. William Paget thus informed him that the 'Protector had penetrated so far into the country that he was only four miles away from Edinburgh itself, and knowing that the whole army of the Scots to the number of twenty-four thousand men was advancing towards him, he had decided to be beforehand with them and to occupy a mountain which stood between the two armies'.[2] When Somerset 'heard that the enemy was approaching', he 'then decided to send the Earl of Warwick with a good body of horse to take the enemy in the rear, and in order to carry out this operation more unobservedly, he took advantage of the wind and had some smoky fires lit'. This turned out to be a good stratagem, because it 'enabled the Earl of Warwick to surprise the rear guard of the enemy who was so completely taken unawares that after making a very slight resistance they took to flight' and 'there were some fifteen thousand of [the Scots] either killed or taken prisoner' on the field.

Furthermore, Admiral Clinton had been as successful at sea as Somerset had been on land. Following the route at Pinkie, a man named John Beton had offered 'to put into the hands of the English all the principal ships of the Scottish realm, of which he was the commander'.[3] This seemed reasonable, inasmuch as Scotland had just suffered a massive defeat and her regent was currently on the run. It would have been expected that the Scots navy, seeing that it was hopeless, would want to surrender honourably. Thus, Somerset made plans 'that Beton should accompany the English fleet for this purpose' to Leith Harbor. However, this was not intended to be a surrender. This was actually a last-ditch effort by the Scots to get the upper hand over at least some of the English forces. Beton had been careful to have the Scottish 'ships anchored in a position where they could only be attacked on one side, and arranged to have the whole of their artillery ranged on that side'. Once Beton and the English were in Leith he asked to be put ashore, and told them 'to approach the Scottish ships slowly' so that he could facilitate the surrender. As the English fleet 'gradually approached the Scots, unsuspicious of treachery, it was received with a great cannonade'. After a pitched sea battle, the English 'forced the Scottish ships to surrender, some of which were brought to these parts and the rest were burnt'.

King Edward was, naturally, overjoyed by the Protector's accomplishment. He wrote to congratulate his uncle, and although all due thanks were given to God, 'most hearty thanks' was given to Somerset as well. The king declared that the 'good success' it had 'pleased God to grant to us against the Scots' had been accomplished by the 'good courage and wise foresight' of the Lord Protector. The jubilant sovereign also asked his uncle to 'thank most heartily, in our name, our good cousin the Earl of Warwick, and all the others of the noblemen, gentlemen, and others' who had fought for England.

The king's forces, ambassador van der Delft told the emperor, had 'now subdued the greater part of the Scottish border country'.[4] What amazed the ambassador was that the English, even with 'the whole of Scotland in the hollow of their hand', were saying that it was 'not the valour of their men that has won them this great victory but the grace of God alone, since the enemy being so powerful and resolute to fight, was nevertheless so quickly defeated and with so little loss on their side.' He was also surprised to hear that Somerset and most of the English forces were being withdrawn and returning to London. He assumed there must be some secret negotiations in the works to hand over Mary, Queen of Scots, who was still safe behind the thick walls of Stirling Castle. He thought it highly 'unlikely that the Protector would leave the enemy's country in the full flood of his success without some sort of treaty'. Nor could van der Delft imagine that the duke would 'leave the whole settlement to the Earl of Warwick'.

Nonetheless, that was exactly what the Lord Protector had done. While John Dudley was literally holding the fort in the hostile territory of occupied southern Scotland, Somerset marched home covered in glory. The aldermen and mayor of London wanted to receive him as a hero 'with much joy', but supposedly he declined. According to contemporary chronicler Richard Grafton, the duke was 'offended therewith, and forbade any such triumph to be made for him, for said he if any things had been done for the honor of the realm, it was God's doing' and not his own.

One has to wonder: with the Queen of Scots almost within his grasp, why did Somerset not stay and push his advantage? After all, as one occupant of London pointed out, Stirling Castle could 'hardly hold out against [the English] force, for the Earl of Warwick is only four miles away, and the Protector with a fine force also; so that it may be captured if desired'.[5] Taking a large chunk of this 'fine force' back to England would doom the efforts of the remaining troops to winkle the queen from her fortress. Moreover, it's not as if the Scots had suddenly stopped resisting. They were waging guerrilla warfare against their occupiers, with some success. Was it because 'winter approached, and the season of the year served not'[6] for fighting? This seems doubtful, since multiple skirmishes between Scotland and England, both on land and at sea, continued until Christmas. So why did the duke return prematurely?

In part, it was probably because he was astute enough not to trust Thomas Seymour or any other ambitious councillor to be alone with the king while he was away. He might also have been spurred to come home because England had tumbled into religious chaos since the reformist proclamations the previous August. The Protestant commissioners given the task of abolishing idolatry had almost immediately turned into zealots. Across the kingdom, churches were being raided and their icons and relics were being smashed to bits in front of a mostly horrified populace.[7]

The bones of a local saint were taken and thrown onto a bonfire in Shropshire. Another bonfire of church images and heirlooms took place in Shrewsbury. A rabble of 'divers curates and other persons' marauded through the churches of Norwich, demolishing anything of which they didn't approve. In Durham, a royal commissioner was recorded to have actually jumped up and down on the church's iconography in his frenzy to wreck it.

Even roods – the life-sized or larger crucifixes set above the entrance to the chancel of the church – were being torn down as idols. If the roods were those with the attendant figures of the Virgin Mary and St John kneeling at the feet of Christ, they were almost certainly doomed. One of the first roods to be ripped down and destroyed after the Protector left for Scotland was the one in St Paul's Cathedral, done as a part of the fanatical purging of its images in early September. Catholics must have considered it Divine Retribution when a workman was crushed to death under the collapsing rood, but this putative sign of God's displeasure didn't give the commissioners a moment's pause.[8] The Protestant commissioners were too sure the Almighty favoured only them to let the death of a workman stop them. The beautiful interior of the cathedral would be sacked by these spiritual Visigoths. All of the 'obits and chantreys were confiscated, and the vestments and altar cloths were sold', after which the 'altar, and chapel, and tombs (all but John of Gaunt's) were then ruthlessly destroyed'.[9]

Almost anything that could be considered artistic or attractive was declared ungodly by the Reformers. The colourful murals on church walls were covered over with whitewash. Tapestries and paintings were incinerated. Rood screens, the exquisitely carved wooden partitions between the chancel and nave of a church, were chopped into kindly. Altars were smashed. Worship of the divine, the most ardent Protestants seemed to think, could only truly take place if there was nothing pretty visible to the human eye.

Not all these assaults on the ornaments of the church were motivated by piety, of course. Many of those who took away the altar cloths and gilded icons and were mostly trying to 'dispossess the church of what property and possessions remained to it, and to share among themselve such booty as could be creditably wrested from the unbefriended hierarchy'.[10] At Greyfriars church in London some miscreants 'pulled up all the tombs,

King Henry VII (circa between 1501 and 1509, attributed to Maynnart Wewyck).

Left to Right: the future King Edward IV as a boy, King Henry VIII, Jane Seymour (circa 1545).

Queen Mary I (after Hans Eworth's original, painted between circa 1600 and 1629).

Queen Elizabeth I as a young teen (attributed to William Scrots, circa 1546).

Queen Katheryn Parr (seventeenth or eighteenth century copy of a lost portrait).

Edward Seymour, Earl of Hertford and 1st Duke of Somerset (circa 1540s).

Thomas Seymour,
1st Baron Seymour of
Sudeley (circa between
1547 and 1549).

John Dudley, Duke
of Northumberland
(seventeenth century
reproduction).

Edward VI as a toddler (circa 1538).

Edward VI (circa 1546).

Edward VI by William Scrots (circa 1550).

A life model of Edward VI produced by artist/ historian George S. Stuart and photographed by Peter d'Aprix.

Edward VI (after 1543).

A shilling (front and back) depicting Edward VI, struck between 1551 and 1553.

Edward VI by Hans Holbein the Younger (circa 1542).

Edward VI (circa between 1545 and 1553).

Edward VI as a young boy holding a pet monkey, by Hans Holbein the Younger.

Edward VI as an infant, from the collection of portrait miniatures in the Rijksmuseum, Amsterdam.

Edward VI giving his permission to John a Lasco for the creation of a congregation for European Protestants in London in 1550.

Edward VI by William Scrots (circa 1550).

Astrological birth chart for King Edward VI, calculated when he was nine.

Edward VI granting a Royal Charter to Bridewell Hospital in 1553.

Edward VI crushing the Pope with 'the worde of the Lord' (circa between 1568 and 1571).

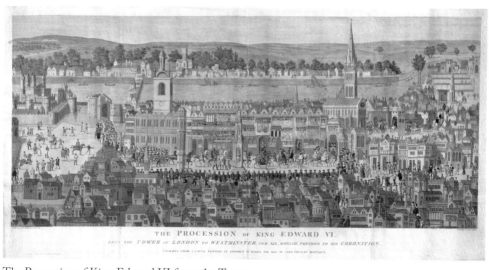

The Procession of King Edward VI from the Tower.

Edward VI as a young boy.

Thomas Cranmer, Archbishop of
Canterbury, godfather of Edward VI.

Lady Jane Grey, heir to Edward VI and
briefly queen of England.

Miniature of Queen Jane Seymour, by Nicholas Hilliard after Hans Holbein.

Lady Jane Grey, copied from a lost original at an unknown date by and unknown artist.

Queen Elizabeth I in her coronation robes (circa between 1600 and 1610 as a copy of a lost original of 1559/1560).

great stones, all the altars, with the stalls and wall of the choir and altar' in order to sell them.[11] Purportedly, even the religiously earnest Somerset 'pulled down the chapel and charnel-house in the Pardon churchyard, and carted off the stones of St. Paul's cloister' because he 'was desirous of building rapidly a sumptuous palace in the Strand'.[12]

Those who disagreed with the vandalism risked condemnation as 'Popish idolaters', and could lose their positions, their property, and their lives. The elderly Bishop of Winchester, Stephen Gardiner, was thrown into the notorious Fleet Prison when he dared to protest the desecration of the churches, and several other bishops would join him there in short order for the same reason. One of those was the Bishop of London, Edmund Bonner. Only the year before Bonner had led the 'children of Paul's School, with parsons and vicars of every London church, in their copes', from St. Paul's to St. Peter's with the bishop 'bearing the sacrament under a canopy; and at the Cross', in a procession before the mayor and aldermen of the city.[13] Now, he was imprisoned for his support of that sacrament's sanctity. The commoners who objected were not spared, either. A man named John Bisse was sent to Fleet for daring to have 'spoken and done inconveniently against the taking down of images abused in the church'.[14] Christians for and against stringent Protestantism were having shouting matches, or even coming to blows, in the aisles of churches. A priest by the name of John Forest was forced to give up his homily in mid-sentence when a congregant with a dissenting opinion called him a 'whoremonger and other misnames' loudly enough to disrupt service.[15]

By November, all but the most fanatical reformers were aghast at what was happening to the churches. Parliament tried to reverse the tide by passing the *Act against Revilers of the Sacrament and for the Communion in both kinds*. This was intended to defend the sacrament, which had 'been most marvelously abused', either due to 'wickedness or else of ignorance and want of learning'. The act also clarified that the sacrament could be administered in either the Protestant or Catholic form 'to any person that will devoutly and humbly desire it'. Anyone caught in depravity against the sacrament would 'suffer imprisonment of their bodies … and make fine and ransom art the king's will and pleasure'. Notwithstanding this defence, Catholicism and traditional religion were attacked almost in the same breath when Parliament then passed the *Act for the Dissolution of the Chantries* in December, which stole the funds that had been given to the church for requiem masses. This theft was theoretically for the 'relief of the king's majesty's charges and expenses, which do daily grow' as a result of the war in Scotland and maintaining Boulogne in France. However, in reality, a 'large part of the chantry endowments eventually went to the harpies who surrounded the young king'.[16]

Meanwhile, Somerset's early removal from Scotland was bearing bitter fruit, with van der Delf reporting that 'the Scots have laid siege to one of the forts held by the English in their country, and that great hopes are entertained of capturing it'.[17] The Scots were ultimately unsuccessful in taking the fort, but it did leave Warwick's forces too busy in defence to lay siege to Stirling Castle and achieve the ultimate goal of capturing Mary, Queen of Scots. Ambassador van der Delft had also heard that Somerset was aware the French planned to reinforce the Scottish resistance, and had therefore begun negotiations with the Earl of Arran and King Henry II of France 'to consent to the new marriage of the little Princess of Scotland, but with the condition that she should not be taken out of the country, and that the forts constructed by the English in Scotland should be dismantled.'[18] As it would so happen, these negotiations were simply a ruse by the Auld Alliance to keep the English complacent while France sent ships and supplies to Scotland. The Scots had also negotiated a betrothal between their queen and the heir to the French throne with England being none the wiser.

Things were not going copaceticly in France, either. There was a fight between the English and French at Boulogne when the occupiers attempted to re-supply the city. Reports of the results varied, but it would appear that at least some of the foodstuff didn't get through. Hungry troops and starving citizens did not make Boulogne more secure. Moreover, in spite of the fact the city was under treaty to return to French hands in 1554, Somerset continued to pour resources into its defence and maintenance. Considering that the Lord Protector was facing depleted royal coffers, continued hostilities in southern Scotland, and a potential civil war over religion in England, it would have been much smarter for him to offer to give the French the city earlier in exchange for cash and cessation of support for Scotland.

Edward VI seems to have been blissfully unaware of any of his country's troubles, at home or abroad. Neither the Lord Protector nor the majority of the councillors seemed to think it wise to 'burden' the king with the whole truth, and made sure the youngster heard more good news than bad. He was therefore able to enjoy a cheerful Christmas with the dowager queen and Thomas Seymour.[19] He may have grown leery of his younger uncle, but his love for his stepmother seems to have remained undiminished. Although his sister Mary had been enraged by Kateryn's early remarriage, Edward does not appear to have held it against her. When Thomas Seymour had tried to coax him into signing a document the previous September, the king had first asked if it was something for the queen, indicating he was willing to sign something if it would benefit his stepmother even if he was cautious about helping his uncle. Kateryn Parr was still a surrogate mother for the little boy, and he had a fiercely strong attachment to her.

Whether Somerset and his wife were able to put aside their animosity toward the admiral and the dowager queen long enough to spend Christmas together with the king is uncertain, but the duke seems to have been with his nephew soon thereafter. January 1548 began with Edward and his whole council at Hampton Court, and on 'New Year's day the king went publicly to mass, which was celebrated with the accustomed solemnity'.[20]

It would have seemed, at first, that everything was now going Somerset's way. He had won a victory against the Scots. He was indisputably the ten-year-old sovereign's beloved and favoured kinsman. He had even secured his position as Lord Protector by bullying the final parliament of 1547 to grant him the authority to rule in Edward's name 'until such time' as the king removed him by a handwritten document 'sealed with the Great Seal of England'.[21] Inasmuch as Somerset himself had control of the Great Seal, it would make it extremely difficult to take the counterfeit crown off his head without consent, even if the king should begin to favour someone else. The duke must have felt clever and reasonably secure.

Notwithstanding his successes, the Lord Protector had actually planted the seeds of his undoing with his attempts to solidify his position. He had made many of the councillors unhappy with his overreach, and fomented the worry that he would try to rule the country through Edward almost indefinitely. Nor were the councillors satisfied with his quasi-kingship. They were aware of how unstable England's gains in Scotland really were, and they knew it was just a matter of time before the French would wrest Boulogne from English control. Few councillors, apart from Archbishop Cranmer, seemed pleased with the way the reformation was being handled. Worst of all, from the point of view of the councillors, Somerset was stingy. He was offering so little wages to the mercenaries he needed to fight his wars that 'no foreigners will come here in search of them whilst they can find service elsewhere'. Perhaps the councillors could have forgiven that, shortsighted though it was, but what they could not forgive was 'the meanness of the Protector' towards themselves, and they were beginning to 'complain of it publicly'.

Thomas Seymour seems to have been angry enough to even plot treason against his brother. One of the first people the admiral hoped to woo to his side was his wife's brother, William Parr, Marquess of Northampton. Somerset had made this task easier for the admiral by alienating Parr beyond endurance for no good reason. The previous April, Parr had petitioned to have his first marriage dissolved. His wife, Anne Bouchier, had run away almost a decade before and had already borne her lover several children, so the marriage was indisputably over. Parr was in love with Lady Elisabeth Brooke and wanted to remarry. He assumed that since Somerset had dissolved his own first marriage for adultery and had remarried, the Lord Protector would be sympathetic. However, the duke had an untapped reserve of hypocrisy of which Parr was unaware. Somerset dithered so long that Parr felt the need to secretly marry Elisabeth Brooke in a clandestine wedding ceremony, to secure the future of the children she might give him. When the Lord Protector found out about the bigamous marriage in February 1548 he went ballistic. Parr was forced to put Elisabeth 'away and never speak to her again on pain of death, in consequence of his having already a wife living, although he has long been separated from her.' Afterwards, the marquess was banished from the court and 'only spoken of secretly' by his friends. As a result, while William Parr was probably not willing to fight in open rebellion against Somerset, he would undoubtedly be looking for a way to take down the Lord Protector when the opportunity arose.

Other men Thomas Seymour hoped to inveigle into a revolt against his brother were Henry Grey, Marquess of Dorset, and Henry Manners, Earl of Rutland. Gery had already allowed the admiral to purchase the warship of his eldest daughter, Lady Jane Grey, who was third in line to the throne, because Seymour had assured him that a marriage between

Jane and King Edward could be arranged. It's unlikely Dorset knew that the admiral was planning an outright uprising, but was ready to back him if the council tried to oust Somerset. The Earl of Rutland was the Warden of the Scottish Marches and had considerable influence in the north, where Somerset's religious reforms were proving unpopular. Again, it is improbable that the earl would have agreed to an armed insurrection against Somerset, but had no motivation to be loyal to the duke either.

Whatever Thomas Seymour had been planning was derailed by a scandal involving him and the king's youngest sister that spring. Lady Elizabeth had lived with her stepmother since the late king's death, and thus was in frequent proximity to the dowager queen's husband. Seymour treated the blossoming girl with undue familiarity, tickling her and letting her see him in his shirt and slippers. It is unclear that the admiral was actually trying to seduce or molest Elizabeth, because the testimony regarding their actions comes mainly from Elizabeth's governess, Kat Astley, who loved gossip and was prone to wild exaggeration. Nevertheless, the admiral's behaviour toward Lady Elizabeth was bad enough that it caused a furore when it became common knowledge. If nothing else, it made Thomas Seymour look like a fool for slapping his wife's teenage stepdaughter on the butt and coming into her bedroom unannounced. Tales grow in the telling, and soon rumours begin to spread that Elizabeth was pregnant with Seymour's baby and had been thrown into the Tower for it.

In reality, the only one pregnant was Seymour's wife, Kateryn. Evidence suggests she didn't really think that her husband and stepdaughter were actually involved in anything illicit, but by May it was clear the scandal was out of control. The only thing to do was to separate Lady Elizabeth and the admiral. Elizabeth was sent to Hertfordshire to live with Sir Anthony Denny and his wife. Denny was Henry VIII's former Groom of the Stool and a good friend of the dowager queen. Moreover, his wife, Joan, was Kat Astley's sister. The king's youngest sister would be safe and well cared for in their hands.

From the letter Elizabeth wrote to her stepmother when she reached the Denny's, the women seem to have parted on good terms. Elizabeth thanked Kateryn for the 'manifold kindnesses received at your highnesses hands' and swore that she was 'replete with sore to depart from your highness, especially leaving you undoubtful of health'. She was also especially grateful to her stepmother for Kateryn's promise 'warn me of all the evils that you should hear of me'. She told the dowager queen that she thanked God 'for providing such friends to me' and that she prayed that God would 'enrich me with their long life'. There is no sign of an apology for wrongdoing, or any hint of guilt, or indication she thought that her stepmother was angry with her.

If King Edward was told about the scandal, he doesn't mention it in his diary or hint at it in his existing letters. There also doesn't appear to have been any active animus against his uncle, which would have surely been extant if the king thought Seymour was trying to meddle with Elizabeth. In April he had been fed and entertained by the admiral when he took the French ambassador on a tour of the *Great Harry*, now rechristened the *Great Edward*, that had been anchored near Woolwich.[22] In July he had added a handwritten note to the bottom of a letter John Fowler sent to Seymour, asking for money and to be 'recommended to the queen' by her husband. These are not the actions of a miffed monarch.

Then again, the king may have been angry with Seymour yet willing to try to smooth things over, since he seems to have been inclined to be a peace-maker at this age. He had recently broken up a mock battle at Greenwich when the fighting grew too heated, and had assured both sides that they had done an equally good job.[23] Edward wouldn't have wanted tension between himself and the husband of the only mother he could remember.

Somerset was livid when the scandal broke, but he had bigger fish to fry than a naughty younger brother. Things were falling apart all around him. He had taken control of the government 'to such an extent, indeed, that very little mention is made of the King and his Court' but everyone was 'beginning to recognise that the reputation of the Court of England [had] greatly come down'.[24] The English were holding onto Boulogne, in spite of the occasional brawl with the French, but it necessitated 'sending every day reinforcements' with less and less money to spend for them. There were also fears of another French invasion of England. Nor were things going well in the north. Troops under the command of Henry Grey had suffered 'a bad reverse' against the Scots, 'having attempted to surprise the enemy, whom they found in larger numbers than they had been led to expect. They therefore were defeated and left some four or five hundred men on the field.[25] The Lord Protector would thus need to make plans to reinforce his men in Scotland as well. He already knew the

French were backing the Scots, but now there were international rumours that King Christian III of Denmark had agreed to help them as well, and was planning to send two thousand soldiers 'and a considerable number of ships'.[26] It was unlikely, but still worrying for England.

Things at home weren't going any better for the Lord Protector. Religious tensions were mounting. Ambassador van der Delft reported that arguments over the '[correct' form of Christianity were 'getting worse and worse here daily', with the English theologians 'so variable that it is difficult to understand what they are driving at; the only thing evident being that they are constantly getting worse, not without sorrow of a large number of worthy folk. To such an extent is this so that in the county of Cornwall they have killed the commissioner sent down in the King's name to introduce the new ordinances.'[27] Moreover, the increasing enclosure of common lands by the gentry, which was driving more and more Englishmen into penury and starvation, was doing nothing to smooth over religious differences.

To make things harder on himself, Somerset was continuing to alienate his most powerful allies for no rational purpose. He made the Earl of Warwick highly vexed by interfering in the internal matters of Dudley's home county. It was nothing of serious importance, merely the refusal to remove a justice and appoint the one Dudley had chosen, and had no benefit that would come close to the disadvantage of insulting his fellow councillor. Noblemen were hypersensitive about their honour, and Warwick did not like being treated to his 'poor credit and estimation' and knowing that there were 'base friends who would smile to see [him] so used'.[28] Dudley confided to William Paget that he was willing to forgive the duke, provided that there was no more disrespect, but if Paget told the Lord Protector about it then Somerset didn't listen.

Disaster struck when the French arrived to bolster the beleaguered Scots in June, landing at Leith and entrenching in Edinburgh. Somerset's advisors warned him that it was dangerous to allow the French to gain a stronghold so near Mary, Queen of Scots, but the Lord Protector was slow to act on their advice. The treasury was already overdrawn supporting costly garrisons to the south of Edinburgh and perhaps Somerset didn't want the expense or the hassle of a major engagement with the French on Scottish soil. He waited until August to begin assembling reinforcements and sending the Earl of Warwick north once more to deal with the situation. This was arguably the biggest mistake of the duke's ersatz reign, because by the first week of August the French had smuggled the five-year-old out of the country and taken her to live with her new betrothed, the heir to France's throne, Dauphin Francis. The whole point of the Rough Wooing, the embodied chance to unite England and Scotland, was now at the French court and engaged to the French prince.

Somerset had utterly failed his king regarding the Scottish matter, but Edward continued to support his uncle's regency. The strongest reason for the king's approval was probably that he was completely in sympathy with even Somerset's most radical reformist policies. Additionally, the Augsburg Interim, intended as a compromise of sorts between traditional Catholicism and the new Protestantism, had become an imperial law on 30 June and had given the king and his uncle another common religious enemy. Evangelical Protestants were convinced the Interim was a back-door attempt to subvert the reforms needed for 'true' worship. This attack on the Reformation must be fought tooth and nail, and Somerset was the man whom the king trusted to help him in this fight. Edward's faith was paramount, and he judged the quality of everyone around him by their loyalty to the reformed church, and in extension to that, their loyalty to him as the head of that church.

Although he was only ten years old, Edward was determined to fulfil the Protestant hopes that he was a new Josiah, and rid his realm of the 'false idols' of Catholic iconography and art. Without a doubt, Protestant reformers embraced him as such. They rejoiced that they had 'a king who is firm, learned, and pious beyond his age'.[29] Archbishop Cranmer called his godson 'most earnestly given to the true knowledge of god', and extolled his desire 'to bring up his people' into the true faith. John Foxe would laud him in the *Book of Martyrs* for 'zealous care ... concerning reformation of Christ's church', and claim that 'nothing can be said enough of his commendation'.[30] Surrounded by like-minded scholars, taught that Protestantism was the only path to God, and praised to the skies for his dogmatic inflexibility, it is little wonder the king was absolutist and fundamentalist.

Chapter Nine

Somerset Loses Control of the King

Kateryn Parr brought a little girl into the world on 30 August 1548, and just six days later King Edward VI lost a second mother to the dangers of childbirth. Although there is no record, either in his private journal or existing letters, of the young king's reaction, he would have undeniably been grief-stricken by the death of the woman who had been so kind to him. It was Kateryn, among all of his adult caretakers, in whom he could have had the most confidence that she loved him simply for his own sake. She had ascended as high as a woman's rank could go, and had no reason to love him other than that she was a loving person. As the dowager queen, she could be close to him in a way even his sisters could not. The court around him was kept so formal that an Italian noted derisively that the Lady Elizabeth had to curtsey to her knee to the floor five times as she approached his table to dine with him.[1] A queen, even a dowager queen, would not need to abase herself so thoroughly. When he ate dinner with other members of his family, even his siblings, they had to sit on a bench far enough away from him that the canopy of state was never over their heads as well. The dowager queen could sit next to him. She may have been the only person in the world who would have dared to hug the little boy, or treat him affectionately. His last remaining link with his parents or the feeling of parental tenderness was gone.

His siblings were likewise heartbroken by their stepmother's loss. His eldest sister had reconciled with the dowager queen just a few weeks before, and Kateryn had named her newborn daughter Mary. Considering how many mother-figures Mary had lost since childhood, and her fragile mental state, the dowager queen's death must have devastated her. Kateryn had continued to write to Elizabeth frequently, letters that the teenaged girl had exclaimed made her 'most joyful'. We know the missives were kind, because Elizabeth replied that she was grateful that 'your grace wished me with you till I were weary' and told her stepmother that if she could stay as long as she wanted 'your highness were like to be cumbered' because she'd never leave. As with Edward, Kateryn Parr was the only mother Elizabeth had ever known. Now, death had left her motherless once more.

In response to losing his stepmother, the king seems to have thrown himself into religion even further, if such a thing were possible. Archbishop Cranmer had finished the first Book of Common Prayer, which would produce the liturgy in English for the first time, and it is inconceivable that he didn't show it to his godson for approval before putting the book before a specially assembled commission in September to endorse it. Somerset and Cranmer had also presented the Act of Uniformity to the Parliament, which would require every church 'within this realm of England, Wales, Calais, and the marches of the same, or other the king's dominions' to use the Book of Common Prayer for its services 'and none other or otherwise'. The abolition of services in Latin in favour of the prayer book was causing a serious ruckus among the more moderate reformists. The king, who had turned eleven years old that October, was keeping abreast of the parliamentary procedures with the attention of a man three times his age, and was displeased by their resistance. When Somerset complained of how Thomas Thirlby, Bishop of Norwich, was refusing to sign off on either the prayer book or the act, Edward told him he was not surprised. This startled his uncle, who asked him why. 'I expected nothing else,' the king replied acerbically, 'but that he, who has been so long a time with the Emperor, should smell of the Interim.'

To the king's satisfaction, the Act of Uniformity passed on 21 January 1549, and the Book of Common Prayer was sent off to the printers. The act, however, certainly didn't represent uniformity. Of the eighteen bishops present in the House of Lords for the final vote, only ten supported it, and several of those assenting votes may have come because Somerset and John Dudley had browbeaten them into submission. Moreover, there were many Christians in the kingdom who preferred to hear the rites in Latin, and they were unhappy to be given no choice in the matter. Rumours flew that Mass was being abolished. Saints Days, which were beloved for the break they provided from day-to-day work, were restricted. There was no longer to be ash on Ash Wednesday, palms on Palm Sunday, or candles on Candlemas. As the churchwardens in Berkshire recorded, 'all godly ceremonies and good uses were taken out of the Church'.[2] This deprivation of spiritual comforts on top of enclosures and other economic hardships naturally caused further social unrest.

Any victory Edward would have felt in the passing of the act was almost surely tempered by dismay regarding the actions of his younger uncle, Thomas Seymour, who seems to have lost his wits after the death of his wife. His mother, Margaret, had come to Sudeley Castle to take care of her new granddaughter and his ward, Jane Grey, which freed the admiral to return to his schemes of usurping the protectorate from his brother. On 16 January he appears to have made an asinine attempt to 'rescue' (or kidnap) Edward from Somerset's control, fleeing into the night after he shot and killed the king's pet dog when it barked. History conveys the impression that he killed his nephew's affections for him with the same bullet.

Men were sent to summon the admiral for questioning the day after he tried to snatch the king from Hampton Court, but Seymour refused to obey. He had the audacity to send word to his elder brother that William Pageant 'must be sent as hostage to his house if they wanted him to answer the summons; and that he must (receive an assurance) that he would return as free as he went forth'.[3] Of course, these shenanigans were not appreciated by the council. They began to gather evidence against Seymour. The admiral 'protested vigorously ... saying he had attempted nothing against the King; on the contrary, that he had the King's confidence and approval' but it didn't stop the investigations. His plot to become Protector in his brother's place soon came to light, along with the damning suggestion that he had 'tried to negotiate his own marriage with the Lady Elizabeth and gain a lever with which to accomplish his purpose'. The charming, foolhardy admiral was subsequently arrested in late February and imprisoned in the Tower.

Thomas Seymour was condemned to death by an Act of Attainder and beheaded on 20 March 1549. He died, as the future Queen Elizabeth famously said, 'a man of much wit and very little judgement'. Nevertheless, there were many who looked askance at his execution without trial, and Somerset's willingness to behead his own brother was abhorred. The Protector may have been counting on the fact he was called 'the goodly duke' by the ordinary people, due to his initial attempts to slow or halt the enclosures, to keep him popular. However, his execution of his brother was beyond the pale of defence even if he had stopped the enclosures altogether. Somerset also tried to ward off criticism by promoting a smear campaign against Thomas Seymour, but it was to no avail. The duke was derided as 'a blood-sucker and a ravenous wolf' and it was said that 'the blood of his brother the admiral cried against him before God'.[4] Later he would try to claim that he had only done it because someone (reputed to be John Dudley) had talked him into it, but that argument elides the fact that he was unquestionably powerful enough to commute his brother's sentence to perpetual imprisonment. Instead, the Protector fled the capital the day before the execution, so he wouldn't be confronted with the evidence of fratricide.

In his journal, the king calmly noted that the admiral had been condemned to death without further comment. Was he secretly upset? Or had he become convinced that the admiral was genuinely conspiring to kill him? Circumstances favour the latter explanation. The men he trusted the most, particularly Somerset and John Dudley, had told him that Seymour was trying to wed Elizabeth, which the king was smart enough to know could eventually lead to the admiral's promotion to monarch. His uncle had tried to remove him from his household by force, and had shot his pet. Moreover, was the dog's death the only one the king blamed on Seymour? If the admiral had been willing to wait the two years of a normal mourning period to wed Kateryn Parr, then the dowager queen would probably still be alive. The king had also, either through coaxing or with a wisdom beyond his age, begun to question the motivation behind Seymour's gifts of money. During the investigation, he had shown no qualms in telling the council about the funds he had been given, or the admiral's attempts to inveigle him to sign documents behind Somerset's back, despite how bad it looked for his uncle. The strongest evidence that Edward believed his uncle to be guilty of treason is that he agreed, with the Lord Protector by his side, that the council could decide Thomas Seymour's fate, giving them 'his surety ... that they could proceed as they required',[5] and then had not intervened when his uncle was condemned to die.

Whatever his feelings toward his younger uncle, the king still appeared to have great faith in, and love for, his uncle Somerset. That was good news for the duke, since his ineffectual leadership both home and abroad meant that only the king's favour stood between him and being ousted from the protectorate. The assault on Scotland had become pointless once

Mary, Queen of Scots, had arrived at the French court, but rather than negotiate for peace he was still pouring men and supplies into the war's insatiable maw. More and more of England's gains were being reclaimed by the Franco-Scots alliance. France continued to supply reinforcements to prevent the English from making renewed headway. The entire conflict had devolved into both sides marauding across the borderlands and destroying as much as they could in a blood-soaked stalemate. Keeping a grip on Boulogne was also proving costly and problematic. The English were able to keep the French from retaking the city in May, but only just barely. The French had destroyed any of the outposts that England tried to build to strengthen their position and, naturally, the native populace within the city were constantly scheming against the occupiers. It was becoming ever more difficult, and increasingly expensive, to maintain supplies for the English garrison with very little to show for the effort.

A civil war over religion appeared to be fomenting within the borders of the realm as well. In the first two years of his protectorate, Somerset had issued enough contradictory proclamations – some tolerant and some intolerant of Catholicism, some progressive and some totalitarian regarding economically relevant policies – that the populace was left uncertain as to whether they were coming or going. Notwithstanding the confusion he had caused, once the Act of Unity had passed he appears to have decided to clamp down on dissension, possibly in an attempt to please King Edward and prove his erstwhile piety. This increased rigidity ignored how unwelcome the new Prayer Book was proving to be with large sections of the populace, and only served to exacerbate the rising tension. He also ignored the input of his fellow councillors, who tried to tell him he was taking the wrong approach to the problem. William Pageant wrote to Somerset, warning him that religious reform should be slowed, or better yet halted, for the time being, due to the unhappiness the Prayer Book was causing. This wise advice fell on deaf ears.

Greed for both authority and prestige was also making the duke act stupidly. He had added 'by the grace of God' to the announcements of his titles and was bluntly acting as the stand-in sovereign for state functions. The palace he was building for himself just outside London was becoming a medieval Disneyland and was devouring everything around it. He confiscated the surrounding houses, including the residences of four bishops, and the Church of St Mary in order to knock them all down and use their components and land to expand his vanity project.[6] When he began to raid St Margaret's Church near Westminster Abbey for its building materials as well, 'the sight of the scaffolding excited such vigorous opposition from the parishioners, that this part of his scheme had to be given up'.[7] Instead he turned his sights on the Church of the Knights of St John, demolishing it and then carting off the stone, timber, and lead to use for constructing Somerset Palace. He even snaffled books from the Guildhall Library in London to make his own library more impressive.

The Protector's biggest mistake, however, was in his own hypocritical religious behaviour. He had not been content to take building components only from the chapel and grounds of St Paul's Cathedral, but had actually destroyed the charnel house as well. This blatant desecration of the dead for venial purposes caused many formerly 'well disposed minds' to develop a 'hard opinion' of him, inasmuch as his 'actions were in a high degree impious' and 'did draw with them both open dislike from men' and God's vengeance'.[8] His allies also scathingly began to note that the duke had grown 'cold in hearing God's word'[9] because he was choosing to enjoy worldly pleasures on Sundays instead of attending reformist services. Perhaps his new dislike of Protestant sermons came from the fact that denouncements of those who 'have for your possessions yearly too much'[10] were becoming progressively common?

Somerset's foolish solution to his shrinking popularity among Protestants was to crack down on those who disliked the new Prayer Book and suspected Catholic sympathisers. As ever, the martyrdom of those supporting the older rites of faith further entrenched resistance. Ambassador van der Delft also warned Somerset that giving Protestants all their own way was dangerous, since 'those who have the gospel only for ever in their mouths ... are the very men who refuse to obey anyone, wronging the whole world in order that they may live according to their own inclinations, which is quite contrary to the Gospel of which they professed to be so fond.'[11] His words would prove prophetic. Moreover, Archbishop Cranmer, supported by the king, was openly determined that the reforms go further, until they stripped away the last vestiges of 'popish' religious practice. These reformist edicts would be enforced regardless of how many Englishmen detested them.

Like Frankenstein, the Protestants created their own monster. The rapid and brutally imposed reforms were the main reasons for the Prayer

Book Rebellion in June 1549. The revolt, centred in Devon and Cornwall, was not an attempt to return to Catholicism or deny the king's role as the head of the church. The rebels were simply demanding that they be allowed to continue using the prayer service from the last decade of Henry VIII's reign. Archbishop Cranmer's liturgical writings are considered masterworks from a modern perspective, but they were too different from the accustomed services to do anything other than antagonise adherents of the preexisting religious rites. Rather than stamping out practices reminiscent of Catholicism, the forcible application of the new Prayer Book merely made the people more determined to hold on to the old ways of worshipping.

Somerset was aware that the West Country uprisings were as much over land enclosures and inflation of food prices as they were the Book of Common Prayer. To his credit, he even understood the injustice of the gentry seizing and privatising lands that were traditionally for common use. In sympathy for the rebel's physical needs, the Protector issued a proclamation on 2 July promising to regulate the price of food, among other things.[12] Unfortunately, what should be seen as compassion for the poor was seen by the Privy Council as treasonous support for those who would overthrow the 'natural' order and have the base rule the elite. One of the 'crimes' Somerset was later accused of when he was removed from the office of Lord Protector was that he, 'had not taken care to suppress the late insurrections, but had justified and encouraged them'.[13] The majority of the council members, including Archbishop Cranmer (who was personally incensed by the burning of his prayer books), urged the duke to take a hard line against the rebels. After ignoring the council's good advice on almost every other topic, Somerset finally heeded their bad advice. He dispatched troops, composed mostly of German and Italian mercenaries, under the command of Baron John Russell, to subdue the rebels.

At almost the same time that the Prayer Book Rebellion broke out in the west, other uprisings were springing up across England. These small rebellions in Essex, Suffolk, Sussex, Hertfordshire, Buckinghamshire, and Oxfordshire were more or less jumped-up riots, and were easily put down by local authorities. Kett's Rebellion, which had exploded in the north, was a horse of a different colour.

While the main cause of Kett's Rebellion was the enclosure of land and the resulting economic hardship, it was just as tangled in religious matters as the Prayer Book Rebellion had been in economic ones. In early July, people in the Norfolk village of Wymondham were illicitly celebrating St Thomas Becket's feast day when the discussion of grievances against the government spilt over into calls for action. The unhappy northerners found a leader in a wealthy yeoman farmer named Robert Kett, and not long thereafter were marching on Norwich with blood in their eyes. Norwich, the second-largest city in England at the time, subsequently fell to the rebels a few weeks later. A frightened Somerset quickly sent another mixture of military and mercenaries to the north under the generalship of William Parr, Marquess of Northampton, hoping to quash the latest rebellion before any more could spring up.

The simultaneous rebellions and poisonous religious atmosphere had so unsettled the country that a rumour also began to spread that King Edward had died. The fears of the king's death were so prevalent that it was 'consequently judged necessary that he should publicly show himself to the people'.[14] The king, therefore, paraded through London 'with a goodly company' from Suffolk Palace to Whitehall on 23 July.

Relieved by the king's obvious health, London was further reassured by news that the Prayer Book Rebellion had been successfully suppressed. The insurgents, outnumbered by superiorly trained soldiers, were crushed at Clyst St. Mary on 5 August, and almost a thousand men had been taken prisoner. Unbelievably, Russell had then slit the throats of the captured rebels later that night.[15] The surviving dissenters had retaliated at Clyst Heath the following day, but they were again decimated by Russell's mercenaries. The rebellion was broken, but Somerset, terrified by the revolts occurring both the west and the north, ordered Russell to continue punitive measures against suspected nonconformists in Cornwall and Devon.

Although the English government had won in the west, things were not going their way in the north. To the shock of the Protector, the council, and London in general, William Parr's troops were soundly defeated by Kett's rebels. John Dudley had been successful in his battles against the Scots, so the council saw the Earl of Warwick as the best hope of putting down the rebellion. Somerset and Warwick had already had a falling out, and the last thing the duke wanted was to give his rival another chance to shine, but he feared the northern rebels more. Therefore, he sent Warwick north with more troops and more mercenaries to take back Norwich and suppress the revolt. After days of bloody skirmishes in the street and one pitched battle outside the city walls, Norwich was recaptured from the rebels on 27 August. Kett was arrested, and would be later tried and hanged for his part in the rebellion. Warwick was hailed as a hero by his fellow councillors and reformists for his successful suppression of the rebellion, but would become a locus of hatred and anti-Protestant feelings in the north.

The Protector's earlier mercies toward the working class still secured him a continued measure of popularity, regardless of his fratricide and the prayer book proclamations. Moreover, the king continued to support him, having dedicated a treatise he wrote that year against the Pope's love for 'idols and devils' to his uncle out of respect for the duke's appreciation of 'the divine word and sincere religion'. Nonetheless, almost no one else in power was terribly happy with Somerset after the disastrous summer of 1549. He was well aware that the council was dissatisfied with his protectorate, and hoped to replace him with the Earl of Warwick. He spent September and early October desperately trying, by every means possible, to keep a hold on his shadow crown. He published tracts accusing some councillors of mendacity, and sent pleading missives to other councillors whom he hoped would be his allies. When that didn't seem to be enough, he issued a summons to his friends and family demanding that they bring him military aid at Hampton Court, where he was keeping the king close by his side. Notwithstanding his efforts to either butter up or bully its members, the council sent him a letter asking him to step down from his position of Lord Protector. Clearly, they hoped to effect a regime change in a calm and peaceful manner, without unduly alarming the populace or King Edward.

Their hopes that Somerset would relinquish power without a fight were in vain. In a last-ditch effort to save himself, he persuaded the young king that his enemies were also bent on Edward's overthrow, and possibly the king's murder. In fairness, Somerset would have almost certainly believed that the Council meant to kill him, and he was therefore fighting for his life. With his neck on the line, he probably convinced himself that he had no choice but to impel his nephew to help him. Believing that his uncle had been truthful with him, King Edward appeared before those assembled at Hampton Court to fight for Somerset and told them, 'he was displeased that an attempt should be made to take his uncle the

Protector away from him, and prayed that all would help him in resisting, for he himself was clothed, and ready to arm'.[16]

In spite of Somerset's seeming willingness to start a civil war and his possession of the king, the bulk of the councillors convened at the Tower and let it be known that they intended to force the duke to step down. Panicked, Somerset grabbed the king and ran for it. The outraged council then 'made its proclamation in which the Protector was declared to be a traitor for having destroyed the kingdom by his avarice, taken everything for himself, unsettled the people, and finally carried off the King in order to make himself sovereign lord of all in defiance of the commands left by the late King, and in spite of the repeated admonitions of the Council.'[17]

These events were indisputably terrifying for Edward, who still trusted his uncle implicitly and believed Somerset's assertions that the council had rebelled. The king would record in his diary how he was rushed away from Hampton Court late in the evening of 6 October to Windsor Castle. It would have been dark, even if some of the company were bearing torches. It would have been cold. The little boy would have been surrounded by the jingling of horses and the noises of armed men, reminding him of his present danger. Observers reported that the young king had carried a drawn sword, crying out, 'My vassals will you help me against those who want to kill me?'[18] It was more than twenty miles to his destination, so he would have had to have ridden for roughly four hours in a constant state of anxiety. He would have been afraid that his company might be assaulted, and would have wondered how he would know friend from foe in the night. His uncle Somerset had let him have very little martial training, and he must have fretted about how unable he was to defend himself. As a Tudor king, he would have been taught the history of the Princes in the Tower, and would have almost certainly worried that he might be the next boy-king to disappear into an unmarked grave.

His arrival at Windsor Castle, 'where watch and ward' was kept over him, wouldn't have ameliorated his fears very much, either. He was still in peril, only now he was behind the walls of a thinly manned fortress. Because they had arrived without preparation, there were inadequate supplies of food and other necessities. For the first time in his life, the king was forced to endure minor deprivations and sleep in a chilly room without sufficient heating. To make things harder, he had caught a cold on the ride to the castle, and woke up the next morning 'much troubled with a great rheum'.[19] He would also quickly come to think of Windsor as his prison, because there were 'no galleries nor gardens to walk in'.[20]

Nevertheless, the young king tried to do what he could to help his situation. The morning after his arrival he wrote a stern letter, probably assisted by Somerset and Archbishop Cranmer, to the council claiming that he knew, 'what opinion you have conceived of our dearest uncle the Lord Protector'.[21] He warned them that 'we do lament our present estate being in such and imminent dangers', and unless they should 'be careful to bring those uproars into a quiet … we shall have cause to think you forget your duties to us'. He vigorously defended his uncle, and told his councillors to consider that every 'man hath his faults, [Somerset] his, and you yours; and if we shall hereafter as rigorously weigh yours, as we hear that you intend with cruelty to purge his, which of you all shall be able to stand before us?' He insisted that the duke 'meaneth no hurt' and reminded them if they were displeased with Somerset's government then it was up to him to decide what to do with his uncle, 'whom you know we love' and who should 'therefore somewhat the more to be considered'. He told them flatly that they should 'in nowise counsel us to proceed to extremities against him, for fear of any respect that might particularly seem hereafter to touch any of you'. He ended the letter by telling them that he was sending Sir Philip Hoby to act as an envoy between them and his uncle, demanding that they 'tender our preservation and the weal of our realm'.

The councillors were mindful that the populace and the monarch had concerns regarding their intentions. They therefore took steps to alleviate the fears of the king and kingdom. They published articles against Somerset for the general public, accusing the duke of mismanagement, malfeasance, and scarring the life out of the king by claiming the council were trying to kill him. These articles moreover pointed out the Protector's imprudence in dragging the king to Windsor 'without any provision there made for his grace', putting the king in 'great fear' and causing him to take 'also such disease as was to his great peril'.[22] They sent missives to the king's sisters, letting Mary and Elizabeth know the accusations against Somerset and assuring them that the whole rumpus was to remove him from his position as Protector without any harm meant toward the sovereign. They also sent the duke a letter via his messenger, Philip Hoby, in an attempt to defuse the situation before it got even worse. They promised him, among other things, that 'on their faith and honours they did not intend, or will hurt [his] person,' nor to 'take away any of his lands or goods'.

Unbeknownst to Somerset, Hoby had an additional letter in his pouch meant for the king's eyes only. The original has been lost to history, but the king recorded in his journal that it accused his uncle of 'faults, ambition, vain-glory, entering into rash wars in my youth … enriching himself of my treasure, following his own opinion, and doing all by his own authority, etc'. Although it assured the king that the council only wanted to depose Somerset because he was abusing his position and taking advantage of his nephew, Edward appears to have been unmoved by their promises and to have remained certain that Somerset was only trying to protect them both.

Notwithstanding the king's remaining suspicions, Archbishop Cranmer and William Paget, who had remained with Somerset, became convinced that Warwick and the other councillors only wanted the best for their sovereign. Ergo, they made plans with the council on how to get Edward away from the Protector. They 'sequestered' the duke from the king so that he could no longer influence his nephew and arranged a date for councillors to come to Windsor. However, they did not inform the king of these plans, in case word got back to the duke. Consequently, when Warwick and a handful of other councillors arrived at the castle on 11 October, the young monarch's first reaction to his liberators was surprise and profound alarm. He had been told so often and so urgently that his councillors meant to kill him that he had no doubt that was what they intended to do. Happily for Edward, he 'was soon afterwards disabused'[23] of these fears by Warwick and the others. They came before him 'most humbly on their knees' and explained their reasons and motivations for wishing to remove Somerset from the protectorate, 'which his majesty did accept in most gracious part, giving their lordships his most hearty thanks'.[24]

Since the royal physician had 'dispraised' Windsor, the councillors offered to immediately escort him back to Hampton Court so he could be made more comfortable, and he gladly accepted. He accordingly left Windsor in a much better state of mind than when he arrived there, and 'he thanked all the company for having rid him of such fear and peril'.[25] He was subsequently able to awake at Hampton Court on the morning of his twelfth birthday well-rested, well-fed, and well pleased with how things had turned out. Paget wrote to the council to tell them that their sovereign was now 'in good health and merry'. Better yet, he had 'with a merry countenance and a loud voice [asked] how your lordships did, when he should see you, and that you should be welcome whenever you come'.[26]

On 13 October the Duke of Somerset's protectorate over the king was removed by the will of the council, and orders were given for his arrest. He was brought into London the following day by no less than three hundred armed horsemen, who were there to both prevent his rescue and safeguard him from the unhappy crowds who now suspected him of being a traitor to their young king. The former protector repeatedly cried out that 'he was no traitor, but as faithful a servant of the king as any man'.[27] Nevertheless, doubts remained. William Paulet, the Lord High Treasurer, wrote that the duke 'was now stayed' but was to be examined by the council 'whereby great questions shall follow'.[28]

Chapter Ten

Edward is Becoming a King in Truth

King Edward likewise rode into London on 17 October 'accompanied by the Councillors and all the nobles of the realm'[1] in order to reassure the people he was alive and well. Wearing a coat of 'cloth of tissue' and bedecked in jewels, he led a magnificent parade of over a thousand horsemen through the streets of the city while the crowds cheered. Reminiscent of his coronation, the route from London Bridge to Temple Bar along which he rode was lined with 'minstrels and singing men' and 'garnished with arras and other decent hangings'.[2]

The city was jubilant. There had been no bloody coup or usurpation of the king's throne. The government had remained essentially stable, and there was no current threat of another civil war. All that the populace had to worry about now were the rising food prices, devalued currency, enclosures, continual plagues of incurable diseases, religious upheaval, and potential rebellions.

The king trusted his councillors once more, but he retained enough good feeling towards his uncle that he demanded assurances of Somerset's safety and treatment. The duke was being treated well, and in spite of many historians assertions to the contrary, there is scant evidence that the Earl of Warwick was plotting to execute the former Lord Protector. It was Thomas Wriothelsey who was inveigling to take over the top spot in the council. It was Wriothesley who set out 'with conservative support to recover the precedence he had lost in 1547 when the protector had sacked him as lord chancellor', and only when John Dudley was threatened 'to be dragged down as an erstwhile supporter of Somerset did he act in self-defence' by seeking leadership.[3] Warwick secured the appointment of Henry Grey, Marquess of Dorset, and Richard Cox, Bishop of Ely, to the council and with the addition of these two new allies he was able to cut off Wriothesley and the conservatives from governance. Once Dudley had control of the council, he could have begun to pressure them to prove Somerset's 'treason' and execute him, king's kinsman or not. Instead,

Warwick worked with the crown to save the duke's hide. The former Protector was able to pay a fine and be released from the Tower with the king's pardon on 6 February 1550.

If Dudley had ever planned on becoming the de facto monarch the way Somerset had, now was his chance, but he did not make the slightest attempt to give himself a similar protectorate. He behaved in the opposite manner, working to gain a consensus with his fellow councillors before implementing policy. Instead of personally holding on to the dry stamp of the king's signature, as Somerset had done, he put Sir John Gage in charge of it. Gage was not only a lawyer, he had been one of Henry VIII's trusted courtiers. He was made the chief gentleman of King Edward's privy chamber, so that he would know if the monarch was aware that the dry stamp would be used. Dudley also increased the number of gentlemen around the king to make sure that no single councillor, including himself, could get the young sovereign to himself and beguile his way into power. From now on there would always be at least three gentlemen of the privy chamber with the king, two of whom would sleep on pallets in his room, and five grooms would always be present. Although Dudley was careful to install men he trusted as the king's grooms, everything was done with Edward's consent. In fact, under Warwick's offices, the young monarch was being consulted more about his own affairs and government than ever before. Additionally, while Dudley did stack the council with Protestant allies, he also appointed those who didn't agree with him as members. He would even go so far as to allow Somerset, who was certain to work against him, to be reinstated to the council in April. This was quite a risk, in that William Paget had already told an ambassador that although the former Protector 'governed us ill … you will see that he will come back into authority as before, and this will happen because there is no one else to take his place'.[4] Moreover, as a duke Somerset would have been given social precedence over all the other council members, regardless of the earl's position as its head. This clearly didn't bother Warwick enough to do anything about it, since he didn't demand further elevation to match his rival's.

Dudley may have been content to remain the Earl of Warwick, but he was careful to reward his close allies who had given him their support. In January 1550, he arranged to have William Paulet, already the Lord High Treasurer, elevated to the Earl of Wiltshire. John Russell was raised from a lord to the Earl of Bedford, and from the steward of Cornwall to the Lord Privy Seal. Walter Devereux, Lord Ferrers, was made a member of council and promoted to Viscount Hereford. Warwick had already installed his brother, Andrew Dudley, and three other Protestant stalwarts as the four chief gentlemen of the king's privy chamber, but now he added to the honours of the king's household. William Parr was given the position of Lord Great Chamberlain, with Baron Thomas Wentworth serving as the chamberlain under him. Finally, Sir Anthony Wingfield, whom the council had trusted to arrest Somerset a few months before, was made Comptroller and put in charge of managing the king's personal expenses.

Most importantly, Warwick's new position as the head of the council ushered in the true beginnings of Edward VI's rule. From 1550 onward, the young monarch would begin to take the reins of power increasingly into his own hands, and would show himself to be as adept at governance as his grandfather, King Henry VII. Only the future Queen Elizabeth I would prove herself to be as canny a Tudor monarch as her brother had been.

The king continued to love and support his uncle Somerset, even after the debacle in October, but he quickly came to enjoy the new freedoms instituted by Warwick and the revamped council. Dudley did not make Somerset's mistake of treating Edward as a malleable child to be cosseted and controlled. The monarch was still young, but he had such substantial intelligence that he was older in thought than in years. Warwick took the boy's brains into account and gave him an increasing say in his own affairs and government. Giacomo Soranzo, the Viennese ambassador, wrote that the earl 'supplied him freely with money, appointing a Lord Privy Purse (*un tesoriero suo proprio*), recommending him to make presents, and show that he was king'.[5] More importantly, Warwick 'made him acquainted with all public business, and chose to have his opinion, in such wise that his commands might then be executed without delay'.[6] It is a measure of Edward's perspicacity that even with his newfound freedoms he was judicious enough 'that he would never do any act, either of grace or justice, without the approval of his council'. This almost preternatural prudence made him 'so popular with his councillors and the whole country that there is perhaps no instance on record of any other king of that age being more beloved, or who gave greater promise'.[7]

Warwick also gave Edward more autonomy over his own body. Whereas Somerset had kept the king practically wrapped in swaddling, the earl, 'who was a soldier at heart and by profession … changed the King's studies accordingly'.[8] Dudley let the king start his marital training, so he could learn how to 'handle his weapons, and to go through other similar exercises'. Like most boys of his social class, the king was eager to begin, and 'soon commenced arming and tilting, managing horses, and delighting in every sort of exercise'. Although Edward would never evince his father's prodigious athletic prowess, he liked 'drawing the bow, playing rackets, hunting, and so forth, indefatigably'. As much as he enjoyed these liberties, observers noted admiringly that the young king was nonetheless careful to 'never neglect his studies'.[9]

The king's newly granted rights to participate in more risky activities does not indicate that Warwick wasn't determined to take good care of him, however. The court protocols remained fanatically devoted to preserving Edward's well-being. To keep away the pestilence thought to travel in foul odours, his chambers were constantly kept 'as sweet as they may be'.[10] His food, clothes, and even the cushions on the seat of his toilet were all tested for poisons before coming into contact with the king. His yeomen of the guard were increased from one hundred men to four hundred, plus an additional sixty men-at-arms who had been tested in real battles abroad. If he wanted to go outside, or even walk along the palace galleries, the guards and the king's personal ushers had to check the area carefully first to make sure there were no dangers lurking. His bed also had to be checked, both under it and among his coverlets, for sabotage and hidden assassins. In any house he visited, the chambers for his private use could not have separate doors into back gardens or courtyards, lest someone sneak inside for nefarious purposes. Not even letters or gifts could be given to the king without being vetted for clandestine poisons.

There were also attempts to protect the king's mind from subjects or ideas that might upset him 'before the steadiness of mature age'. Cynically, this could be seen as an attempt to prevent him from learning that Catholicism was not evil or how badly his subjects were faring under the new enclosure laws. It's certainly true that John Gage stopped someone from giving the king a tract regarding the abuses of the poor by the rich. Nevertheless, there seems to have been at the very least a mixed motivation, and a genuine desire to shelter the twelve-year-old boy from the harshness of reality. The king was supposedly reading a historical chronicle when he came across a reference to his father's execution of a finance minister who had served under King Henry VII. Not knowing that this man was Edmund Dudley, the king asked Warwick about it. Rather than explaining that his father had been unjustly beheaded, Dudley told his sovereign not to burden his 'youthful and tender mind' with such dark matters, and distracted Edward with an archery session.[11] If the anecdote is true, then there were two possible reasons that Warwick would have acted as he did. Historians antagonistic toward the earl claim that he did not want to bring 'forward what be neither profitable or honorable for himself',[12] but it is equally likely that Dudley did not want to scrub any of the gloss from Edward's hero-worship of Henry VIII.

In spite of how beneficial the king was finding Warwick's guardianship to be, Somerset's ineptitude had left the government up to their eyeballs in alligators and Dudley was getting all the blame as president of the council. His efforts to stabilize the kingdom were often greeted with hostility, especially in regards to his suppression of dissent and rebellion. There were constant rumours of further peasant uprisings to match the country's religious turmoil, and the council tried to crack down on 'unlawful assemblies' by authorising whatever force the king's officers deemed necessary to break them up. This only made people angrier, of course. Warwick and the council were also continuing to push the hardline Reformist beliefs that were causing distress for much of the population, having declared that they would 'further do in all things ... whatsoever may lend to the glory of God and the advancement of his holy word'.[13] The government's insistence on controlling private worship pleased the young king, but it poured fuel on the flames of discontent among moderate Protestants and those who longed for a resurgence of the old faith.

It had become undeniable that England didn't have the resources to deal with international skirmishes on top of internal strife. It was especially problematic in the light of ambassadorial warnings that France 'now flourishes, and [King Henry II] is young and lusty, and of mind to do great acts'.[14] It was doubtful England could hold on to Boulogne if the French made another determined attack. Having discussed matters with Dudley and the other members of the council, the king therefore issued an official 'instruction' that his ambassadors should 'treat and conclude upon a peace' with France. This instruction stipulated that if 'the French commissioners should require Boulogne ... and all such grounds as was of late conquered by our late father' it would need to be returned in order to secure the peace, then English commissions were authorised to 'agree and assent thereto' in the king's name.[15] In exchange, they were to try to get payment for the city, as had been agreed previously, and get the French to hand over Mary, Queen of Scots, to the English. Since everyone knew that the French were unlikely to relinquish the Scottish queen, the instructions basically told the ambassadors to at least get as much money out of France as they could. Moreover, once it was clear that Mary was off the table, then they were to open negotiations for Edward's marriage to the French king's eldest daughter, the five-year-old Elisabeth of Valois.

The commissioners of peace were able to do their jobs with commendable speed, and the Treaty of Boulogne was made on 29 March 1550. It accomplished several things, including bringing a halt to the Rough Wooing. The English promised to withdraw from the land they still occupied in Scotland, destroy the remaining fortifications they had built to pacify the locals, and resume commerce between the nations immediately. The treaty also negotiated that England would receive large sums of money to return the city of Boulogne to French control in May, four years earlier than agreed in the Treaty of Camp. It additionally set up an exchange of 'hostages' between England and France, which was more of a chance for youthful nobles to spend some time in a foreign court than anything else. Several of the king's friends and former schoolmates went to spend a few months at the French court in turn, including Henry Brandon, Henry Fitzalan, and Henry Stanley. As a mark to the crown's continuing favour toward the Seymour family, the Duke of Somerset's eldest son was among the young men chosen to go.

To celebrate the arrival of the French ambassadors who had come to ratify the treaty, Edward hosted multiple entertainments, including lavish suppers, dancing, musical performances, pageants, and several hunts. The king seemed especially pleased to take them to 'the baiting of bears and bulls', a spot that a modern person would find revoltingly cruel but which delighted Tudor audiences. They also joined the king in dining with his uncle Somerset, who had been released from the Tower and marginally restored to grace, and 'afterward went into the Thames, and saw both the bear hunted in the river, and also wild-fire cast out of boats, and many pretty conceits'.[16] He and the ambassadors were moreover treated to a mock naval battle, where men would 'stand upon the end of a boat without hold of anything and [run] one at another until one was cast unto the water', which 'pleased and amused' the king very much.[17]

Edward would likewise enjoy having the French hostages at his court, inasmuch as they were another excuse to stage elaborate events and to frolic. The new imperial ambassador, Jehan Scheyfve, reported that a water-pageant had been held at Greenwich in which 'four or five boats took a certain castle, and the king was very much pleased and amused by it ... he has a natural liking and taste for all sorts of warlike sports'.[18] The king also went 'to see the games of tilting of French and English gentlemen, together with some Italians and Spaniards'.[19] During the three hours he spent watching the sport, he was reported to be in 'close conversation' with one of the Frenchmen, so they had evidently become very friendly in a short space of time. The French guests also reciprocated by hosting events of their own, and the 'games provided by the Frenchmen here, on water and on land ... [gave] great satisfaction'[20] to both the participants and those watching them.

One of the hostages who came to England, Francois de Vendome, Vidame de Chartres, became the king's particular favourite. The Vidame was charming, boisterous, and amusing – the perfect man to show the somewhat stuffy young monarch how to relax and have fun. The appealing Frenchman was often in the king's company, and would coax Edward 'away from his books and his master's lessons, saying to him: 'What need has your Majesty of so many books?'[21] He would then drag the king away for a day of sport and revelry. The king also recorded in his journal that he enjoyed a 'great supper' his friend hosted with games, fireworks, and 'divers masques'. One of the masques had been especially fine, featuring 'fifteen or sixteen of the first noblemen, several being dressed in gold and silver cloth'.[22] Better yet, the king's good friend, Henry Brandon, who had recently returned from France, 'was among them, dressed up as a nun'.[23] King Edward would become a saint-like figure among later Protestants, but those future Puritans would have been aghast to see the kind of frivolities and frolics the monarch enjoyed.

While the court was engaged in revelry, the former Lord Protector continued to steadily redeem himself to the king and council, so that almost all of his lands were restored to him by the first week of May. Just a few days later, he was elevated once more to the role of a Gentleman of the Privy Chamber, and was able to easily interact with his royal nephew again. Furthermore, no one on the council was attempting to punish him for his earlier transgressions against them. The new imperial ambassador, Jehan Scheyfve, noted that although Somerset 'goes very little to court as yet ... everybody without exception pays him great respect, and there is no doubt that he will win back his foremost place'.[24]

Warwick was unquestionably going above and beyond to reconcile with Somerset. The two men were in 'close communication' and were seen 'visiting each other every day'.[25] Rumours had soon begun that the duke was 'again to assume the head of government, and that this will be brought about by the hand of the Earl of Warwick', and that they intended 'to make common cause and do as they please in all things'.[26] The reason for their collaboration was supposedly to 'abolish totally the practice of the ancient religion, so hated and calumniated by the earl and spurned by' the duke. The scuttlebutt of an alliance between them seemed to have been accurate when Dudley arranged for his eldest son to marry Somerset's eldest daughter, Anne Seymour, on 3 June. The wedding was such a big deal that even the king even attended, writing in his journal that after the ceremony 'a fair dinner was made', followed by dancing, and later he sat with the ladies in a specially constructed sunshade 'made of boughs' and watched several gentleman run courses on the tilting field.

Dudley could also see that the duke was on the brink of destroying himself, and made every effort to save him. Warwick cautioned him that 'the whole of the council is in suspicion',[27] fearing that Somerset was trying to get back his title of Lord Protector. 'Alas,' the earl wrote in exasperation, 'what means my lord in this wise to discredit himself ... considering how his late governance is yet misliked?'[28] The former Lord Protector had gotten away with a de facto kingship once, but Warwick knew that neither he nor the council could let the duke off the hook again so easily if he tried to renew his previous authority. Showing 'most plainly the inward grief of his heart with not a few tears', the earl warned him that he would 'so far overthrow himself as shall pass the power of his friends to recover'.[29] Sadly, Warwick's advice would fall on deaf ears.

Perhaps one of the reasons Warwick was working so hard to keep the king's uncle on the council was because of the civil discord beleaguering the realm. The average Englishman, 'far from recognising the ex-protector's incompetence',[30] still thought of him as 'the good duke'. This popularity meant that Somerset might be able to deescalate potential riots, so that Dudley didn't have to quell any more full-blown uprisings by force. Mini-rebellions were popping up all over the kingdom in response to the government's religious amendments, but Warwick was between a rock and a hard place regarding church matters. The evangelical zeal of the king made it nigh impossible for the earl to soften any reforms without incurring the royal wrath. A boy-king was still a king, and must therefore be obeyed.

Nor could Dudley do much about the enclosures that were causing so much deprivation and hardship among the lower classes. The crown's coffers were empty, and the only way to refill them was taxes, and taxes on the gentry required that the gentry have profits to be taxed. Sheep, with their marketable meat and wool, were by far the landowners best money makers. Ergo, more and more land which had been held in common was not being fenced in to raise sheep. Even if Warwick could have seen how barbarous it was to make the majority starve so the few could be profitable (and there is no indication that he *did* see it), attempts to restrict the enclosures would have caused a rebellion among the councillors who were profiting from it. Just talking about halting the enclosures had already cost Somerset the protectorate. Warwick was not in the happy position of being a king's beloved uncle, and if the council put him in the Tower he might leave it a head shorter than he had gone into it.

When news of possible insurrections began to spread that summer, the best that Dudley and the council could do was try to put out the fires wherever they saw smoke. John Russell, William Herbert, and Somerset were sent 'each to his own quarter to keep them under and check them in their disobedience'.[31] Additionally, a 'great number of staves, batons and ammunition of war [were] sent to the various parts of the country for that purpose'.[32] These uprisings were unlikely to have any real effect, in that the rebels had almost no weapons and were ' unable to hold communication together or assemble more than ten together', but it was a frightening sign of how unstable the country was becoming.

Rebellions at home weren't the only thing worrying the king and his council. There was also the continued fear of a possible invasion of

Catholics from abroad, hoping to put Mary on the throne in Edward's place. A French ambassador to Spain, Sebastien de Laubespine, the Abbot of Bassefontaine, reported that the English were afraid Emperor Charles V would declare Mary the rightful monarch, on the accusation that 'the present King was the schismatic son of a schismatic father, born of a woman who had not been married according to the rites of the Roman Church'.[33] There was theoretically an imperial plot to wed Mary to the emperor's son, who could 'then wage war against England for her' and assume the rule of England as her husband. It is hardly astonishing that the king should therefore begin to give a great deal of thought to improving fortifications and shoring up England's military weaknesses.[34] He would keep detailed records of his ideas and plans for his realm's defence in his diary, evidently determined to keep his subjects safe from Catholicism physically as well as spiritually.

Edward and the council decided that the king should make a more extensive summer progress than usual, hoping to calm his subjects by appearing before them in various places and to 'subdue them by showing them clemency'[35] for their small rebellions. Starting in late July, he first travelled to Syon House, a home owned by his uncle Somerset, where he ate dinner before continuing onward to Windsor. For security's sake, he would sleep in royal residences during his procession, staying in the palaces of Guildford, Woking, Oatlands, Nonsuch, and Richmond. While in Surrey that August, he summoned his eldest sister to an audience in Woking Palace. Notwithstanding that it was a command from the king, Mary baulked. She knew her brother had found out that she had almost tried to escape England the month before, and was 'suspecting some harsh usage to her person'.[36]

Earlier that spring Mary had become profoundly afraid that the king and his council would deny her the right to hear Catholic mass in her own home. She begged imperial ambassador van der Delft to help her, saying that if anything happened to Edward then she 'should be far better out of the kingdom', because as soon as he was dead she would be killed by the councillors to prevent her from taking the throne. She assured the ambassador that the councillors were 'wicked and wily in their actions, and particularly malevolent towards' her.[37] Weeping, she told van der Delft that she 'must not wait till the blow falls', and was 'quite resolved to withdraw elsewhere', rather than to stay in England where she expected at the very least 'to suffer as I suffered once during my father's lifetime'.[38] Although she was not actually being persecuted at the time, van der Delft could not assuage her fears that the council would be moving against her at any moment. She was terrified that her little brother, who was growing older and more fanatical in his beliefs every day, would soon force her to choose between martyrdom and her soul. Mary assured the ambassador that she was willing to die for her faith, but she greatly preferred to live.

Moved by her obvious distress, van der Delft promised to help smuggle her out of England and into the imperial court. He wrote to the emperor that they had already accomplished step one of the plan, which was to move her to 'a house only two miles distant from an arm of the sea'[39] to await the rescue ship. He said the princes would be joined in the fight by 'four of her ladies whom she trusts more than the rest', and three other gentlemen from her household.

The plan that the ambassador had hatched was a good one, and probably would have worked if van der Delft had not become ill and if Mary's comptroller, Sir Robert Rochester, had not done all he could to prevent her from leaving. Rochester was aided by Mary herself, who panicked and dithered until it was too late. Jehan Duboys, the captain of the ship sent to liberate Mary, reported that she had said, 'I am like a little ignorant girl, and I care neither for my goods nor for the world, but only for God's service and my conscience', but had decided that 'if there is peril in going and peril in staying, I must choose the lesser of two evils'. However, rather than leave, she began to fret about leaving the rest of her household, which was 'composed of good Christians who may, in my absence, become lost sheep, and even follow these new opinions. Thus might I incur God's censure, which would be a heavy grief to me'. Then she talked herself into fleeing again, telling her comptroller, 'I had better go, so be it in God's name; for I know of no danger in going that will not be as great or even greater' than staying. Nevertheless, she still hesitated, saying that she would prefer to stay in England if she could live and serve God as she had always done. She was afraid to stay, however, because the council might release a new anti-Catholic edict that would make her life not worth living. Mary was also worried about making the emperor angry if she didn't go, having 'so often importuned his majesty on the subject'.[40]

An unmistakably exasperated Duboys wrote that after Mary conferred again with her principal woman of the bed-chamber, they all appeared to come to a decision, and she turned to him saying 'that she could not be ready before the day after next, Friday; but that she could then leave her house at four in the morning under the pretext of going to amuse herself and purge her stomach by the sea, as her ladies did daily'. Unfortunately for the captain, who had finally gotten a concrete answer, that's when the comptroller came back and told Mary, 'I see great danger', and that she had better depart at once,' which frightened Mary into doing the opposite. Duboys said that they all continued to debate the best course of action 'in great perplexity', with Mary repeating, 'but what is to become of me?' all the while. Finally, he told them that they 'must come to some decision, for it was beginning to get dark, and once the watch was set I should be unable to go'. While Mary continued to wail, 'but what is to become of me?' the captain and the comptroller agreed that within ten or twelve days a servant named Baker, who could be trusted, would be sent to tell Duboys 'the exact day when they could be ready to put the plan into execution immediately upon the arrival of our ships'.[41] Unfortunately, no one ever came to indicate to the valiant Jehan Duboys where or when another attempt to extract Lady Mary from peril could be made, and the entire escape plan had to be scuppered.

If Mary had left England it would have been a terrible blow to Edward and the Reformists. The worry that she would be used as an imperial figurehead in the restoration of Catholicism in England would have become almost unbearable. As it was, when the king and council found out that what had almost happened, they were 'so angry about it that they had written to all their ministers resident in foreign courts what a wrong the Emperor had wished to do them, instructing their representatives to report it to all Christian princes and potentates'. In essence, the king and his council were vexed enough about Mary's near escape that they were willing to cause an international incident by tattling on the most powerful monarch in Europe.

The best way for England to protect itself from an incursion by a foreign power was to strengthen its navy. English domination of the briny deep was still more than a century away, but the island nation had already garnered a reputation for seamanship. Edward, a lover of all things martial, enthusiastically supported the council's ideas of refitting and strengthening the navy under the newly appointed Lord High Admiral, Edward Finnes de Clinton. The Royal treasury paid out money for timber and coal, as well as money to 'shipwrights, caulkers, sawyers, labourers, captains, masters, mariners, and gunners serving His Highness in the wars ... and also for the charges of transportation of His Highness's ships from Portsmouth to Gillingham ... [and] the provisions of certain munitions for the furniture of sundry His Highness's ships appointed to serve by sea.[42] The king was also a frequent visitor at Deptford, the first Royal Navy Dockyard, to see that the royal money was being put to good use. In fact, Edward went to the docks so often that High Street had to be paved, because it was 'so noisome and full of filth' that it was difficult for the king to 'pass to and fro to see the building of his Highness's ships'.[43]

Although one of the purposes for these new and newly refitted ships was ostensibly to fight pirates off the English coast, the navy was to indulge in piracy as much as fight it. If a 'legitimate' naval vessel was to overtake a ship sailing under a French flag, the captains had privately been assured that the goods on board those French ships were booty. They had been told they could help themselves under the guise that, 'they have been spoiled before by Frenchmen and could have no justice, or pretending that the victualles or things of munition found in any such French ships were sent to aid'[44] England's enemies. The goods aboard Russian, Swedish, and Spanish ships were likewise vulnerable to being illicitly confiscated, regardless of any formal treaties between the English and that nation. In the spirit of 'if you cannot beat them; join them', foreign traders found it in their best interest to become trading partners with English companies if they wanted respite from English pirating.

The king and council were more concerned about a form of piracy on land – price gouging. Inflation of the costs of food had become untenable, and hunger was rife. The price of flour had doubled, and the size of the half-penny bread loaf had correspondingly shrunk. This was bad news indeed, since these loaves were the main source of calories for the working class and poor. Their meagre wages could no longer provide them with enough to eat. Worse, soldiers returning from their posts in Boulogne had flooded London. They not only competed with the other labourers for both jobs and food, but they were also actually forming groups to 'set upon the citizens and their houses and take there such booty and spoil as they can lay hand upon'.[45] Worst of all, some merchants and farmers had taken to hoarding grain so they could profit even more by inflating the price of bread further. To try to provide some relief for the food crisis, Edward's government issued a proclamation that all local justices should 'look in their quarters what superfluous corn were in every barn, and appoint it to be sold at a reasonable price'.[46] These justices were also required to go to the markets with the excess grain, to make sure it was actually being sold at an acceptable cost. Moreover, no more foodstuffs were to be shipped out of the country for sale, with the exception of supplies going to the English citizens in Calais. The government also established a nightly patrol in London, in the hopes of controlling the unruly soldiers infesting the city. These efforts were probably too little, compared to the damage enclosures were causing, but at least they were something.

The king moved to Richmond in October, where Edward received the unwelcome gift of a serious illness for his thirteenth birthday. By the beginning of November, ambassador Scheyfve was reporting that although the news about the king's indisposition was being 'kept very secret', his 'recovery was despaired of' and that even 'the physicians had given him up'.[47] The secrecy surrounding Edward's health has had the regrettable side effect of leaving no historical record of what ailed him, so the reason for his sickness remains a riddle. We know that it wasn't smallpox or measles, since he would report contracting those diseases in 1552, or the flu, since the 'catarrh' wouldn't hit England until later in the decade, but that doesn't narrow it down much. The young king could have had any one of several ailments – from diphtheria to typhoid – which would have been severe enough to panic his doctors and councillors.

It was a terrible time for the monarch to get sick. There was a general feeling of discontent throughout the realm because of church reforms, the cost of food, and the scarcity of money even among the relatively well to do. Religious animosity had become so bad that the council was afraid that in the event of a foreign assault on England, too much of the populace would yield to the invaders 'instead of rousing themselves to ward them off, in the hope of getting the upper hand of their opponents at home'.[48] Nor was it only a Catholic incursion by the Holy Roman Empire that they feared. There was also profound concern that the French king might be planning an offensive into England, because he knew 'how weakened and powerless the kingdom has become because of the divisions between the nobles and those who govern'. Although no one believed Edward could 'remedy any of these troubles owing to his tender age', he was a figure around which people could rally. Moreover, if he died and Mary came to the throne, Catholicism would come with her, and the Protestant councillors would probably lose everything – including their lives.

It's no wonder that ambassador Scheyfve was reporting that there were 'deep causes of discord among the members of the Council' in the wake of the king's illness. Somerset, in particular, was trying 'win over the people, which he had not tried to do before'. No one knows if he wanted the additional popularity because he was going to try to be able to hold the throne for a Protestant successor, or if he was planning to exchange the title of duke to sovereign. Warwick was also said to be scheming to become the new king. There was the rather fantastical rumour spreading that he was going to divorce his wife so he could marry the king's younger sister, Elizabeth, 'with whom he is said to have had several secret and intimate personal communications'.[49] In reality, there is no evidence that either the earl or the duke were manoeuvring politically for any reason other than that they wanted to survive the upheaval after the king's death.

Fortunately for his councillors and his kingdom, Edward recovered from his mystery malady. The young king was clearly still in good overall health at this time, since the lack of modern antibiotics or medical treatments meant he could count only on his own immune system to survive. He was well enough by Christmas to join his court celebrations at Greenwich, restore his councillors to a reasonable level of political equilibrium.

Chapter Eleven

Edward's Reign Begins

E dward would truly begin to exert his authority as king in 1551. He may not have been steering the ship of state on his own yet, but it was obvious that he had his hand on the tiller and was already tacking the sails toward the policies he favoured. Like his father, he believed that he knew appropriate theology his subjects should embrace, and was determined that they worship the way he wanted them to. He believed that Satan himself was behind 'super-stitiousness and idolatry', and the 'bringing in of popery and naughtiness' to England.[1] These beliefs naturally resulted in deeply-held bigotry toward Catholics and those who did embrace the most strenuous styles of the Reformation.

Frankly, the young king was giving every sign that he would have become as much of a religious purist and fanatic as his elder sister, Queen Mary I. If so, would he have been remembered as Bloody Edward for executing Catholics, the way his sister is remembered as Bloody Mary for having Protestants burned at the stake? It's unlikely. The king's gender and the fact his religious views carried the day in England have probably prevented such an untoward nickname. There is also a chance that he would have mellowed with age. The king had the same formidable intellect as his sister Elizabeth, who would famously declare that she had no wish to open windows into men's souls, and he might have eventually tried to embrace religious moderation the way she did.

For the present, however, King Edward was indisputably a zealous Protestant. Contemporary apostolic Reformers thus saw the king, literally, as a godsend. There could never be enough praise for the king who, by 'abolishing idolatrous masses and false invocations, reduced against religion to a right sincerity'.[2] They boasted to one another that the king 'supports and encourages pure religion and godly and learned men to the utmost of his power, and would effect much more if his age allowed him'.[3] They lauded him for ordering preaching during weekly sermons, and bragged that he 'received with his own hand a copy of every sermon that he hears, and most diligently requires an account of them after dinner from those who study with him'.[4] Archbishop Cranmer pridefully claimed that his godson was 'a youth of such godliness as to be a wonder to the whole world' and 'orders all things for the advancement of God's glory'. Never had there been such a pious king, and if there had 'ever existed a Josiah since the first that name, this is certainly he'.[5]

With such fulsome feedback from his fellow reformists, it is no surprise that Edward had become such a rabidly evangelical teenager. For clandestine Catholics and those who missed the beauties of the older liturgies, the changes to church services were already radical enough, but the king would go further. His opinions became more extreme, and edged ever closer to a Lutheran rejection of transubstantiation. He would eventually come to agree with Nicholas Ridley, Bishop of London, that even altars were objectionably papist and demanded that churches replace them with simple communion tables. Strict reformists, such as the king, had decided that the only thing a church needed was a prayer book, surplice, tablecloth, bell, and cup for communion … and they were wavering on the need for a bell.

Edward seemed to believe that it was his duty to 'save' his eldest sister from her doctrinal errors. In January, he and some of his council sent for the Lady Mary, to discuss the whispers that had reached the court saying she was practicing Catholic rituals in her household. When she was confronted, Mary burst into tears because her brother, whom she loved and honoured 'above all other beings, as by nature and duty bound',[6] had been told evil things about her. The king didn't seem to notice that this response was not actually a denial, because he began to cry with remorse for having hurt his sister's feelings. He told her to dry her eyes, and promised that he thought no harm of her. Mary was then convinced, as she would explain to the imperial ambassador, 'that thenceforward my poor priests ran no danger in saying the mass within my house'.

Notwithstanding the lady's certainty, the king was far from giving up on his quest to convert his sister. His council sent her a letter on the 17th of the same month, accusing her of breaking the laws and the king's commands by stubbornly clinging to the old ways of celebrating mass. Mary wrote a letter telling them that 'my faith and my religion are those held by the whole of Christendom, formerly confessed by this kingdom under the late King, my father, until you altered them with your new laws'.[7] Furthermore, while her brother may have been the boss of her, they were not, and she didn't have to listen to them. As for the king, she trusted that 'when he reaches years of greater understanding, that he will not be wroth against me', when all that she wanted was for things to be 'left as the late King his father left it, until his Majesty has reached the age to judge for himself'. She also rebuked the councillors, telling them that she didn't think it was right that the king 'should be robbed of freedom by laws and statutes on spiritual matters passed during his minority', and only God knew 'whether his majesty may not take it amiss in time to come'. Mary then declared that this was the 'final answer to any letters you might write to me on matters of religion'. She then closed the letter with a guilt trip for councillors, who were cruel to bother her when they knew she was in fragile health, and if they could see 'what pain I suffer in bending down my head to write and in considering the answer I have to give you, for love and charity you would not wish to give me occasion to do it'.

Although the councillors, in awe of Mary's royal status as King Henry VIII's daughter, might have backed down after such a castigation, it only made her brother angry. Edward sent a sharp letter to tell her that he had seen the councils 'good and suitable admonitions, and your fruitless and wayward misunderstanding of the same',[8] and had decided to write to her himself in the hopes of persuading her to behave even if the council could not. He was greatly displeased that she, his very own sister, 'in whom by nature we should place reliance and our highest esteem, wish to break our laws and set them aside deliberately and of your own free will; and moreover sustain and encourage others to commit a like offence'. She may have been promised to be allowed to practice the old faith in several ways, but that obviously did not give her the right to let others practice heresy with her. The only reason he was letting her get away with hearing Mass in the first place was because he loved her, and had hoped to bring her around to the true religion with enough patience. She was, he told her irately, making two serious mistakes in regards to her circumstances. The first was that she was 'using and perpetuating the use of a form of worship to the honour of God, which in truth is more like dishonour'. Her rejection of the true paths to righteousness was sheer pigheadedness on her part, and he was shocked that she didn't love him enough to see reason. Her second mistake was to think she could just break his laws with impunity. He had 'suffered it until now, with the hope that some improvement might be forthcoming', but if she kept doing it, how much longer did she think he'd put up with it? What was particularly egregious, he said, was that someone of her royal status was doing it, and therefore lending 'colour to faction among the people'. He might be young, as she had pointed out, but he was old enough to see that if he were 'to grant you license to break our laws and set them aside' then it would 'be an encouragement to others to do likewise'. She should be warned that her continued disobedience could diminish the great love he felt for her. Additionally, she had offended him by 'objecting to the use of our authority for altering matters not changed by our father', because he possessed 'the same authority our father had … without diminution of any sort'. He cautioned her sternly that she had better not be 'so bold as to offend again in this matter', since her 'own writing might bear witness' against her. After this allusion to putting her on trial, he ended the letter with a postscript reiterating that he loved her, but that he *would* see his laws strictly obeyed, and any lawbreakers *would* be watched and denounced.

Mary responded to his letter by claiming that it had caused her 'more suffering than any illness even unto death'. But she insisted that she was doing nothing wrong, that she had been promised by both himself and her father that she could enjoy the old faith in her own household, and she beseeched him again to wait until he was older before he made judgment on spiritual matters. She implied that his council was poisoning him against her, but God knew how loyal she really was to her brother. She ended her letter by begging the king 'for the love of God' to let her at least practice the modified Catholicism of their father, and if he would not, then she was prepared to die for it. In sum, unless he was willing to execute her, nothing would stop her from worshipping as she pleased.

Unwilling to behead his sister, the new Josiah turned elsewhere to enforce his reforms. He therefore enthusiastically supported the council's proclamation in March 1551 to confiscate all the remaining church plate and vestments in his kingdom for the crown's secular disposal. Not only would this eradicate the terrible scourge of idolatry and attractiveness from English places of worship, it would also help refill the bankrupt royal coffers. The council were not shy about the reasons the government was ransacking the vestries, either. The proclamation point-blank stated that the ornamentation was being looted from churches 'for as much as the king's majesty had need presently of a mass of money'.[9] Even the bells in the steeples could be seized. This despoiling of the churches was seen as so extreme that even some of the hardline Protestant commissioners actually 'baulked at so breathtaking an act of sacrilege'.[10]

This final raid on the church was a bridge too far for the king's eldest sister. In a flagrant display of rebellion, on 17 March, the Lady Mary processed into London surrounded by scores of knights, gentlemen, and ladies, and every one of them had their black prayer beads prominently displayed before the crowds. There were few things so blatantly Catholic as rosaries, and Edward's government had banned them as manifestations of idolatry. If Mary had carried a banner saying 'I love Pope Julius III' and pulled a wagon full of saints' icons, she could not have made a bolder statement regarding her own faith.

Next in line to the throne or not, her audacity was breathtaking. She was courting a stay in the Tower, perhaps with an added visit to the headsman, and she knew it.

Word of her arrival came before her, and by the time she got to court, preparations had been made to receive her. She was met by the king's comptroller, Sir Anthony Wingfield, 'and led by him towards the king, who was awaiting her with the entire council, to the number of twenty-five, in a certain gallery'.[11] Her brother greeted her with kind civility, and Mary judiciously paid him all due reverence as her sovereign. She apologised for having been so long between visits, but explained she had been unwell. After some initial small-talk, 'the king led her, unaccompanied by any of her ladies, into his chamber, where she was surrounded by the Councillors'.[12] The time of reckoning was at hand. Edward, however, was going to find it as hard to bend his sister to his will as it had been for their father to bulldoze Mary's mother, Katherine of Aragon.

The king began gently, saying only that 'that he desired to remind her of the letters that both he and his council had sent to her' regarding the old faith. Mary defended herself by reminding him yet again that when he first came to the throne, he and his councillors had given her the right to practice the modified Catholicism of Henry VIII. She also brought up the fact that her cousin, Emperor Charles V, was presently England's ally, and if she were denied the right to hear Mass, he might become England's enemy. This was perhaps foolish of her, because King

Edward was no more pleased to be threatened with a foreign potentate than their mighty sire had been. Mary must have read the room, because she switched tactics, pitifully protesting that she was innocent of any wrongdoing. She promised that she had never stirred up trouble over the old faith, and swore that she prayed daily for the king's health and the kingdom's peace. She repeated that age might change his mind, because although he knew much 'riper age and experience would teach him much more yet'. Edward, who was just as fond of being talked down to as any other Tudor monarch, 'retorted that she also might still have something to learn, for no one was too old for that'.

Now the council stepped in to chastise the king's sister. They accused her of disobedience, even though Henry VIII's will ordered her to 'obey ordinances and submit to the council's instructions'. They insisted that they weren't trying to hurt her. picking on her; they 'felt themselves bound by the will, and obliged to execute its provisions' and bound to obey their present king. She sweetly assured them that she was perfectly aware that they were all doing their best. Nevertheless, she was 'confident that the late King had never ordered anything in the least prejudicial to the king, her brother, because of the paternal love he bore him, and it was reasonable to suppose that he alone cared more for the good of his kingdom than all the members of his Council put together'. This discomposed Warwick, and he blustered, 'How now, my Lady? It seems that your Grace is trying to show us in a hateful light to the king, our master, without any cause whatsoever'. She denied that was her intent, but 'they had opened the matter and pressed her so hard, she was unwilling to hide or dissemble the truth'.

Having defanged the council, she addressed her brother. Tearfully, she said that 'in the last resort there were only two things: soul and body. Her soul she offered to God, and her body to his majesty's service, and might it please him to take away her life rather than the old religion, in which she desired to live and die'. Edward, who loved his sister despite his impatience with her obstinate refusal to adopt what he thought of as the true religion, quickly responded that he wished for no such sacrifice. He told her acerbically that he was not trying to constrain her faith, but simply wanted her to obey him and to stop trying to rule for herself.[13] Considering that she had just gotten away with parading rosary beads through the city and had not agreed to stop her household Catholic services, Mary thought it best to quit while she was ahead. She therefore very humbly begged her brother to 'excuse her from coming to Court any more on this occasion because of her illness, and to give her permission to depart, which he did'.[14]

The king had hoped to convince his sister to do the proper thing and submit to his higher authority, but that wasn't happening any time soon. All of Henry VIII's children had inherited his fierce intractability, and although they could talk their way around almost anything, none of them knew how to back down.

He also had to decide what to do with his less troublesome younger sister. Although Elizabeth was supporting his religious reforms, the rumours that Warwick had wanted to marry her had highlighted another set of problems. A king's sister was clearly too dangerous to leave lying around where any power-hungry Protestant might pick her up. A new ambassador, an ardent Scots reformer named Sir John Borthwick, was therefore dispatched to Denmark with instructions to negotiate a wedding between Elizabeth and King Christian III's eldest son, Prince Frederick.

His sisters were soon to be the least of his problems, however. The warmer weather of spring brought with it another outbreak of the dreaded sweating sickness. Historians and epidemiologists remain uncertain what this illness actually was, but it was indisputably deadly. It started in the northern part of the realm, and quickly swept south, 'whereof a great number of people died in a small time', especially in London.[15] As the name implies, when the disease was contracted the patient began to sweat profusely, and many died within hours of evincing symptoms. One of the oddest aspects of the illness was the fact it seemed to affect only the English. The contemporary chroniclers were perplexed 'that God had appointed the said sickness only for the plague of Englishmen', and noted that most of the victims that 'died thereof were men and not women nor children'.[16] The illness also reportedly 'followed the Englishmen, that such merchants of England as were in Flanders and Spain, and other Countries beyond the sea were visited therewithal, and none other nation infected thereine'.[17] The sweating sickness would ravage the kingdom until autumn, and then disappear again as suddenly and mysteriously as it had come.

The young king was also greatly stressed about the state of English currency, which had been watered down and debased by his royal father to the point where it was worth only a fraction of what it had been a decade ago. He appears to have educated himself regarding the matter and had a better awareness of the economic influence of the coinage than most of his councillors.[18] What was needed was to align preexisting money with the value of its precious metal content and to mint new, more trustworthy coins. Edward understood both why this was necessary, and how it could be used for the crown's advantage. The king wrote in his journal that 'it was appointed to make twenty thousand pound weight for necessity somewhat baser, [in order] to get gains [of] £160,000 clear, by which the debt of the realm might be paid, the country defended from any sudden attempt, and the coin amended'.[19] The king understood that the cost of coin production was defrayed by the relative worth of the coinage minted, and his plans 'were both logical and correct ... historians should see them as yet another proof of his penetrating grasp of the intricate policies with which his government wrestled'.[20] The young monarch, who was showing himself to be as fiscally savvy as King Henry VII, was no ordinary thirteen-year-old boy.

The king and his council issued proclamations in July and August that debased the coinage, which was really the only reasonable option available to them. However, since economics and currency were complex issues few people had the educational background to comprehend, this was met with great umbrage by the commoners. People were understandably upset by the sudden reduction of their coins' value, especially when it coincided with rising food costs. When the 'murmurings of the people against the depreciation of the currency have recently come to the Council's ears, and they have issued express orders to the mayor and sheriffs of London to call together the people of that town, and explain to them that everything that has been done with the currency has been dictated by zeal for the public good, with the object of placing it once more on the old footing.'[21] In spite of this good-faith effort by the government, the populace was still angry and confused. The main target of this public vexation was John Dudley, which even the imperial ambassador thought was unfair. Jehan Scheyfve had never been a fan of Warwick's, but he nonetheless wrote to the emperor that the English were doing the earl 'a great injustice, for he was most careful and vigilant in his solicitude for the country's welfare.

Consequently, such opinions ought to be rejected'.[22] His dislike for the president of the council still shone through, however, because he followed up his praise with the assertion that Dudley's good works were 'of course a scheme, for Warwick is trying to make himself out very humane, in order to gain all men's hearts, and particularly those of the populace, thus hoping to make his reign permanent'. Scheyfve added that some courtiers feared that the earl would succeed in gaining popularity, and 'in the meantime he is ruling absolutely, and all posts and offices are being given to [his] creatures'.

This accusation of power-hoarding was almost as unfair as blaming Dudley for the debasing of the coinage, because the earl was handing over more and more control of the government to his teenage sovereign almost every day. Edward was growing up, and had begun to undertake an active role as monarch and as a man. The young king was not only 'learned to a miracle'[23] in academic topics and religion, he had an innate grasp of statecraft that dwarfed the abilities of most men. For one thing, he understood that to be taken seriously he needed to show both his subjects and the ambassadors of other nations that he was no longer a small child. He needed to make public displays of his nascent adulthood. One of the manliest things a noble youth could do was to show off an ability for martial sports. Accordingly, the king decided he would no longer sit out of the sun on the sidelines and simply watch the mock battles, as he had done at the wedding of Warwick's son to Anne Somerset. He would learn to compete in tournaments, as his father had done. Ambassadors soon began reporting that the king was practising 'the use of arms every day on horseback, and enjoys it greatly'.[24]

One of his first public attempts in a tournament occurred at an event he hosted at Greenwich. The king issued a challenge, saying that he and a team of fifteen members of his chamber would 'run at base, shoot, and run at the ring' against any seventeen gentleman volunteers. The king's team, all wearing black silk coats 'pulled out with white taffeta',[25] ran 120 courses against the opposing player, who were decked out in yellow. Edward acquitted himself well in spite of the fact his team lost on overall points. He would never be the natural athlete his father had been, but the fact he was participating in tourneys at all counted heavily in his favour. A month later the king entered the field again, and 'tried his skill five or six times with the other young lords',[26] including a turn at sword-play. When the French ambassador complimented him on his growing prowess, the king modestly replied that 'it was a small beginning, and as time passed he hoped to do his duty better'.[27] The king ran the ring again at Blackheath just a few weeks afterwards, and then dined on board one of his carracks at Deptford.[28]

Edward was also keenly aware that it was also time to arrange a royal wedding. He needed to marry early and to a woman with a substantial dowry. He therefore sent William Parr, Marquess of Northampton, to France to bestow the Order of the Garter on King Henri II and to begin the formal negotiations for a bride. Although there had been some former discussion of an Anglo-French union, no serious steps had been taken and England's king was considered a single ready to mingle among the crowned heads of Europe. What had spurred the young monarch to look toward France, his long-standing enemy, for his future wife? It was unlikely that the French could offer a significantly better dowery for their candidate than the imperial coffers could provide. Perhaps the king's spat with his sister, and her unwise implication that he risked war with the Holy Roman Empire if he thwarted her, had made him decide to disoblige the emperor by choosing a French alliance? Whatever his motives for seeking a French princess to wed, the king knew that the emperor would attempt to prevent a match between England and France if he could. Thus, the wedding negotiations needed to be kept hush-hush. William Parr, whom Edward called his 'honest uncle', had been chosen for this task in large part because he was one of the few people Edward trusted to be both shrewd and secretive.

Parr first made another attempt to get Mary, Queen of Scots, back from the French. Unsurprisingly, the French refused, 'saying both they had taken too much pain and spent too many lives for her'.[29] That is probably no more than Northampton had expected, but it did put the French in the position to be placating rather than placated. In consequence, Henry II was the first to suggest that his eldest daughter, Elizabeth of Valois, would be a good wife for the king. Elizabeth was pretty, sweet-natured, and shy, which were all ideal qualities for a royal wife. Moreover, since she was only six years old the young couple would have time to grow up together before the marriage would really begin. Parr reported this offer back to his king, and after some struggle to obtain the best possible dowry, Edward agreed.

Both countries were still trying to keep the potential marriage under their hats when the French sent envoys in July to give Edward the Order of Saint-Michel and to finalise some aspects of the betrothal contract. That summer's outbreak of the sweating sickness was continuing to blight the streets of London, so the ambassadors were lodged at Richmond Palace and entertained at Hampton Court. Human nature being what it is, news of the impending marriage had quickly leaked out and within weeks of the French envoy arriving the courtiers were 'talking quite openly, and as if of a settled matter, of the marriage between the King of England and the daughter of France'.[30]

Edward's reactions to his forthcoming marriage offers a unique insight into the king's personality. Although he seems to have been initially reserved and cautious, he showed himself to be both caring and good-humoured once some level of intimacy was established. The king's calm formality upon receiving the Order of Saint-Michel had created such an impression of coldness that his council felt compelled to tell Northampton to 'explain to the French King the high gratification of their master, which was perhaps not so apparent to the Ambassador'.[31] The council was almost desperate to assure King Henry III that their young monarch was pleased as punch about the medal and the engagement to Elisabeth of Valois, but he was naturally 'of such modesty that in his most gladness hath not much outward show thereof'. Moreover, the council explained, because 'French speech being not natural to him', their sovereign could not 'so abundantly express the joy of his heart as if he should have answered in his natural speech as the French King did in his'.[32] Clearly, the king was not one for broadcasting his excitement, and his council was worried that his lack of enthusiasm might have offended the French. In contrast. when the French ambassador was leaving Richmond a few weeks later the king spontaneously and affectionately gave him a diamond ring 'for my memory'.[33] He had obviously come to like the ambassador as an individual, and wanted him to have evidence of the goodwill between them. This was almost certainly a genuine gesture of friendship, since the king seems to have had no instinct to use false tokens as a way to manipulate the emotions of others. Warwick had to remind Edward to show off his possession of his fiancée's miniature portrait to the ambassador, so it could be 'reported in France as a token of the king's gallantry'.[34] A naturally serious boy, it seems as though the monarch had to get to know someone well in order to warm up to them, and overt displays of emotion or the deliberate misdirection of his feelings were not his forte.

Further proof that Edward did not wear his heart on his sleeve – regardless of how deeply he felt about something on a personal level – is found in his behaviour upon learning of the death of two of his closest friends, Henry and Charles Brandon. The sons of the late Duke of Suffolk and his fourth wife, Katherine Willoughby, were almost the same age as the king and had been brought up with him as his companions and schoolmates. Henry Brandon, the present duke, was a particularly close friend. The boys had been taken to Huntingdonshire to escape the sweating sickness in London, but it found them in the countryside refuge and carried them off within hours of each other on 14 July 1551. The king received the news of their loss shortly after the French ambassadors arrived, which goes a long way toward explaining why he had trouble showing enthusiasm regarding his engagement. It is hard to put on a happy face when two of your closest childhood friends have just died.

Edward wasn't allowed to take any time off to deal with his sorrow. It was his duty as king to entertain and charm the French representatives. For the next three weeks, that is exactly what he did. He welcomed them to his court, attended pageants with them, gave large feasts in their honour, gifted them with expensive presents, gambled with them, played his lute for them, went hunting and shooting with them, and even joked with them about the inferiority of English food.[35] He was the perfect host, and impressed the ambassadors so much that they described him as 'an angel in human form'.[36] Notwithstanding his facade of cheer, the minute the French envoys left, Edward enclosed himself away in his privy chambers 'surrounded by seven or eight gentlemen', where he remained 'almost in hiding' while he processed 'the shock and surprise he received' at the news of Henry Brandon's death, 'for the King loved him dearly'.[37] Edward, in spite of his historical reputation, was far from coldhearted or unloving. He was simply a masterful stoic from a very early age. His profound ability to hide his emotions when he needed to should not be conflated with the absence of those emotions.

Even as Edward grieved, the business of the kingdom had to be taken care of. It was time to let the cat formally out of the bag regarding his betrothal to Elisabeth of Valois. The council sent a message to the imperial ambassador assuring him that the upcoming union 'had been negotiated without any prejudice to the treaties and friendly relations existing between' the Holy Roman Empire and England, and the 'was minded to observe and continue the treaties in all respects'. The excessive assurances that England's alliance with France shouldn't give the emperor any worries immediately caused the emperor to start to worry, of course. Why would the English bend over backwards to claim they weren't plotting anything with the French, unless they were plotting something with the French?

It was as if the king and his council were fed up with the imperial attempts to interfere with English affairs, and wanted to make the emperor nervous about a joint Anglo-French attack on imperial territories. The king also clamped down harder on Mary in retaliation for past imperial blackmail on her behalf. The alliance with France meant that the teeth had been metaphorically pulled from any threat of imperial invasion, and Mary no longer had any leverage for her demands. Edward met with his council in August, determined to do something about the recalcitrant former princess allowing her entire household to hear mass against the law and the king's own commands. As a result, three of Mary's most important household officers – Sir Robert Rochester, Sir Francis Englefield, and Sir Edward Waldegrave – were arrested and summoned before the council. The men of Mary's household were told that since she was so 'fixed and obstinate in a religion repugnant and contrary to that observed in England'[38] it was their duty as the king's subjects to stop the lady's chaplains and ministers from celebrating Mass or any other Catholic service. This would, the councillors reasoned, 'avoid disturbing the lady herself, and also the scandal that might arise if any orders were to be issued to her directly'. When her gentleman returned to Mary's household and told her what they had been ordered to do, she 'told them flatly that she forbade them to execute their charge, for she was mistress in her own house, and they were not to meddle with religion or her conscience'. She considered it 'very strange and unreasonable that her ministers and servants should wield such authority in her house', and she told them that she would write directly to the king and take responsibility for their refusal.

Mary's gentlemen, under the false impression that they could flout the king's authority in favour of their mistress's wishes, obeyed her, and were subsequently arrested on 23 August. A few days after they were incarcerated in the Tower, it was Lady Mary's turn to face the music. She received a formal visit at her residence in Copped Hall from the king's Lord Chancellor, Richard Rich, accompanied by Sir Anthony Wingfield and William Petre. They were there to install Wingfield as her household's new comptroller, and let her know in no uncertain terms that her sovereign had forbidden her chaplains to say mass for anyone other than herself. They told her about the king's 'dissatisfaction and resentment ... when he saw how firm and pertinacious she remained'. He had given her many chances to amend her behaviour because he loved her, but now 'the prick of conscience and solicitude for his kingdom's welfare, which depended upon implicit obedience of all his subjects, none excepted, to the laws and statutes of the realm, forbade him to put up with her behaviour any longer'.[39] In short, Edward was fed up to the back teeth with her defiance.

Mary should have realised how irritated the king was with her and bent her knee to his commands, but as she had done with her father, she assumed her close familial relationship with the monarch would prevent the royal wrath from falling too heavily upon her. She foolishly decided to stick to her guns. First, she trotted out her old arguments regarding theoretical promises made to her and the king's youth, but having heard it all before, the councillors were ready with hard retorts. She then tried to bully them into backing down with a bout of hysterical pathos, declaring she would 'lay my head on a block and suffer death'[40] before she would forgo the Catholic service, but they were unmoved and repeated the king's commands. Mary, unwilling to admit that she was defying her sovereign, deflected the blame. She insisted that her brother didn't really want her to give up the old faith; this was all a ploy by Warwick and her enemies on the council to destroy her. The councillors then showed her the letters patent from the king commanding her to submit to the law of the realm like every other subject. Stymied by reality, she told them she couldn't deal with the letters at the moment because she was too ill. She berated the royal deputies for their cruelty toward a weak and fragile woman, and declared that 'if I shall chance to die, I will protest openly that you of the council to be the causes of my death'.[41] She then ran away to her privy chamber to be comforted by her ladies, while the men of the household were rounded up and told 'general and particular prohibition

... particularly to the chaplains'. There would be no plausible deniability, or insistence they were obeying their mistress, to save the chaplains if they were caught saying Mass for anyone other than Mary.

To ensure that her chaplains would not be forced to use the Book of Common Prayer for her household at a later date, Mary dismissed them from her service the following day. She also reported her predicament to the imperial ambassador, in the hopes Scheyfve could sway the king or council. Both a stalwart Catholic and deeply partisan toward the former princess, the ambassador went before the council and pleaded with them on her behalf. He reported that after 'they had listened attentively to my words, the Earl of Warwick spoke, and said that my proposal was so important that they must report it to the King and consult his Majesty; and to this he limited himself'.[42] Scheyfve, assuming that Dudley was the real power behind the throne, tried to cajole him into making his own decision in favour of Mary, telling the earl that he was 'sufficiently informed of the king's intentions, and it was not necessary to consult him further'. However, Warwick pointedly replied 'that the King was now so old that he wished to concern himself with all the public affairs of the kingdom; and at this they rose to go to his majesty'.[43] Scheyfve tried once more to convince the councillors that they, not the king, were the ones in charge of the kingdom and they could let Mary have her mass without having to bother Edward with this little trifle. This flattery fell flat, and William Parr accused the ambassador of wanting them to let the Lady Mary 'remain in the old religion until the king came of age', and that Scheyfve was falsely implying that Edward had already agreed to it earlier. Before the ambassador could reply, Warwick interrupted him and told him he was wrong to think the council would decide such matters on their own, because they 'held the King to be as much of age as if he were forty'. The young sovereign may have only been thirteen, but his genius and his judgement had made him an adult in practice, if not in years.

Edward was clear in his reply to the ambassador. He was not only irked by the repeated reappearance of a topic he considered closed, he was suspicious that the emperor was having Scheyfve pester him just to be annoying. The king was completely indifferent to the suggestion that letting Mary have mass in her household would make her imperial cousin very happy. The emperor would just have to learn to live with disappointment. Scheyfve then tried to at least get Mary's gentlemen released from the Tower, on the excuse that they were simply being imprisoned to hurt their mistress. This didn't fly either. The young monarch told him that far from being unfair or cruel to Mary by taking away her loyal servants, he 'had done nothing but according to a king's office herein, in observing the laws that were so godly and in punishing the offenders'.[44] Without question, the king had decided his sister would be brought to heel.

Mary might have tried to continue to defy the king, but when war broke out yet again between France and the Holy Roman Empire that September, Mary realised that with the emperor too busy to help her she had no choice except to capitulate. Bitterly, and while still blaming Warwick for her situation, she began keeping her devotions separate and private. She never seemed to truly recognise how adamant her brother was in regards to religion, even after Stephan Gardiner was stripped of his bishopric and imprisoned indefinitely for defending the old faith.

Chapter Twelve

Religious Reform and Troublesome Relatives

It is evident from reading Edward's journal and letters that he was motivated to religious reform by a sincere desire to do the right thing, and that desire additionally spilt over into secular governance. He was now old enough to understand the breakdown of law and order in his lands, and to be appalled by the lax administration of justice within his realm. He could see England was ill, but how could he heal his nation? Accordingly, the king wrote an essay that sores of his kingdom must be cured with eight medicines or plasters:

1. Good education; 2. Devising of good laws; 3. Executing the lawes justly, without respect of persons; 4. Example of rulers; 5. Punishing of vagabonds and idle persons; 6. Encouraging the good; 7. Ordering well the [economy and trade] 8. Engendering friendship [between factions] in all the parts of the commonwealth.[1]

The entirety of the king's essay, published posthumously in 1557, revealed that he truly understood the importance and duties of statecraft. Warwick was right; Edward was as much of an age as if he were forty.

Unquestionably, the king and the council were trying their best to help the common people through these trying economic times. They had continued in their attempts to fix England's devalued currency. Edward wrote in his journal that he was concerned the great London merchants were not giving a proper exchange for the new coinage, and had decided that new farthings, half-pence, and pence should be minted 'to serve for the poor people'.[2] He and the council had also issued a proclamation ordering that certain essentials, such as butter and cheese, could only be sold at a reasonable price, even though it would not be 'fully so good cheap as it was when the coin was at the perfect'.[3] Moreover, he and his councillors had begun to compose laws to bring before Parliament that were aimed at alleviating the suffering of labourers and the impoverished.

The king's biggest blind spot was for the good works that had been done by the Catholic Church. His loathing of anything 'papist' meant that he and his council actually destroyed several Catholic charities that had cared for the infirm or ill.[4]

The teenaged monarch was more of a forward long-term thinker than his father had ever been, so he had also given due thought to how to improve English trade, and thus the English revenue. He had become determined to try to make Southhampton a great 'mart', a centre of commerce to rival Antwerp, 'for as a market doth enrich a town, so doth a mart enrich a realm'.[5] As well as boosting the economy, the great mart would cut out the middleman for English trade, lowering the price of imported goods and making them more accessible to the common people. Since the Flemmings had managed to set up an international market while 'having but very little commodities',[6] he thought it would be much easier for England to create one when they already had more to trade. His ideas to bring the great mart into existence were ingenious, and economically sound. Taxes would be lower there than in other marts, to lure traders across the realm, and merchants would be allowed to travel freely to and from Southampton. The mart would also be made the only place a particular commodity could be sold, making it a trade centre from the start. The residents and merchants of Southampton would be given extra liberties, 'and if money may be spared, some must be lent to them to begin their trade'.[7] Once the southern mart had been well established, the king planned to have another built in the north, at Hull.

At the beginning of October, court scuttlebutt had it that the king was planning a slew of promotions for those he considered worthy, and on the 11th those reports were proven true. He swore in his personal friends, Barnaby Fitzpatrick and Robert Dudley, as two of the six gentlemen of his privy chamber. He knighted another of his privy gentlemen, Henry Neville. He also knighted his former nursery chamberlain, William Sidney, and his tutor, John Cheke, who became one of the thirty-five members of the expanded council. His secretary, William Cecil, who would later go on to become a key player in the reign of Queen Elizabeth I, was knighted as well. Those whom the king judged to be suitably devout Reformers were likewise given rewards. Long-standing council member, William Paulet, was elevated from the Earl of Wiltshire to the Marquess of Winchester. William Herbert, the newly-created Baron of Cardiff, was additionally made the Earl of Pembroke. Henry Grey, Marquess of Dorset, whose wife was the oldest surviving child of Charles Brandon and the king's aunt, Mary Tudor, was invested as the Duke of Suffolk *jure uxoris*. Most importantly, the king's trusted advisor, the Earl of Warwick, became the Duke of Northumberland.

It has been suspected by many historians that Dudley was given his promotion in order to deal with the king's troublesome uncle, the Duke of Somerset, who had never forgiven the men who had displaced him from his protectorate. The fact that England was doing better under Warwick's leadership had only rubbed salt in the duke's wounds. Somerset had been plotting against the president of the council for months, and may have even attempted to assassinate the earl the previous April.[8] Warwick had suspected the duke, but had no proof. Nevertheless, he was sure enough about Somerset's perfidy that he excluded him from his confidence, and thus from much of the council business. Somerset began to complain that it was 'strange' that things should 'come before the council, and I not hear of it',[9] yet his political ostracisation was all his own doing. He became dependent on William Paget and Henry Stanley, Lord Strange, to keep him in the loop regarding council business. He had also tried to meddle in his nephew's betrothal to Elisabeth of Valois. He had coaxed Lord Strange, who was a member of the king's privy chamber, into suggesting to Edward that Somerset's young daughter, Jane Seymour, would make a much better bride than a French princess. However, all that his interference accomplished was to make him more unwelcome at court and get Henry Stanley into hot water. Seething about his political lockout, Somerset then tried to capitalise on his popularity as the 'good duke' to spread the word that Dudley was the sole reason for the country's socio-economic difficulties, 'causing a great murmur among the commons'.[10]

Earlier that month, news seems to have come to light that Somerset had been plotting with a handful of allies to overthrow the council. Thomas Palmer, who claimed to be one of the duke's co-conspirators, ratted out the whole scheme to Northumberland and the council. According to Palmer, the king's uncle planned to invite Dudley, William Parr, and Henry Herbert to a banquet, where they would be murdered by the duke's men. With them out of the way, the council could be brought back under Somerset's control, he would resume his governance of the king's person, and be reinstated as Lord Protector. Whether or not Palmer was telling the truth about the duke's misdeeds remains a subject of historical debate, but the earlier behaviour of the king's uncle gave every indication that at the very least he intended to keep trying to displace Dudley and regain power. Somerset's ceaseless skullduggery could have tested the patience of a saint, and Northumberland was not a saint.

On 17 October, only two years since he had last been arrested for potential treason, Somerset was once more imprisoned in the Tower. This time, the duke would find no mercy from either the council or his nephew. Like his brother, Thomas Seymour, he would wait in vain for a powerful relative to save him.

The arrest of the 'good duke' resulted in a 'great unrest' in London and the countryside, 'kept alive by the hatred borne towards the Duke of Northumberland and his party by many lords, and, above all, by the commons, who are saying quite openly that the Duke of Somerset is being unjustly accused, and that the other party deserves punishment much more than the prisoners.'[11] Those who disliked Northumberland also accused him of keeping only 'his creatures' around the king, in order to prevent Edward from learning of the calumny perpetrated against his uncle. However, there is evidence written in the king's own hand that showed him to be well aware of the indictments against Somerset.

The former Lord Protector was put on trial at Westminster Hall in early December, and King Edward recorded the event matter-of-factly in his private journal and a letter to Barnaby Fitzpatrick. The duke insisted that he had never intended to harm his nephew, or planned to commit treason. Nevertheless, he seemed to confess he had designed the murders of Dudley, Parr, and Herbert, or at least could not deny it absolutely. Furthermore, the Earl of Arundel had admitted that he and Somerset had planned to seize Northumberland to 'answer and reform things',[12] but he swore there was no plan to harm them physically. As a result of the testimony given against the duke, the lords 'acquitted him of high treason, and condemned him of treason felonious, and so he was adjudged to be hanged'.[13] Somerset then gave thanks to the lords for allowing him to have an open trial to defend himself, and begged Dudley, Parr, and Herbert to forgive him 'for his ill meaning against them, and made suit for his life, wife and children, servants and debts'.[14]

In spite of the testimony by Thomas Palmer, William Crane, Sir Miles Partridge, and Lord Strange that Somerset was planning to reclaim his protectorate by force, it would prove 'impossible to persuade the people or impress it upon them ... that Somerset really tried to lead such an enterprise'.[15] Londoners gathered outside the hall shouting 'God save the duke'.[16] The cries of Somerset's supporters were so loud that they were 'heard at Charing cross plainly',[17] and when the axe representing condemnation of high treason was withdrawn, the rumour quickly spread that the duke was acquitted of all charges.

Historians have traditionally been no less partisan in their praise or condemnation of Somerset than people were on the day of his trial. For those on Team Somerset, the denunciation of the duke was orchestrated by the dastardly Northumberland as a means to keep his hold on the king, and no evidence of malfeasance is to be believed. Even the depositions of his co-conspirators are taradiddles and fabrications. The imperial ambassador claimed that Northumberland had 'worked through a third person' until Somerset had 'confessed the whole plot, compromised the prisoners and other notable personages, and signed his confession with his own hand'.[18] The king's apathy toward his uncle was likewise chalked up to Dudley's cleverness in making sure Edward only heard the slanders against Somerset and never anything in his defence. For those on Team Northumberland, who were notably fewer but no less enthusiastic about the topic, Somerset brought his destruction down on his own head by his earlier overreach and later machinations to regain his former authority. Northumberland had tried to make peace with his rival for more than a year, but when he was given enough rope, Somerset hanged himself.

After a few weeks' grace to put his affairs in order, Edward Seymour, the Duke of Somerset, who once wore England's shadow-crown as Lord Protector, was led from his prison and executed on 22 January 1552. The king, formerly an ardent supporter of his uncle, had signed the death warrant with a steady hand and had merely noted in his journal that, 'The duke of Somerset had his head cut off upon Tower hill between eight and nine o'clock in the morning'. Why was Edward so blasé about Somerset's execution, when he had been so protective of his uncle two years before? For one thing, we cannot be sure he was really unmoved. The king was not one to display his feelings, and there is no way of knowing if he felt any private turmoil if he didn't make a note of it. When he first heard the charges against the duke, he was thought to be so 'deeply distressed' that he had 'become very thin and weak'.[19] Perhaps the young king's affection had truly cooled into indifference for his uncle. He was not stupid, and he would have realised that his uncle had been using him to rule the kingdom in the years after Henry VIII's death. That might have been excused, if Somerset had been doting and warm toward the king, but the duke had been too busy to be tender toward his orphaned nephew. Perhaps the king had come to think that Somerset had always viewed him mainly as a lodestone for power, and did not believe his uncle had ever really loved him. The deposition of Lord Strange, who detailed how Somerset had asked him to spy on the king, may have been the last straw that turned Edward against the duke. There might have been a festering resentment that his uncle had once kidnapped him. Maybe, in hindsight, the king had come to distrust the motivations behind the execution of Thomas Seymour. It is possible that he now believed that his uncle had actually planned to kill members of the council in order to have control over him again. Or it could be that the king was disgusted with the duke for growing 'so cold in hearing God's word ... [he] would not distrain himself to go from his gallery to his hall for the hearing of a sermon'.[20] Whatever the reason for it, Edward appears to have believed that his uncle deserved his fate.

Nonetheless, it should be noted that even if the king had been heartbroken by his kinsman's putative betrayal or execution, he would have hardly shown it. He had turned fourteen shortly before Somerset's arrest, and had ceased his formal education with tutors in order to focus all his attention on governing his country. Edward was not yet legally an adult, but in his time period teens his age were treated socioculturally as young men, rather than boys. He was still being advised by his councillors (as all kings were, regardless of their age), but he was already the penultimate authority on any policy decisions. After all, his father had been only seventeen when he had become the king, and he had ruled without a regent. In his role as an adult monarch, Edward needed to maintain a facade of mature control, especially before foreign dignitaries.

While Somerset had awaited his trial in the Tower, his nephew had been busy entertaining Marie of Guise, the Dowager Queen of Scotland, who had come to further strengthen the new diplomatic ties with France, as well as the peace between England and the Scots. The king was engaged to a French princess, and France was now openly at war again with the Holy Roman Empire. The king and his council, all too aware of how busted English finances were, wanted to remain neutral rather than commit to the expense of another war, yet they also wanted to keep ties with France firm, which would keep the emperor anxious not to provoke England. It was up to the teenage sovereign to pull off this balancing act with gestures of friendship to the French envoys without making promises or commitments. He seems to have walked this fine line with aplomb, because Marie of Guise would say she had 'found more wisdom and solid judgment in young King Edward than she would have looked for in any three princes that were then in Europe'.[21]

As sovereign, Edward needed to dazzle his own courtiers and subjects, as well as visitors. Whether he felt like it or not, the king hosted open-house festivities at Greenwich for the Twelve Days of Christmas. He appointed George Ferrers as the Lord of Misrule, who contrived 'sundry sights and devices of rare intention', as well as 'diverse interludes and matters of pastimes', which the king then rewarded with 'princely liberality'.[22] There were also sporting contests, tournaments, plays, masques, and banquets to celebrate the yuletide. Presents were exchanged for New Year's Day, and the young monarch was given falcons, greyhounds, and mastiffs, as well the usual gilt cups and bowls. He seemed to be particularly pleased with the dozen fine horses and two mules sent to him from France by his future father-in-law, King Henry II. All in all, the king seems to have enjoyed himself, inasmuch as he wrote to Barnaby Fitzpatrick in January to tell him that that the holiday had been 'been well and merrily spent'. The letter, which described some of the tilts that Edward had seen and the flooding in Essex, did not mention that his uncle Somerset had been executed shortly before the missive had been sent.

After Somerset's death, it became popular (and remains popular to the present day) to credit Northumberland with all manner of deviousness. He was suspected of plotting the execution of Archbishop Cranmer, and rumoured to have 'conversed in secret about certain English prophecies according to which the King of England will not live long'.[23] Most of all, he is charged with having exerted undue influence over his teenage king. Notwithstanding the persistence of these accusations, the historical evidence does not confirm any of them. The duke was indisputably a trusted and beloved councillor, but Edward took orders from no one. The king was a 'lad of quick, ready and well-developed mind; remarkably so for his age',[24] and if he had ever been anyone's pawn, there was no doubt that he now knew who wore the crown. His journal, letters, and essays all paint a picture of a monarch who was completely aware of his responsibilities and the intricacies of statecraft. If he thought someone was attempting to mitigate his authority, he didn't hesitate to rebuke them sharply. When a member of his council failed to rubber-stamp one of his commands, he 'marveled' angrily that anyone would have the gall to 'refuse to sign that bill, or deliver that letter, that I had willed anyone about me to write'.[25] He pointed out that it would be a great impediment to him if he had to send for the council every time he made a decision, and he would 'seem to be in bondage'.[26] He clearly had no intention of suffering his hands to be metaphorically tied by his council. Moreover, the letters written by Northumberland and other councilmen to their king were expressed in terms of fulfilling his will, making it clear that he had the last word on the matter. For all his youth, Edward VI had the same implacable commitment to his sovereignty as any Tudor monarch before or after him.

Nevertheless, a large chunk of Edward's subjects continued to blame Northumberland, but not the king, for the death of Somerset. People seemed to have forgotten that Somerset was power-hungry enough to murder his brother and had sent mercenaries to kill Englishmen on their own soil. He had become sainted in the public imagination for his offer to at least *consider* doing something about the enclosures. As a result, the dislike of Northumberland became so intense that the man could not win for losing. A simple misprint on the new coinage was speculated to be some sort of conspiracy against the king on the duke's part.[27] The imperial ambassador wondered if his sincere attempt to play peace-maker between France and the Holy Roman Empire was a sly distraction while the duke's oldest son secretly mustered troops to assist the French. The duke was believed to be the one behind the king's sister, Lady Elizabeth, refusing to wed the Earl of Pembroke, William Herbert. Even the king's new freedoms were held against Northumberland, with claims that the duke had only done it 'to cause the king to forget the Duke of Somerset as quickly as possible'.[28]

The growing animosity toward Northumberland among Edward's courtiers had little to do with Somerset, however. Rather, it was the result of the fears that he had become too powerful, and too influential. Some of the king's gentlemen, therefore, began to use every opportunity to slander the duke, much to his frustration and dismay, in the hopes of bringing him down a peg or two. The constant disparagement of Northumberland may have borne fruit. During a game of archery Edward mocked the duke for missing his shot, telling him he had 'aimed better' he had 'cut off the head of my uncle Somerset'.[29] Notwithstanding the gibe, which may have merely been an example of gallows humour, the king continued to favour the duke and rely on his advice more than any other councillor's.

Another reason that Northumberland was so unpopular was due to the backlash against the crown's increasingly strident push for the English to become fully Protestant. People were unhappy that they were losing so much of their old forms of worship, and they wanted someone to blame for it. Since the sovereign was excused on the grounds of his youth, Northumberland became the target of their ire. Even the king's own words were not sufficient proof that he, rather than the president of his council, was the actual driving force behind the radical reforms. Instead, it was rumoured that the duke was sneaking into Edward's rooms in the dead of night to corrupt his thoughts, so when the king spoke people were tricked into believing that his ideas had 'proceeded from his mind and by his invention'.[30] The king's eldest sister, Mary, in particular, seemed to think that the breach between herself and her brother regarding religion had been caused, or at least aided, by the duke.

Northumberland was also being blamed by the general populace for the increased taxes and the economic stagnation the country was bogged down in. England was in a staggering amount of debt, and only revenue would alleviate the crisis, but no one wanted any of the needed money to come out of *their* pocket. This is a completely understandable point of view for the poor and working class, who could barely eke a subsistence living, but there is no real excuse for the incessant grumbling of the rich regarding taxation. The king tried to lead by example, and was cutting back his expenditures everywhere he could. The imperial ambassador reported that all the 'crown expenses are being diminished, even to the king's table'. The mounted artillery that Edward was so proud of was disbanded because it cost too much to maintain. He also stopped 'paying his ministers and officers, except those abroad', whose salaries he continued 'for the sake of his reputation'.[31] The king's thriftiness is in complete contrast to the behaviour of Henry VIII, who had maintained his extravagant spending even as his kingdom was beggared by useless wars. Edward was more of a responsible adult at the age of fourteen than his father had been at fifty.

Chapter Thirteen

The King's Health Begins to Fail

At the beginning of April, the fragile ecosystem of the court was briefly disturbed when the king developed a serious illness. Edward wrote in his journal that he fell sick with measles and smallpox, but it is unlikely that he would have survived an onslaught from both diseases at once even if he had perfect health. Considering that he developed pock-marks on his face, so that he 'did not wish to show himself to strangers'[1] for more than a week, he had probably contracted smallpox. The king fortunately recovered from his illness without any major complications, and by the end of the month he 'was convalescent and very cheerful'.[2] He removed to Greenwich in the first week of May, and was soon entertaining ambassadors and dignitaries once more. He also made sure his subjects could see that he was well once more. He rode through Greenwich park to review a 'goodly muster of his men of arms', and rode to Blackheath with his guard 'in their jerkins and doublets' to compete in a tournament, where he 'ran at the ring' with other young lords and knights.[3]

The king had resumed his participation in matters of state as well. It appears that he agreed, or may have even been the instigator, of the council policy attempting to set England up as a neutral peacemaker between warring continental rulers. In June, he sent letters of congratulations to both the king and queen of France for their nation's recent victories against the imperial armies, but on the very same day, he also sent letters of congratulations to the emperor and Mary of Hungary regarding their victories over the French. The king additionally wrote a letter around this time to Henry Clifford, Earl of Cumberland, supporting a match between the earl's daughter, Margaret Clifford, and Northumberland's fourth son, Guildford Dudley. Margaret Clifford's mother was Eleanor Brandon, the youngest daughter of Charles Brandon and Mary Tudor, which meant that Margaret was sixth in line to the throne at that time. Although this union was backed by the duke's allies on the council, the fears among several high ranking lords that a wedding between Margaret and Guildford put John Dudley a little too close to the throne won out, and the potential marriage was kaput.

Edward was also busy making arrangements to go on summer progress in July, the way his father had often done. His trip would take him in a wide loop, first to Devon in the south, then westward through Wiltshire, and finally homeward to Windsor Palace. The main purpose of such a progress was for the king to be seen by the people who were geographically constrained to areas farther from London, and he continued to deal with governmental issues via courier, but the teenage monarch managed to squeeze some fun and relaxation into his travels as well. Edward was a deep thinker, but that didn't mean he was a stick in the mud. He enjoyed his trip and staying in the homes of some of his courtiers, where he had 'both good hunting and good cheer'.[4] In Sussex he visited Sir Anthony Browne's estate, Cowdray Park, and was 'marvelously, yea, rather excessively banquetted'.[5] In Hampshire, he was entertained at Warblington Manor, the home of Sir Richard Cotton, and had such a good time that shortly afterwards he made his host the comptroller of the royal household. He also called on his Lord Treasurer, William Paulet, at Waltham Palace, which impressed him as a 'fair, great old house'.[6] He also inspected the fortifications at Plymouth and found them inadequate, but he thought the town itself was 'handsome, and for the bigness of it' had some nice houses. He was feasted there by the town's most prominent citizens, many of whom 'kept costly tables'. At Salisbury, he was greeted by twenty-four aldermen in crimson gowns, along with several other of the town's best citizens, and was given a gilt cup filled with gold coins. While in Wiltshire, the king paid a visit to William Herbert at Wilton House. The Earl of Pembroke welcomed him there 'with great magnificence', serving him dinner in 'vessels of pure gold … and all the members of his household, down to the very least, in silver'.[7] When he left, the earl gave the king a parting gift of a 'very rich camp-bed, decorated with pearls and precious stones'.

The young monarch had returned to Windsor by mid-September, having cut his pleasant journey a few days short in order to deal with matters of governance. He had apparently been delighted by his summer progress, telling a friend he had been happily 'occupied in killing of wild beasts, in pleasant journeys, in good fare, [and] in viewing of fair countries'.[8] It is good to know that Edward had been so delighted that summer, because his first significant progress would, unfortunately, turn out to be his last.

As the days became shorter, the king's working hours became longer. He continued to facilitate international trade in an attempt to revitalise the kingdom's economy, shipping 'great quantities of cloth to flanders', and sending well-guarded shipments of goods to Spain as well.[9] There were also plans afoot to call back as much of the country's currency as possible, possibly to recast it with a higher content of precious metal and increase its relative worth. Additionally, he and his council were making every effort to broker peace between France and the Holy Roman Empire, while each country was making every effort to drag England into the war on their side. Edward skilfully navigated the fine line between amity and alliance with both. When the imperial ambassador hinted that the emperor was displeased with England's close association with the French, the king 'only replied that the friendship was in the interest of both countries, and he would not fail to maintain it'.[10]

Shortly after his fifteenth birthday that October, Edward welcomed Gerolamo Cardano,[11] a famous Italian polymath, to his court. Among his many talents, Cardano was an astronomer/astrologer, and had been asked to cast the king's horoscope. Since he was also a noted physician, his visit has given rise to speculation he had been summoned because the king's health was failing. While there certainly might have been some early warning signs of an underlying problem with Edward's constitution, Cardano may have been invited because he had dedicated his last book, *De Varietate Rerum*, to England's erudite sovereign. The king was also an avid amateur stargazer, so he may have simply wanted to meet such a renowned astrologer.

Cardano described the king as being 'of a stature somewhat below the middle height, pale-faced with grey eyes, a grave aspect, decorous and handsome'.[12] Edward had a 'somewhat projecting shoulder blade', which wasn't bad enough to be a deformity, although it may have been the reason why he 'carried himself like an old man'.[13] He also thought that the king was reasonably healthy, being short-sighted and a little hard of hearing but not a 'sufferer from fixed diseases'.[14] The Italian scholar, however, was much more impressed by the king's incredible intellect than his rather mediocre physical form. He found the monarch to be 'of so much wit and promise' that he could comprehend anything.[15] He noted that Edward spoke several languages, but that his ability to speak French and Latin were 'singularly perfect'. He was astounded by the king's understanding of logic, natural philosophy, music, and praised him for having a love for all 'liberal arts and sciences'.[16] Cardano was amazed to find that such a teenager was able to ask rational and pointed questions about the nature of comets, and was so quick to understand the explanations he was given. The king was even good at playing the lute. Not only was the young monarch brilliant, he had a 'disposition worthy of so great a prince'.[17] When 'a kingly majesty required gravity, there you should have seen him a sage and an old man, and yet gentle and pleasant also'.[18] In fact, Edward was so extraordinary that the physician wasn't sure people would believe it. He wrote defensively that although it 'might seem a miracle of nature, to behold the excellent wit and forwardness' of such a young king, he was not speaking 'rhetorically, to amplify things, or make them more than the truth is ... the truth is more than I do utter'.[19] Perhaps it was wishful thinking that caused the astrologer to erroneously forecast a long life for the Tudor sovereign?

The precocious king was seeking to secure a path for his realm in religious matters, as well as in secular ones. His aversion to what he considered papist idolatry had only increased as time passed, and his support of Archbishop Cranmer's reformist theology strengthened. On 1 November, the second Book of Common Prayer was brought into use in England's churches. This latest version of the prayer book moved even farther away from traditional forms of worship. The Eucharist was no longer called the Mass, and references to the body and blood of Christ were replaced with the words 'Take, eat, in remembrance that Christ died for thee'. Just as shocking was the fact that the Order for the Burial of the Dead had been reduced to a simple memorial service that ignored or outright negated the long-held beliefs regarding Purgatory, or the need for intercessory prayer.

Predictably, there was an immediate uproar regarding its use. For those who preferred the old faith, or at least some vestiges of it, Cranmer's altered sacraments were more blasphemous than reformed. For the hardened Protestants, the prayer book wasn't quite reformed enough. If the definition of a good compromise is indeed a situation in which no one is really happy, the second Book of Common Prayer was a *very* good compromise. Edward, however, was determined that his godfather Cranmer's liturgical compositions would become the bedrock of the Anglican service, and the churches were ordered to continue using it.

Notwithstanding that the prayer book was Cranmer's brainchild and had full backing from the king, the English blamed the Duke of Northumberland for it. He was the national scapegoat, and so it is unsurprising that he had become depressed and ill. His stomach hurt so badly he couldn't eat, and he was miserable. He wrote to Edward, begging to be released from the council and allowed to retire to the country. He said that because of his poor health he had 'neither understanding nor wit ... nor body apt' to perform his duties for the king as his 'heart and will desireth'.[20] Since anything he did was construed as a nefarious plot, his desire to relinquish his power merely served to 'enhance suspicions' against him and gave the other councillors 'grounds for fear'.[21] Even his absence from the council due to his poor health was cause for alarm, and it was rumoured that 'he was meditating some step, which may perchance be a radical change in both spiritual and temporal dignities, and a creation of new dukes and earls'.[22] Mistrusted regardless no matter what he did, the melancholy Northumberland wrote to William Cecil about his unhappiness. The duke lamented that although at night he goes to 'bed with a careful and weary heart ... no man scarcely had any good opinion of me' and even while he was so sick in mind and body he was 'not without a new evil imagination of men'.[23] He would be happy to die, the duke confessed, if it wasn't for the 'children which God hath sent me'.[24]

In spite of Northumberland's pleas, the king refused to dismiss him from service. Edward had become too accustomed to his good advice and intelligent analysis to give it up. It's hard to blame the king for this, since England's recovery under the duke's guidance had been steady and strong. The second prayer book was received grudgingly, but there had been no open rebellion. The currency had been shored up, which meant the kingdom's economy was improving and food was becoming more affordable. There was no war to drag the country into a financial deficit or to kill its men. All of the crown's foreign debt had been paid off, and England's international credit was on the mend. Even the fraught relationship between the king and his eldest sister had calmed down after Mary finally acceded to the laws physically, if not in spirit. Nevertheless, most of the population still detested the Duke of Northumberland, and saw him as the root of all their remaining problems. In another letter to William Cecil, the duke said his only comfort was knowing 'with what zeal, faith, and truth' he had served the king, and 'so shall I most please God and have my conscience upright, and then not fear what man doth to me'.[25]

The duke was not free, but for the time being he was too sick to come to court, so he couldn't attend the Christmas revelries at Greenwich. The other councillors, however, were present and most participated in the various festive events. George Ferrers was once more appointed as the Lord of Misrule, and once more his 'devises' were over-the-top and well-received.[26] Minstrels, jugglers, acrobats, jesters, and a small fife-and-drum band of boys dressed in Turkish garments were allowed to roam the palace. There were multiple events scheduled for the daylight hours, including sports, games, hunting, hawking, and a ridiculous tournament of fools riding on hobby-horses led by the Lord of Misrule himself. Twelfth Night was particularly spectacular, with a debut of the 'triumph of Cupid' featuring masked ladies of the court as Venus and her attendants, along with many costumed gentlemen as Mars and his merry men. Even the chancellor and seven other councillors, 'arrayed in apparel accustomed', were part of the elaborate production.[27]

The king enjoyed the presentation so much that there were almost immediate arrangements to put on a play for him on Candlemas. However, by the end of January, the plans had been delayed for a few weeks because the king was feeling unwell. By the middle of February, it had been put on a more lengthy hold, by occasion that his grace was sick, and the show thereof deferred until after Mayday.[28] The fifteen-year-old formerly healthy King Edward VI was dying.

Chapter Fourteen

Edward's Attempt to Secure the Succession of Lady Jane Grey

Initially, it was thought that perhaps the 'fatiguing joyousness' of the season, and an overindulgence of rich food, had temporarily injured the king's health. He didn't seem to be that sick. He could perform royal audiences, and he still attended sermons regularly. In late January, Bishop Nicholas Ridley came to Westminster and preached a 'godly exhortation to the rich, to be merciful to the poor, and also moved such as were in authority to travel by some charitable way and means to comfort and relieve them'.[1] The king's beliefs were sincere, and he seems to have been determined to follow the tenets of the Christian faith as well as enforce them. He was already feeling unwell and feverish, but he nevertheless summoned Ridley after the sermon to discuss how he might devise a way to help the greatest number of his impoverished subjects. The bishop, 'being amazed to hear the wisdom and earnest zeal of the king',[2] hesitated for a moment but finally told Edward that the best way to assist the impoverished was to order the mayor of London to convene a council and organise some relief through the city's infrastructure. Taking this advice, the ailing king immediately wrote a letter for Bishop Ridley to take to the mayor. Pleased to do the personal bidding of the king, the worthies of London were able to suggest several possible solutions, including charitable hospitals and a rudimentary attempt at welfare in the form of small weekly stipends to lepers. The king's health had deteriorated badly by the time these recommendations reached him, but he was not only willing to grant charters and governmental authority to these charities, he 'required that he might be accounted as the chief founder and patron thereof'.[3] In spite of the always shaky state of the royal finances, Edward donated some of the crown's lands to fund, among other things, Christ's Hospital in Newgate Street, St. Thomas's Hospital in Southwark, and Bridewell Hospital on the banks of the Fleet River.

Shortly after he had spoken with Bishop Ridley, it had become apparent that the king was suffering from a serious illness. He had developed a 'touch, strong, straining cough' and notwithstanding the best medical treatments available and the hardiness of his youth, 'it daily increased by dangerous degrees'.[4] Worse, it wasn't only 'a violence of the cough which did infest him, but wherewith a weakness … which showed plainly that his vial parts were most strongly and strangely assaulted'.[5] He was also showing some peculiar symptoms that confused the royal physicians. They could see he was suffering from something other than the ordinary form of tuberculosis or pneumonia, but they didn't know how or why. The lack of a sure diagnosis fostered a growing rumour that the king had been poisoned. As was now customary, Northumberland promptly became the chief suspect. Whispers began that the duke had administered the poison to the king by giving him 'a nosegay of sweet flowers which was presented to him as a great dainty on New Year's Day'.[6] That the duke had not been at Greenwich did nothing to stop the gossip, because fact had always played very little part in the public antipathy toward him. Supporters of the old faith, and therefore of Lady Mary, also promoted these misgivings about him whenever possible, since he was seen as the real reason for the king's evangelism. Meanwhile, reformist zealots like John Knox did not defend him because they saw him as too lenient on continued papist idolatry. The attacks by the Protestants were an especial source of pain for the duke, who grumbled to William Cecil that he had 'for twenty years stood to one kind of religion'[7] despite the personal dangers to himself, and was now being chastised by his fellow reformers on top of everything else.

Notwithstanding that he was still recuperating from his own illness, the beleaguered Northumberland nevertheless returned to court so he could assist his ailing sovereign. The duke was therefore present to greet Lady Mary when she arrived for a long-promised visit to her brother at Westminster on 17 February. Her attendance at court would mean that the cat would be out of the bag regarding the king's indisposition, but to delay or put off her visit would have aroused too much suspicion that Edward was being deliberately isolated by his councillors. They decided to split the difference and tell Mary on the evening of her arrival in London that the king had been 'attacked by a fever' and was sick enough that his sister 'could not see him for three days'.[8] She was nonetheless 'honourably received and entertained' by the Northumberland and the other councillors, and when she was finally able to see the king he spoke to her 'very kindly and graciously … making no mention of matters of religion'.

Once he knew that the king was ill, the imperial ambassador, Jehan Scheyfve, was quick to speculate on the nature and reason for the disease. He claimed that Edward seemed 'to be sensitive to the slightest indisposition or change, partly at any rate because his right shoulder is lower than his left' but that some 'make light of the imperfection, saying that the depression in the right shoulder is hereditary in the house of Seymour'.[9] The late Duke of Somerset had the same condition, but 'he only suffered inconvenience as far as it affected his appearance, and his shoulder never troubled him in any other way'. However, 'about a year ago the King overstrained himself while hunting, and that the defect was increased'. He also reported that the king's life was thought to be in danger, but he believed that the doctors were mostly exaggerating to cover their butts in case the monarch was actually sicker than he seemed. Nevertheless, the king was suffering 'a good deal when the fever is upon him, especially from a difficulty in drawing his breath, which is due to the compression of the organs on the right side'. Scheyfve also gave his gleefully macabre opinion that the malady was 'a visitation and sign from God', to punish the king for leaving the Catholic faith.

Although the king had become very weak and had lost a lot of weight, he rallied enough to open Parliament on 1 March. The only concession he made to his infirmity was to move the opening to Westminster, so he didn't have to go very far to attend. The king walked into chapel under his own steam, remained seated upright for the entirety of Bishop Ridley's sermon, and 'with divers lords received the communion'.[10] Then he went into his great chamber with his lords and sat under his cloth of estate while some of his ministers spoke to the audience on his behalf. The speech was kept short, and immediately after 'the lords departed … because the king was sickly'.[11] The king would once again appear in his royal seat in the waiting chamber of Westminster thirty days later, this time to give his assent to the acts passed and to dissolve the Parliament early, but his health remained poor.

As spring advanced, Edward began to go into his park at Westminster whenever the weather was nice enough which seemed to make him feel a little better. His physicians decided that since fresh air was benefiting him, he should be moved a bit closer to the countryside. The teenage monarch was therefore taken by the royal barge to Greenwich on 11 April, and as his flotilla passed by the Tower he was saluted with 'a great shot of guns and chambers, and all the ships shot off guns all the way to Ratcliffe'.[12] Alas, the move did not seem to help him. He continued to become weaker. The imperial ambassador was told by 'a trustworthy source' that the monarch had been coughing up matter that was 'sometimes coloured a greenish yellow and black, [and] sometimes pink, like the colour of blood',[13] which had confounded his physicians.

Edward knew he was gravely ill, and knew that he needed to choose an heir in case the worst should happen. He did not want his half-sister Mary to reign after him, because there was too much risk that she would attempt to turn England toward 'popery' again. He gave serious consideration to naming the Lady Elizabeth, his 'sweet sister Temperance',[14] as his heir, yet in the end, he decided that he really couldn't skip over one sister for theoretical illegitimacy but not the other. Additionally, while he approved of her Protestant theology, he also believed Elizabeth's mother Anne Boleyn had been a trollop, adulteress, and perhaps even a witch who ensorcelled his father. To think otherwise would mean that his father had committed judicial murder that his mother had been complicit. Even if he had come to terms with his father's brutality, his mother had been presented as saintly to him his entire life. He would have thought of her as a perfect model of womanhood. It would have been much easier for him to assume that Anne Boleyn was a monster and therefore Elizabeth could not be queen.

If neither of his sisters could be allowed the crown, then according to kinship it should have fallen to a descendant of Henry VIII's oldest sister, Margaret Tudor, who had married James IV of Scotland. That would have made Mary, Queen of Scots, his successor, but not only was she Catholic, she was engaged to the heir to the French throne. Once Mary had his throne, England would be annexed to France in all but name. He could never agree to that. Therefore, he took the example of his father's will and named the descendants of his younger aunt, Mary Tudor, as his potential heirs. Only Mary Tudor's daughters had lived to adulthood and the eldest, Frances, had married Henry Grey, who had become the Duke of Suffolk through her when her half-brothers had died. For some reason, Edward skipped over his first cousin and chose her eldest daughter, Lady

Jane Grey, to be next in line for the throne. The most likely reason for the preferment was because Jane Grey, like her father and the king, was well-known to be a devout and uncompromising reformist.

The king wrote, in his own hand, the first draft of what he called 'My Devise for the Succession' naming Jane Grey as his heir. The exact date he started this document is unknown, but it was possible he was working on it as early as February 1553 and it had certainly been written by April.[15] It has been commonly assumed that Jane's nomination was a ploy by Northumberland to wed her to one of his sons and rule through them, but there is no evidence that the duke had any influence over his sovereign's choice of successor. Nor were Jane and Guildford Dudley engaged to each other when the king became sick. Guildford was the fourth surviving son of the duke, and would have had no aspirations – or hope – of marrying someone with Jane Grey's bloodlines under normal circumstances. Their betrothal seems to have occurred *after* the king had the idea of naming Jane to wear the crown next. Just as the devise was Edward's brainchild, the decision to wed Jane to Northumberland's son appears to have been his idea as well. Moreover, there were difficulties in securing the marriage between Guildford and Jane that only the king could surmount. For one thing, Jane's parents were less than thrilled with the idea. It wasn't just that Guildford was not much of a prize for a daughter they had once hoped would marry the king. What was worse, from Henry Grey's point of view, was that the groom's family were not reformist enough. The Duke of Suffolk was as enamoured of the new religion as the king himself, and the Dudleys lacked his zealousness. It was only the fact that Edward was determined for the match, and no one could gainsay the king, that finally sealed the deal. It seems that the duke was the man the king trusted the most to assist the new queen to uphold Protestantism and govern the realm, and the best way to secure his place near the throne was to make him Jane's father-in-law.

Northumberland knew what kind of ruckus news of the engagement would cause, even though most people were unaware that Jane Grey was the chosen heir. He was already accused of being the secret king; what would people say when they knew his son had married into the royal line? Things would become especially dicey when the court discovered the forthcoming wedding between his brother, Andrew Dudley, and Jane's cousin Margaret Clifford.

To assure the court that he wasn't power-mad, he arranged another marriage to a rival successor that would put his potential supremacy in jeopardy. The next in line to the throne after Jane was her sister, Katherine Grey. The duke's main rival for primacy in the Council (and thus one of the men who trusted him the least) was William Herbert, Earl of Pembroke. In complete contradiction to his own best interest, Northumberland facilitated a union between Pembroke's eldest son and Katherine Grey. To understand how vulnerable he was making himself with this match, 'one only has to look at the threat Katherine would pose to Queen Elizabeth in the 1560s to realise the danger she would have posed to Jane and Guildford'.[16] The duke also attempted to mend fences with Lady Mary, both 'to earn her favour and show that he [did] not aspire to the crown'.[17] Rather than imprison her for his own safety, he was 'assiduous in his offices' to the king's sister, and even arranged for her to have 'her full arms as Princess of England, as she used to bear them'.[18]

If John Dudley was scheming to rule England with a puppet queen, he was really, *really* bad at it.

The duke had done everything he could to prove that he wasn't trying to usurp royal authority for himself, but most people remained convinced that he was a spider in the middle of a web of evil plans. When news of Jane Grey's betrothal to Guildford Dudley became public, most of the English had no doubt that he had 'formed some mighty plot' to seize power.[19] A rumour began that his eldest son, now the 2nd Earl of Warwick, was planning to divorce his wife and marry the king's youngest sister, Lady Elizabeth. Additionally, the duke was suspected of making secret alliances with France, probably in the hopes that the French would help block an imperial rescue when he arrested Lady Mary. The populace also became certain that he was conspiring to prematurely wrap King Edward in a shroud and take the throne, and began 'crying God save the king and defend him from his enemies'.[20]

Northumberland was no threat to the king, but Edward's life was nevertheless in danger. At the end of April, his desperate doctors had gone to the council and 'requested very earnestly to be allowed to summon others of their art to consult with them and receive the assistance of their knowledge'.[21] Scheyfve reported to the emperor that it was 'held for certain' that the monarch would die, because he was 'suffering from a suppurating tumour (*apostème*) on the lung'.[22] The king was 'vexed by a harsh, continuous cough' and 'a slow fever upon him that never leaves' that had rendered his body 'dry and burning'.[23] His belly was also swollen, and he was 'beginning to break out in ulcers'. His condition was so bad that the grapevine began to claim he had already died and the news was being concealed, which led to three people having their ears torn off for spreading falsehoods about the king.

The May Day jousts were cancelled due to the king's illness, but he unexpectedly seemed to rally a few days after that. Dudley wrote to William Cecil on the 7th, to give him 'the joyful comfort ... that our sovereign lord doth begin very joyfully to increase and amend', leaving his physicians with 'no doubt of the thorough recovery of his highness'.[24] A week later the council cheerfully informed the French ambassadors that 'the king's health was so much improving that he would be able to relieve them at the end of three or four days'.[25] Edward was deemed to be sufficiently restored by the 17th, and formally greeted the ambassadors. The audience was kept short, however, because the king was still physically weak and impaired by his ceaseless coughing. During this time, Edward felt well enough to send Jane Grey 'presents of rich ornaments and jewels' for her upcoming wedding, and to sign 'certain articles concerning religion' aimed at setting some limits on 'the diversity of sects' sprouting from the Reformation.[26] He also sent his eldest sister 'a table diamond, with a pendant pearl',[27] perhaps to thank her for the letter she wrote congratulating him on his convalescence, or perhaps because he was feeling guilty he had written her out of the succession.

For a short while after Jane Grey's wedding to Guildford Dudley in the latter half of May, it seemed that the king was getting better. In the first week of June, he even received some visitors into his sickroom, including Sir Thomas Gresham, who had been his chief economic adviser and the main architect in saving England's currency. The king also saw his old schoolmaster, John Cheke, who delivered books to him in person. Cheke would write to the author about how 'kindly and courteously' the sovereign had received them, and how much he esteemed them, but warned that since 'the king's majesty, debilitated by a long illness, is scarcely yet restored to health' there would probably not be a royal letter of thanks forthcoming soon.[28]

Alas, the hopes of the king's recovery were unfounded. By the middle of the month, it had become obvious that Edward's mysterious illness was still killing him. He was 'wasting away', and his body had 'begun to swell, especially his head and feet'.[29] There was a profusion of ulcers on his scalp, and physicians decided to shave his head so they could apply plasters. He could not rest except when he was 'stuffed with drugs, which doctors call opiates'.[30] When he coughed, the sputum he brought up was 'livid, black, fetid, ... [stank] beyond measure ... [and] if put in a basin full of water it sinks to the bottom'.[31] It was generally reported that the king might survive for 'two months more, but he cannot possibly live beyond that time',[32] and the canard that he was being slowly poisoned was steadily gaining traction in the public imagination.

Suspicions that the Duke of Northumberland was the poisoner, or was at least involved in 'some mighty plot'[33] against the king and Lady Mary, shifted into overdrive. No one believed these accusations against him more than the imperial ambassador, Jehan Scheyfve. Even the duke's kind treatment of Mary, and the fact he had 'granted the people of London ... divers gratifications', were perceived as signs of his Machiavellian cunning. According to the ambassador, there was 'nothing more obvious than the duke's plan'. He had been 'keeping the king-of-arms busy for some time past making ready his claim and descent' while 'strengthening his position', and was now 'planning a new Parliament to help him in the execution of his designs'. He was also thought to be plotting to kill Edward Courtenay[34] in order to prevent a marriage between the Lady Mary and her Plantagenet cousin. Furthermore, Scheyfve warned, the duke might be thinking of getting rid of his present wife and forcing Lady Mary wed him. This would not only secure him the throne, it would lessen the chance of rebellion against him. Although the duke was 'hated and loathed for a tyrant' and 'only able to command obedience by terrorising the people', Mary was a well-loved figure to whom the populace would submit willingly. However, even the ambassador thought this allegation was implausible. It was more likely, in his opinion, that the duke would 'wait until the king died, or was near death, and move to suddenly arrest Mary's most powerful allies, and 'throw them into the Tower ... under colour of preventing any possibility of disturbances'. This would give him the chance to 'send a body of horse, secretly and by night', to tell Mary her brother had died, and pretend they were summoning her to London to take her crown. Then the dastardly duke would imprison her and claim she was 'not a proper person to succeed, by bringing up against her claim the declaration made by Act of Parliament in her father's reign and her more recent, disobedience towards the king, her brother, and his council'. It might also 'be asserted that her accession would mean a violent change of policy and the total ruin of the kingdom, because of her religion'. While the debate was ongoing, the duke and his men 'would keep a close watch on' Lady Mary, 'then perhaps poison her'.[35] There was moreover no doubt that the King of France would 'do his best to enable Northumberland to carry out his designs, particularly with the object of preventing the Princess from coming to the throne'.[36]

In spite of Scheyfve's semi-hysterical conjectures about the duke's designs, the person actually trying to keep Mary off the throne was her younger brother. Edward was ailing badly and in a lot of pain, but he was determined to prevent the return of Catholicism to England. He was sure that the best way to do that was to exclude his eldest sister from the line of succession. After Jane Grey had wed Guildford Dudley, the king's next step was to make his cousin's inheritance as secure as possible. On 11 June he experienced 'a violent hot fever, which … left him weak and still feverish', but he nevertheless ordered the Judges of the King's Bench to come to Greenwich the next day to make his will. These were the best legal experts and lawyers in England. He knew he was dying, and he was resolved that Jane Grey's position as heir would be watertight.

The judges were completely discombobulated when the king commanded them to draft a will with Jane Grey as his successor. Edward had kept his plans private, and very few people had been aware that he was making his cousin his heir – not even Jane herself. The judges weren't sure what to do, or how to respond. Was the young king able to legally circumvent his father's will? Moreover, if Mary and Elizabeth were barred from the line of succession, there was a real risk that the King of France would try to claim the crown for his future daughter-in-law, Mary, Queen of Scots, who was the descendant of the old king's elder sister. Like smart lawyers everywhere, of every era, the judges decided to play for time. They said they needed a day or so to think about it and confer.

As could be expected, the news that the king intended to make Jane Grey his successor quickly spread among the courtiers. Most people were as gobsmacked by the idea as the judges had been. Even after the king's plans were known, the imperial ambassador believed that the possibility of Jane becoming queen was so remote that the Duke of Northumberland had no plans to rule through her as her father-in-law. He speculated that the duke was more likely to use the king's sister Elizabeth as a route to the throne by marrying her to either his son or himself. Nevertheless, Scheyfve assured the emperor, despite the fact no one 'is able to find out exactly what he is planning to do; and it seems he will be guided by events … there is no doubt that he is aspiring to the crown'.[37]

On the 14th, the judges came before the council to give their opinion on Edward's plan for succession. Probably due to the king's youth, the lawyers explained that they were deeply concerned that it would be considered treasonous to overturn Henry VIII's will. Instead, they proffered, why not make Lady Mary heir with the proviso that she would do nothing to change the current stance on religion? Their refusal to do the king's bidding in this matter reportedly infuriated Northumberland, who called the Chief Justice a traitor and offered to take off his doublet and fight them in his shirt. The council then dismissed the legal experts and demanded that they come the next day to hear what the king had to say about their nonsense.

It's likely that the judges weren't expecting the king to confront them in person when they returned, but that is exactly what he did. Although Edward was physically suffering from fever, and was 'unable to keep anything in his stomach, so he lives entirely on restoratives and obtains hardly any repose',[38] he found the strength to rip the King's Bench a new document holder. The indisposed monarch greeted the baulking lawyers with 'sharp words and angry countenance'.[39] He told them that Mary would 'provoke great disturbances' and 'it would be all over for the religion whose fair foundation' he had laid out through so much effort.[40] Furthermore, his sisters had been declared bastards for good reasons and were, in his judgment, both undeserving to be 'numbered among the heirs of the king our beloved father'.[41] Seeing that he was 'so earnest and sharp', the judges decided that they had no choice but to write up the will he demanded and sign it.[42] As a precaution, however, they did ask him to give them a pardon under the Great Seal in case things went wrong later, which he did. Then the king, in spite of being so ill that his doctors had told him he would probably be dead by the time of the next full moon on the 25th, made the judges draw up the letters patent in his presence.

The dying monarch was deeply committed to Jane's ascendancy, and was determined to make everyone acquiesce to it. His legs had become so swollen that he had to continually lie flat on his back in bed, but he didn't let that stop him from securing agreement to his will. One of the toughest nuts to crack would turn out to be his godfather, Thomas Cranmer. The archbishop had been a good friend of Somerset's and blamed Northumberland for the Protector's death. Therefore, he was incredibly reluctant to endorse a will that would set Northumberland up as father-in-law to the queen. Cranmer was also genuinely troubled by conscience. He had promised to obey Henry VIII's will, and it put Lady Mary next in line to the throne. Was it legal, or ethical, to set that will aside? The council had assured him that 'the king was fully entitled to override his father's settlement',[43] but that did not remove all his doubts. He wanted to talk to his godson about it face to face. He then met with Edward, who personally affirmed that everything was in order. He assured Cranmer that the Judges of the King's Bench had agreed 'that the act of entailing the crown, made by his father, could not be prejudicial to him, but that he, being in possession of the crown, might make his will thereof'.[44] Still uncertain, Cranmer begged to be allowed to talk to the judges himself, just to make sure. The king consented, and when Cranmer spoke with them they all confirmed 'that he might lawfully subscribe to the king's will by the laws of the realm'.[45]

Edward put his final signature on his will, with his own hand, on 21 June. The final draft of the document was additionally signed and witnessed by one hundred and two people. Those that signed included every member of the Privy Council and all but one the Judges of the King's Bench.[46] Granted, some of the many who did sign the will, especially those who yearned for a return of the older forms of worship in the churches, were probably not thrilled about Mary's exclusion, but they had nonetheless put their quills to paper and legitimised it. The king's Great Seal was then applied to the will, and it was as official as official could ever be.

Notwithstanding concerns for the king and how his will was to be enforced, the general mood at council appears to be one of relief. The ambassador from France, Antoine de Noailles, found the council 'more content and easy in their minds than he had seen them since his arrival', and he thought this atmosphere of relief had arisen from 'the satisfaction taken by the lords on finding themselves agreed'[47] in their course of action. Even the council members most resistant to the idea of the new succession, such as William Paulet, Marquess of Winchester, and Henry Fitzalan, Earl of Arundel, had come around in the end. The ambassador also noted that parliament had been put off until the following September, probably so it could convene when it needed to confirm Jane Grey as the rightful queen after the king's death.

Edward had used his last weeks on earth to name Jane Grey his heir in a legally binding manner. After his death, Jane Grey would be the lawful queen. He could breathe his last in the certainty that anyone who disputed his will and tried to take the crown from his cousin would be considered traitors.

The last week of June was essentially a death watch over the king, with his passing predicted almost daily. His physicians had decided that he was 'without the strength necessary to rid him of certain humours'[48] which were killing him. Even when he did succeed in ejecting matter from his lungs, the stench indicated putrefaction from within. On the 24th, the imperial ambassador reported that it was predicted the king would die within days, because he had 'not the strength to stir, and can hardly breathe. His body no longer performs its functions, his nails and hair are dropping off, and all his person is scabby'. His condition was so abominable that his doctors had taken the extreme step of allowing a woman physician to try 'administering certain restoratives, though not independently'[49] of the male medicos. She was most likely one of the doctors known as the ladies of Salerno, famous healers who had attended the Schola Medica Salernitana in Italy, which accepted female applicants. She was almost certainly a Catholic, but the reputation of the ladies of Salerno would have outweighed objections to her religion.

Although it was predicted that he would die before the end of June, through either the efforts of the lady healer or his own stubbornness, the monarch made a brief rally. Hearing that his subjects 'were murmuring and saying he was already dead, and in order that his death, when it should occur, might the more easily be concealed',[50] the king also made what would be his final appearance at his window on the first day of July. People could see he was alive, but he was 'so thin and wasted that all men said he was doomed'.

Word had also spread about his last will and testament, 'with its clauses of exclusion', which had been 'written by the king's own hand'.[51]

Moreover, his council had signed and sworn to observe it, although the imperial ambassador insisted this was 'rather out of fear than for any other reason'. Regardless of why it was signed, for Lady Mary and her allies, this was horrific news. The Duke of Northumberland was 'still behaving courteously towards the Princess, as if nothing were about to happen', her supporters were convinced of 'the dangers with which the duke's ambition and avarice menace the Princess Mary', and that he planned to seize her as soon as the king died. Moreover, most people thought since the will naming Jane Grey heir had the council's backing, there was little chance of the king's eldest sister getting the throne. Therefore, her champions snuck her away from her residence at Hunsdon in the night, and helped her make her way to Kenninghall, in Norfolk.

On the night of 6 July 1553 King Edward VI passed away, a victim of a painful and protracted illness that lasted for months. His last words reportedly had been, 'Lord have mercy upon me, and take my spirit'.[52]

Chapter Fifteen

What Killed the Tudor Boys?

The Tudor world had lost a promising young monarch, but *what* had killed him? It was recorded that the 'disease whereof his majesty died was the disease of the lungs, which had in them two great ulcers, and were putrefied, by means whereof he fell into consumption [tuberculosis], and so hath he wasted, being utterly incurable'.[1] A Venetian ambassador would also claim that Edward was 'seized with a malady, which the physicians knew to be consumption'.[2] Most people still assume that tuberculosis was the cause of the teenage king's untimely demise. However, several of the royal physicians appeared to think that he had something other than tuberculosis, and those who believed that he did have TB thought it was the strangest form of the disease they had ever seen. Although he had the frequent cough, general fatigue, and the extreme weight loss that gave consumption its name, his other symptoms did not match the common indicators of the illness. TB almost always takes much longer to kill a patient, often years or even decades, and Tudor physicians would have noticed its onset if Edward had shown signs of contracting it before 1553. The king experienced a lack of appetite, but he also had persistent nausea and vomiting that usually doesn't occur with TB. Moreover, the disease does not cause the hair and nails of the sufferer to fall out, or scabs to form all over the body.

The oddity of the king's infirmity had already stirred up hearsay that he was being poisoned, and shortly after his death, accusations of his murder flourished. Of course, fingers were pointed most often at John Dudley. The Duke of Northumberland was a 'monster', and rather than reveal the evidence of his heinous crime, he had secretly buried the king 'in a passock adjoining the palace', and had put 'a youth not very unlike' the dead sovereign in the coffin for the people to see.[3] Some suggested that the duke had become impatient for the toxin to finish Edward off, and had the sovereign 'secretly destroyed by violence and a dagger'.[4] Others speculated that his sister Elizabeth had sent him a poisoned letter.

The imperial ambassador was afraid that Lady Mary would likewise be suspected in her brother's death, since she was with him when he was first known to be ill.[5] Meanwhile, the Protestants who supported Northumberland argued that a Catholic cabal had been the 'authors of so great wickedness, for they have expressed no signs of sorrow, and no inquiry has been made respecting so great a crime'.

Modern historians are fairly sure that Edward wasn't murdered, but there is still debate about the underlying reason for his death. Jennifer Loach has argued persuasively that the king died of a suppurating pulmonary infection, the result of acute bilateral bronchopneumonia.[6] A suppurating pulmonary infection would have certainly caused many of the king's symptoms, and would have been fatal without antibiotics. Furthermore, when the infection spread to the pleural cavity it would have probably progressed into septicemia and renal failure, causing the king's nausea and hair loss.[7] Chris Skidmore also believes that Edward's later symptoms arose from septicemia and renal failure, but he supports the theory he was initially suffering from reactivated tuberculosis.[8] The young monarch could have contracted TB years before his death, and it could have lain dormant until reawakened by his bout of measles or smallpox a few months before.[9] While both of these postulations are plausible, there is enough doubt in the diagnoses that the speculation about his death continues.

A seldom mentioned, but significant, clue as to the disease that killed the young king is the fact his uncle, Arthur Tudor, and his half-brother, Henry Fitzroy, died of a nearly identical mystery ailment.

Henry Fitzroy, Duke of Richmond, was the illegitimate son of King Henry VIII and a lady-in-waiting named Bessie Blount. Until the birth of Edward VI almost twenty years later, Fitzroy was the only proof Henry VIII could provide that he was capable of siring a son, and the boy was dearly loved by the king for that reason. Shortly after his seventeenth birthday in June 1536, the otherwise healthy duke became sick. Information about what was ailing the teen is scant, in part because the king tried to hide the news of his illegitimate son's failing health. Nonetheless, some descriptions of the teen's illness were leaked. By early July, the imperial ambassador at the time, Eustace Chapuys, reported that 'the King's bastard son ... cannot according to the prognostication of his physicians live many months, having been pronounced in a state of rapid consumption'.[10] A letter to John Dudley by his agent that month also disclosed the same rumour. Two weeks later Chapuys wrote to the emperor again to reveal that King Henry had lost all 'hope of the Duke of Richmond, whom he certainly intended to be his heir and successor',[11] living much longer. Additionally, the king's son appears to have been aware that he was dying, because he started giving away things he valued to his friends and family members. Henry Fitzroy died on 23 July, only a month or so after the first signs his health was in jeopardy.

The disease afflicting King Edward VI sixteen years later would be 'judged to be the same' as the one that had killed his half-brother.[12] Since the details of Fitzroy's death were not recorded with the same exacting attention as the king's, there must be the considerable assumption that the contemporary physicians were aware of facts regarding the duke's illness that didn't make it into the historical record. Fitzroy seems to have developed a pulmonary illness in the last half of June, similar to the 'feverish cold' that would trigger the king's decline in 1553. The duke's illness must have included weight loss, fever, and a chronic cough or no one would have thought it might be 'rapid consumption'. However, if it was consumption, it was indeed rapid – unbelievably so, in fact. Even the fastest form of TB will usually take at least two years after the first signs of infection to kill a patient. It would be far-fetched to think it could cause Fitzroy's death in just a few weeks. Moreover, since there is no evidence that the young duke had recently recovered from the measles, the theory that the TB had been dormant and then reactivated does not apply in this case.

The exact reason for the death of Edward VI's uncle, Arthur Tudor, is also unknown. A contemporary source records that on 27 March 1502 he became ill with a 'deadly corruption … a most pitiful disease and sickness'.[13] A Spanish physician who was with the prince at the time diagnosed him as having 'tisis', a Spanish catchall word covering everything from pulmonary tuberculosis to any wasting, feverish disease the produced ulceration of some bodily organ'.[14] Arthur died on 2 April, only a week after his initial symptoms.

The pulmonary nature of the prince's disease has led to the assumption that his death was the result of consumption.[15] This is unlikely, because his illness moved much too fast to have been TB. Correspondingly, the prince probably didn't die from the sweating sickness, because his illness moved much too slowly.[16] Whether it ended in renewed health or in a grave, sweating sickness was over in a day or two. Influenza and/or pneumonia could have believably killed the prince in a week, but it is unbelievable to think his physicians wouldn't have recognised and named either condition.[17] Likewise, his doctors would have easily spotted the symptoms of the bubonic plague and reported it as the cause of the prince's death. Testicular cancer has been given as another explanation for Arthur's rapid decline, but the odds are good that his doctors would have understood that he had cancer and recorded their treatments for it.[18] Tudor physicians were aware of cancer and its progression, and knew to look for 'morbid swellings that were hard, spread quickly ... and eventually produced ulcers that corroded the flesh'.[19] Health care professionals, past and present, can also recognise the 'cancer smell' that comes with end-stage cancer, 'which somewhat resembles the scent of lilac or jasmine, mixed with an intolerably fetid odor',[20] or 'rotting flesh, but even more pungent'.[21] Arthur's doctors would have known the disease for what it was, even though they were helpless to treat it.

Not only did all three Tudor teens die of something that was very like, but not *quite*, tuberculosis, they were in a similar state of health prior to their final illness. Many people still think that Edward, Fitzroy, and Arthur were physically frail as children, but this is due mainly to a Victorian error that continued unchecked into the twenty-first century. There is little, or no, contemporary evidence that would suggest any of the Tudor boys were particularly delicate or sickly.

A French ambassador had described Edward as being very tall for his age when he was four years old. This is a strong indicator of good health, because the human body directs physical resources toward repair before growth. Furthermore, the future king overcame childhood malaria, as well as measles or smallpox, and any of those diseases can easily kill a strong child, let alone one with an underlying weakness. Edward was also physically active as a teen, enjoying hunting, tennis, and other sports which required physical verve. It is true that he was never described with the same glowing terms ascribed to his father, but few teens could ever be the athletic paragon that a young Henry VIII had been. Other than the imperial ambassador's snide comment that Edward would never be very good at jousting, there is no hint that he wasn't as strong or fit as the rest of the young men at his court. His inability to dominate the tilting field was probably due more to his slight build (as shown in his portraits) than any other reason.

Henry Fitzroy was likewise considered healthy. Perhaps even more so than his half-brother would subsequently be, since he had a more robust frame. His caretakers assured Cardinal Wolsey in 1525 that he was 'in good and prosperous health, and as towardly a young prince as ever hath been seen in our time'.[22] When Fitzroy was a little older, he and his friends spent their time in 'adolescent delight ... a constant round of tennis, jousting, hunting, dancing, and flirting'.[23] The decision to postpone the consummation of his marriage in 1533 might be considered a signal that there was concern for his health, but it was more likely to have been a medical precaution advised for any teenage groom. Male vitality and health were believed to be reduced by the expenditure of sperm, and there would have been a fear that such a young man would wreck his constitution with too much sex. Henry VIII had consummated his first marriage while he was still in his teens, but his circumstances were different. He needed an heir as soon as possible, and as king, he did not have to heed medical advice. Some historians have pointed to Fitzroy's sudden recall from Wales as an indication he might have been unwell, but it was probably just political paranoia on the part of his father.

Arthur Tudor's health may have been a more complicated affair. As with his nephews, he was described as a blooming child. When he was eleven years old, he was described by a visitor to his father's court as being tall and gifted with 'singular beauty and grace'.[24] He may have lacked the hefty physique of his little brother Henry, but there is no description of feebleness by anyone who saw him at close range. His future mother-in-law, Queen Isabella of Castille, wrote that she would 'rather be pleased than dissatisfied' if he postponed intercourse with Katherina of Aragon due to his 'tender age',[25] but that was a normal medical precaution for the time. Queen Isabella also protested against the newlyweds travelling to Ludlow castle near the Welsh border, preferring that the young couple remain at the English court for at least a year, but she didn't say it was because she was worried about the groom's health.[26] King Henry VII obviously considered his son physically fit enough to return to Ludlow Castle. If his father believed him to be healthy, then it is plain that Arthur's physicians had not noticed any problems with the prince's constitution.

Nevertheless, the Spanish attendants who saw Arthur familiarly during his brief marriage to Katherina of Aragon tell another tale. Almost two decades after the event, a member of the wedding party swore that Arthur's 'limbs were so weak that he had never seen a man whose legs and other bits of his body were so small'.[27] Since none of Katherina's attendants had written her parents with a warning or suggestion that the groom was anything less than in fine fettle, this seems to be a case of confirmation bias in hindsight. Arthur had died; QED there *must* have been signs he was unwell and now they could 'remember' those signs. Perhaps the prince had recently had a growth spurt, which can render a teenage boy's body almost ridiculously bony, and the memory had become exaggerated after his death. Or had the prince actually become ill during the trip to Wales? Had he actually been experiencing the slower decline his nephews would later evince?

In sum, Arthur Tudor, Henry Fitzroy, and Edward VI seem to be normatively healthy boys who each died in their mid-teens of a progressive and fast-acting pulmonary disorder that resembled tuberculosis, but did not have a normal presentation of that disease. It is highly unlikely that all three teens were struck down by a bizarrely fast form of consumption, or pulmonary infections, or reactivated tuberculosis. Instead, the similarity of their deaths would be more readily explained by a genetic, heritable factor not previously considered. Taking the various historical details into account, non-classic cystic fibrosis becomes a very plausible cause of the death of the young Tudor royals.

Most people are at least passingly familiar with cystic fibrosis (CF), although probably still think of it solely as the deadly disease that can – and does – kill infants and children. In layman's terms, CF messes up the body's ability to breathe and digest food. In medical terms, the disease is an inherited autosomal recessive disorder resulting in a mutation of the cystic fibrosis transmembrane regulator gene (CFTR gene).[28] There are over 1800 mutations of this gene, and they are not created equal in terms of health.[29] Alterations in the gene have been associated with conditions as mild as a runny nose, and as serious as fatal respiratory and pulmonary issues. Moreover, environmental factors can affect how badly the CFTR gene mutation will affect a patient.[30] Among those many mutations are those that cause 'mild' forms of cystic fibrosis, referred to as atypical types.

Cystic fibrosis has long been typed as either typical, in that it was diagnosed in infancy and childhood and affected multiple organ systems, or atypical, in that it was diagnosed in adolescence or adulthood and manifested in only one or two organ systems. However, advancements in medical knowledge have revealed that CF is more varied than previously thought. The development of 'new CF diagnostic criteria based not only on sweat chloride values but genetic screening and nasal ion transport measurements, have made the diagnosis of CF less straightforward for many clinicians'.[31] These new, more nuanced, diagnostic tools led physicians to the discovery of non-classic CF, a type of the disease that could present atypically in adolescents and adults with the same multi-organ manifestation as typical CF.[32]

Patients with non-classic CF often appear to be reasonably healthy as children. The respiratory problems they experience as they reach adolescence and adulthood will usually be misdiagnosed as asthma, chronic bronchitis, or emphysema, and almost no physician other than a pulmonary specialist would suspect they had a form of cystic fibrosis. Nevertheless, these patients are actually suffering from the same 'respiratory symptoms and chronic airway infection with typical cystic fibrosis pathogens, such as *Pseudomonas aeruginosa* and *Staphylococcus aureus*, as well as nontuberculous mycobacteria'.[33] Although their pulmonary problems are usually less severe than in more typical CF cases, they can still develop advanced bronchiectasis – a condition in which the bronchial tubes in the lungs are abnormally enlarged.[34] Mucus easily builds up in these abnormally wide airways, making them prone to infections and generally causing the patient to experience recurrent bronchitis and other such diseases of the lungs. As teens and adults, non-classic CF patients usually start to present with a chronic productive cough and other pulmonary issues, as well as weight loss and intermittent fever.

There is a wide spectrum of symptoms in patients with non-classic CF. They will often experience milder, more treatable issues with their health, but they can also develop the same 'typical respiratory symptoms, significant lung dysfunction, and infection with mucoid *P aeruginosa*'[35] as patients with the classic form of the disease. Usually, children with non-classic CF will seem to be healthy, except for occasional bouts of bronchitis, well into adolescence and adulthood. However, this facade of well-being is deceptive. Their lungs are becoming irreparably damaged over time. Studies indicate that focal bronchiectasis often occurs even in young non-classical CF patients with apparently normal lung function.[36] Bronchiectasis is a serious and incurable condition requiring a barrage of anti-inflammatory medication and antibiotics to control, with the possibility of surgery in severe cases.[37] Untreated, bronchiectasis can cause abscesses in the lungs and death via respiratory failure, lung collapse, or heart failure. Even with modern medical care, the progressive obstructive lung disease associated with bronchiectasis can result in death for children and adults.[38]

Thanks to advances in medical care, such as antibiotics and surgery, most non-classic CF patients are likely to live to adulthood or old age. Unfortunately, none of these modern life-saving treatments were available to the Tudors. Ergo, if Arthur, Fitzroy, and Edward had all inherited a similar genetic mutation causing non-classic CF, then they could have been relatively healthy as children but have had undetected pulmonary deterioration. By the time they reached their mid-teens, the damage would have been extensive enough that just one more infection (viral or bacterial) would tip the scales toward their demise. Once their bodies and immune systems were weakened more optimistic infections could occur, as well as complications such as septicemia and renal failure. The chronic cough, struggle to breathe, and the 'wasting' effect of malabsorption of food due to the thick mucus obstructing the digestive system were all symptoms exhibited by the dying Tudor adolescents. The bronchiectasis would have also looked a lot like tuberculosis to their physicians, albeit with oddly rapid progression.

Furthermore, non-classic cystic fibrosis would clarify why Edward got ulcers on his skin, a puzzling feature of his illness that cannot be explained by tuberculosis, bronchiectasis, septicemia, or renal failure. The most common culprit behind the chronic airway infections in non-classic CF patients is the pathogen *Pseudomonas aeruginosa*. Nowadays, *P. aeruginosa* can usually be treated successfully with antibiotics. However, the king's physicians had nothing to keep the *P. aeruginosa* from running amok. A long-standing infection of *P. aeruginosa* would have opportunistically spread to other systems in his body, such as his skin, as his immune system weakened. One of the things this bacterium can do is cause hemorrhagic and necrotic lesions with red and irritated skin surrounding them, which would account for the ulcers on the king's body.[39]

Non-classic CF could also be a clue in the long-standing historical whodunit (or who *didn't* dun it) of whether or not Katherina of Aragon and Arthur Tudor consummated their marriage. Cystic fibrosis, in and of itself, is associated with infertility but not erectile dysfunction. However, all types of cystic fibrosis are by their nature chronic obstructive pulmonary diseases (COPD) and advanced COPD *can* cause erectile dysfunction.[40] One of the most common forms of COPD is chronic bronchitis, which involves a long-term cough with mucus eroding lung function and oxygen uptake. Both cystic fibrosis and COPD are associated with chronic airway inflammation that can also inhibit oxygenation of the body.[41] If the inflammation is severe enough and continues long enough then the patient can become both hypoxemic and hypoxic. Hypoxemia occurs when there is insufficient oxygen available in the arterial blood supply, while hypoxia describes the lack of oxygen in the body's tissues due to hypoxemia.

In one of the ironies of physiology, hypoxemia causes coughing and the coughing counterproductively leads to hypoxia. Hypoxia engenders sweating, wheezing, cough, shortness of breath, and discolouration of the skin. Hypoxemia and hypoxia also make a patient incredibly weak, easily tired, and can cause erectile dysfunction.[42] With current breathing treatments and medications, erectile dysfunction doesn't become a problem until male patients with CF are middle-aged. In the Tudor time period, the lack of antibiotics to combat chronic bronchitis means that COPD could have easily affected Arthur in his teens, in that the hypoxemia and hypoxia would have been more pronounced at a younger age.

The lack of wedding-night copulation is a subject of debate, largely because the one person who knew for sure was Katherina of Aragon and the cultural inability to take a woman's word regarding sexual matters and assume she is telling the truth still exists, albeit subconsciously for the most part.[43] Katherina herself was adamant the marriage was unconsummated. She swore, despite what she believed would be the endangerment of her immortal soul if she were lying, that she had become a widow while she was 'intacta et incorrupta', i.e untouched and pure.[44] Those who believe that Katherina was lying base their arguments largely on the papal dispensation for her betrothal to Henry VIII, which said the marriage had 'perhaps' been consummated, and testimony against her given in a court, the Legatine Court at Blackfriars held over the summer of 1529, that Henry had summoned specifically to help him find reasons to dissolve his marriage.[45]

Evidence against Katherina's post-nuptial virginity presented at Blackfriars included the fact that Katherina's young husband shared her bed several times and remembrances of what her groom had claimed after the wedding night. Arthur's body servant, William Thomas, testified that after he had helped the prince get ready for bed, he then 'conducted him clad in his night gown unto the Princess's bedchamber door often and sundry times … and that at the morning he received him at the said door … and waited upon him to his own privy chamber'.[46] Furthermore, it was recalled that Arthur had bragged that he had accomplished his marital duties, insisting that he had been 'in the midst of Spain'.[47] However, if the groom had been *incapable* of consummating his marriage due to chronic hypoxia, his claims to the contrary could have been merely bravado born from embarrassment.

Additionally, not all the evidence given at Blackfriars supported the argument for consummation. Nicholas West, the Bishop of Ely, testified the widowed Katherina had told him more than once that she was still a virgin.[48] Furthermore, Katherina was able to wrest an unspoken admission from Henry VIII that she had been a virgin when she had wed him. Kneeling at his feet like the most humble of wives, Katherina swore before all those assembled that she had been, 'a true maid, without the touch of a man' when she married the king, and told Henry 'whether this be true or no, I put it to your conscience'.[49] The king's response was a ringing silence rather than refutation. A final piece of evidence that indicates that Katherina was telling the truth is that Henry VIII's annulment tactics began to focus on the idea that exchanging vows was enough for a couple to be married *even without consummation*, which suggests he knew Katherina had not had sex with Arthur.[50]

As the English had done at Blackfriars, the Spanish held a tribunal in 1531 at Zaragoza to hear witnesses from the wedding night. Spanish witnesses testified that the nuptial sheets were spotless and Katherina herself told her ladies she was worried her frail husband would never be up to the task of lovemaking.[51] Juan de Gamarra, who had been a serving boy for Katherina and had stayed in her antechamber on the night of her marriage to Arthur, said that 'Francisca de Caceras, who was in charge of dressing and undressing the queen and who she liked and confided in a lot, was looking sad and telling the other ladies that nothing had passed between Prince Arthur and his wife, which surprised everyone and made them laugh at him.'[52] Katherina's doctor was also reported to have said that Arthur 'had been denied the strength to know a woman' because of ill health.[53]

If Katherina's first marriage went unconsummated, which seems to be the likeliest scenario given her testimony, then there was probably a physical reason behind Arthur's inability to have sex with his bride. Chronic pulmonary disease and hypoxia as a complication of non-classic cystic fibrosis is a plausible explanation for Arthur's theoretical erectile dysfunction, and one which closely aligns with the evidence given by the Spanish attendants and the manner of the prince's death a few months later.

Typical cystic fibrosis is an autosomal recessive, which means both parents must give their offspring a copy of a CFTR gene with an established severe mutation that causes null functioning. If a child inherits a mutated gene from one parent and a normal CFTR gene from the other parent, then that child will not develop the disease. In contrast, non-classical CF does not always require the presence of two severely mutated CFTR genes. It can occur when the patient has inherited a gene with a severe mutation from one parent, but a gene with a 'mild' partial loss of function mutation from the other parent.[54] It may also be present when the genes inherited from each parent each have milder mutations that allow residual functioning.[55] Most significantly, non-classic CF can occur when there is only one, or even no mutation of the CFTR gene.[56] This means that factors 'other than mutations in the CFTR gene can produce phenotypes clinically indistinguishable from nonclassic cystic fibrosis caused by CFTR dysfunction'.[57]

In brief, this means that Edward VI, Henry Fitzroy, and Arthur Tudor did not necessarily need to inherit a CFTR gene with a severe genetic mutation from each parent. They may have only needed to receive one mutated gene from a common family member, or may have had a genotype that didn't require a mutated CFTR gene at all to express non-classic CF. Considering the inbreeding among the royal families of Europe, there is also every likelihood that all three boys had comparable genetic profiles.

Arthur Tudor was descended from the Plantagenet king Henry II through three of his paternal great-grandparents, and through all four of his maternal great-grandparents. Clearly, if there was a recessive mutation of the CFTR gene in the Plantagenet DNA, Arthur had multiple chances of inheriting it from both parents. Arthur's younger brother, Henry VIII, also bred back into the Plantagenets to father his sons. Both Fitzroy's mother, Bessie Blount, and Edward's mother, Jane Seymour, were maternally descended from Henry II. Although the mutuality of their ancestors was not as extreme as Arthur's, there were still multiple ways a recessive gene could have been passed on to Fitzroy and Edward through the Plantagenet bloodlines.

The mutations causing cystic fibrosis are also surprisingly common in white populations descended from Northern Europe. As many as one out of every twenty-five members of that population are carriers of the genetic mutations that cause classic CF, and even more might be carriers of genetic mutations that will present as non-classic CF.[58] In fact, hundreds of thousands of people 'who have recurrent sinusitis or unusual forms of lung disease such as nontuberculosis mycobacteria, aspergillosis, recurrent pancreatitis, biliary disease in their liver or males who present to infertility clinics with aspermia'[59] may actually be suffering from milder forms of non-classic cystic fibrosis.

Additionally, there may be a link between cystic fibrosis and the theory that Henry VIII was positive for the Kell blood group.[60] The Kell blood group locus is close to the cystic fibrosis locus on chromosome 7. The CFTR gene is located on the long (q) arm of chromosome 7 at position 31.2 and the Kell cytogenetic location is also on the long (q) arm of chromosome 7 at position 33.[61] While research on any connection between blood type and propensity (or resistance) to disease is still in its infancy, there are already some 'clear examples of protection against infectious diseases from inheritance of polymorphisms in genes encoding and regulating the expression of ABH and Lewis antigens' on red blood cells, 'particularly in respect of *Helicobacter pylori*, norovirus, and cholera infections'.[62] Furthermore, available evidence suggests the surviving disease 'is the most significant selective force affecting the expression of blood groups'.[63] As with CFTR gene mutations, the Kell blood group is found more frequently in Northern Europeans than any other population.[64] It is plausible that the relatively high percentage of Northern Europeans who are positive for the Kell antigen is connected to the prevalence of the CFTR genetic mutation in the population.

There is a final irony if the Tudor teens died from complications of non-classic cystic fibrosis. Roughly 90-95% of males with CF are infertile, and even the mildest form of the disease causes obstructive azoospermia as a result of the congenital bilateral absence of vas deferens.[65] Arthur Tudor, Henry Fitzroy, and Edward VI were all born in the expectation that they would sire their own sons in the future and further the dynastic ambitions of the Tudors. King Henry VIII is remembered by history as a murderous tyrant due to the extremes he went to in securing a male heir, yet it would have all been for nothing. His sons would not have been able to provide him grandchildren, and his efforts to prevent a daughter from inheriting his throne deprived him of his genetic continuance through the female line as well. With a probable inheritance of the Kell positive blood type, the Tudor royals might have already been predestined to reproduce only through their female offspring, but a genetic legacy of CFTR mutations would have sealed the deal.

Chapter Sixteen

The Aftermath of Edward's Death

When Edward died on 6 July 1553, Jane Grey became the new English monarch as had been outlined by his wishes. As was customary after a sovereign's death, the members of the Privy Council got all their ducks in a row in order to establish the reign of a new monarch. Northumberland was sent to secure the Tower where the royal artillery and coffers lay, and on 10 July 1553, the sixteen-year-old Jane Grey was proclaimed queen without a fuss. The English government, the Anglican Church, ambassadors and foreign courts all recognised her as the rightful queen and Guildford Dudley as her king consort.

At this time, Mary was still just the king's bastard sister and technically a fugitive. From her Catholic stronghold in the north, she and her supporters began gathering troops to challenge Queen Jane's place on the throne. Mary was able to secure the defection of several nobles who were jealous of Northumberland's potential power to her cause, including William Herbert, Earl of Pembroke, who threw his recently acquired daughter-in-law Katherine Grey out of his home as a sign of his solidarity to Mary. On 19 July Mary rode into London at the head of an army of Catholic loyalists and took the throne. Jane, her husband, and any of their supporters were imprisoned. Northumberland was captured, and was executed for following Edward's orders and for all his imagined cruelties and slights to Mary. In September, the Parliament declared Mary the rightful queen and regulated Jane to the position of usurper.

But who was the real usurper? It boils down to whether or not Edward could name a successor that supplanted the heirs in his late father's will. To be succinct, yes he could. Parliament had passed a statute under Henry VIII more than a decade before 'purporting that should the king have no legitimate male children, he can appoint whomsoever he chooses to succeed him on the throne, such appointment and declaration having the same validity and vigour as if it had been made by his own Parliament'.[1] King Edward VI had the legal right to name his successor. It did not matter that Mary had been reinstated in Henry VIII's will. The late king's will did not matter so much as a gnat's tiny poo after the new king chose an heir. Moreover, Edward was no longer a child monarch who could only make decisions through a regent. During his lifetime the Church considered childhood to end at six, and a person could assume adult responsibilities as young as twelve years old. While the 'official' age of majority to write a will in the sixteenth century was twenty-one, the concept of legal adulthood was a bit different for kings. Henry VIII was only seventeen when he became king but there was no attempt to assign him a regent. He was old enough to make adult decisions, including whom he would marry and to whom he would leave his crown in the event of his death. As another teenage sovereign, it was likewise Edward's decision to decide who should rule after him.

Queen Mary I would eventually have her young cousin beheaded on 12 February 1554, as a way to appease imperial fears regarding the stability of her crown and to entice Philip II of Spain to marry her. Guildford Dudley, who was barely out of his late teens and who posed absolutely no threat to Mary's sovereignty, would be executed earlier that day as well. Inasmuch as no one likes to consider themselves as illicit insurrectionists, people are particularly loath to think of themselves as murderers. Queen Mary and her supporters would have needed (both politically and to soothe any qualms of conscience) to make sure the idea that Jane Grey had tried to steal the crown was quickly set in stone. Since history is written by the winners, they were incredibly successful at it. Jane Grey, the lawful heir to the throne, has therefore remained an 'innocent traitor' in the cultural narrative ever after.

It is almost beyond doubt that Mary and her adherents would have sincerely believed that they were good guys doing the right thing. Undoubtedly the recently enthroned queen also convinced herself of the necessity of her actions, since she was doing it on God's behalf to restore Catholicism in England. Certainly, no one was going to tell her any differently if they wanted to keep their heads. Nevertheless, a conviction does not become reality simply because it is strongly believed, and a falsehood that is repeated as a truth for hundreds of years does not actually become a fact. Jane Grey was the legitimate sovereign, and as such she deserves to be remembered as a deposed and murdered monarch rather than a puppet forced to commit treason by her supposedly conniving father-in-law, the Duke of Northumberland.

The kerfuffle over the crown naturally delayed the king's funeral. Edward VI was finally laid to rest on 8 August 1553 at Westminster Abbey in the Lady Chapel, near to the remains of his paternal grandparents, Henry VII and Elizabeth of York. The day before the funeral the lead coffin containing his embalmed body was processed through the streets of London, allowing the grieving population a chance to say goodbye to their sovereign. The funeral chariot was draped with cloth of gold and pulled by seven horses under a canopy of blue velvet. The surviving gentleman of his privy chamber and members of his council accompanied his body, bearing banners symbolising his heritage, including the Welsh dragon and the badge of Owen Tudor, the Lancastrian greyhound, and a lion to represent his father. The coffin was topped by a carved effigy of the young king and inscribed with the words, 'Edward the sixth by the Grace of God King of England, France and Ireland, Defender of the Faith and on earth under Christ supreme head of the churches of England and Ireland and he migrated from this life on the 6th day of July in the evening at the 8th hour in the year of our Lord 1553 and in the 7th year of his reign and in the 16th year of his age'. Since the king had actually still been fifteen years old when he died, one has to wonder if this inaccuracy would have bothered the meticulous and erudite monarch if he had known.

Inside the abbey, Archbishop Cranmer waited to perform the funeral service, which Queen Mary had graciously allowed to be a Protestant rite from the 1552 Prayer Book, in accordance with the king's beliefs. The walls of the Lady Chapel were hung with black velvet, with more black cloth runners laying in the aisles. The king's hearse, with its thirteen branched pillars of carved wax, was further adorned by seventy-two yards of draped black velvet.[2] As the mourners wept, many with tears of genuine sorrow, the coffin of what would be the last Tudor king was lowered into a white marble vault beneath the altar of the first Tudor king. As the Italian astronomer Cardano said, 'not only England, but all the world', had cause to lament the loss of a young man with such 'ingenious forwardness and amiable sweetness'.[3]

With Edward's death, the hopeful star of the Reformers for a Protestant realm seemed to wink out as well. In the end, however, Queen Elizabeth I would rise and England would become firmly established as a Protestant stronghold in Europe. Moreover, nationalism and Protestantism became deeply entwined, so that the late king would become venerated as an Evangelical paragon and icon who had 'saved' England from the Catholic Church for several centuries after he had passed away. The turbulent years of his reign were erroneously described as halcyon days of 'tranquility' due

to the 'excellent virtues and singular graces' of the young monarch.[4] John
Cheke wrote that every one of the young monarch's religious achievements
'would be considered as a great action in other men', but were as nothing to
him.[5] John Foxe would claim that there was never a sovereign 'more highly
esteemed, more amply magnified, or more dearly and tenderly beloved of all
his subjects' than Edward VI.[6] In 1630, John Haywood's biography of the
king declared that 'besides his excellent beauty … [and] sweet humanity
… high virtues sparkled in him, especially clemency, courage, care, and
knowledge in affairs of state'.[7] Nineteenth-century historians would
likewise laud the teenage monarch's 'mild disposition, his intelligent mind
… his unfeigned piety, his patriotic spirit, and his ambition of doing good'.[8]

In spite of the high regard for the king, plans to build him an elaborate
tomb never came to fruition. That is just as well, since Puritans destroyed
the altar above his crypt in 1644, and they would have probably also
smashed a memorial too. His grave would be left unmarked until 1966,
when a stone was inlaid in front of the altar bearing the inscription: 'In
memory of King Edward VI buried in this chapel this stone was placed
here by Christ's Hospital in thanksgiving for their founder 7 October 1966'.
The small plaque that marks his burial site is usually ignored by the stream
of visitors eager to see the final resting place of the more famous Tudor
monarch, Queen Elizabeth I, who is interred in the same chapel. Perhaps
the fact that the 1552 Book of Common Prayer has been in continuous use
(with a few modifications) by the Anglican Church since its conception is
enough of a memorial. It is certainly one that the devout king would have
appreciated more than an ornamental and magnificent tomb.

The changing fashions in cultural and academic interests mean that
Edward has largely been forgotten about outside Tudor historical circles.
His reign, when it is mentioned at all, is treated as an unimportant
stopgap between the more interesting tenures of his father and half-
sisters. It seems a pity that a young man with such amazing abilities, who
had the potential to have been one of England's greatest kings, now lies
in uncommemorated obscurity. In the few years that he was sovereign, he
created religious changes that have affected his realm until the present day,
salvaged the nation's currency, managed to briefly extricate his country
from the endless European wars, laid the groundwork for the publishing
industry by allowing printers to produce books at a formally unknown
rate, and made a good start at reestablishing England's international
trade and credit. King Edward VI was a remarkable sovereign, and he
deserves to be remembered with appreciation.

Notes

Foreword
1. Orme, 2003.
2. Kramer, 2012.

Chapter 1
1. Weiss-Amer, 1993.
2. Licence, 2014.
3. Metzler, 2006.
4. Wallis, 2010.
5. Ibid.
6. Leland, Vol.4; 179
7. Wriothesley, 1875.
8. L&P, Vol 12 (ii), 911.
9. In spite of later historical rumours, there is no evidence to support the idea that Jane was given a cesarean section or that Henry commanded the midwives to save the baby at the expense of the mother's life.
10. On a personal level, it bothers me that a man who did everything he could to encourage the usurpation and murder of Anne Boleyn had the audacity to hold her daughter in his arms.
11. Loach, 1999.
12. Skidmore, 2009
13. L&P, Vol. 13(ii).
14. Kramer, 2012.
15. L&P, Vol. 12(ii).
16. Ibid.
17. Perlman and Carusi, 2019.
18. L&P, Vol 12(ii).

Chapter 2
1. L&P, Vol 12 (ii).
2. CSP, Spain, Vol 5.
3. Nichols, 1721.
4. Skidmore, 2009.
5. Ibid.
6. L&P, Vol 14(ii).
7. L&P, Vol 13(i)
8. Skidmore, 2009.
9. Nichols, 1857

10. MacCulloch, 2001.
11. L&P, Vol 13(i)
12. Skidmore, 2009.
13. Licence, 2012.
14. Andrews et al, 2008.
15. Jones, 2013.
16. Pointon, 2009.
17. Nichols, 1857
18. Stewart, 2000.
19. Ives, 2004:105
20. Scarisbrick, 1997.
21. Skidmore, 2009.
22. L&P Vol 14(i).
23. Ibid.
24. Ibid.
25. L&P, Vol 14(ii).
26. Mueller, 1933.
27. Stewart, 2000.
28. Skidmore, 2009.
28. Furdell, 2001.
29. Loach, 1999.
30. Das et al, 2018.
31. Furdell, 2001.
32. Hutchinson, 2011.
33. Nichols, 1857.

Chapter 3
1. L&P Vol 18(i).
2. L&P, Vol 18(i).
3. Clifford, 1809.
4. Ibid.
5. L&P, Vol 18(ii).
6. Clifford, 1809.
7. L&P, Vol 18(ii).
8. Clifford, 1809.
9. Ibid.
10. Ibid.
11. Woolgar, 1999.
12. Skidmore, 2009.
13. Woolgar, 1999.
14. Woolgar, 1999.
15. Skidmore, 2009.
16. Strickland, 1861.

17. Nichols, 1857.
18. Ibid.
19. Clifford, 1887.
20. Ibid.
21. L&P, Vol 18(ii).

Chapter 4
1. Strickland, 1853.
2. L&P, Vol 18(i).
3. Porter, 2010.
4. Halliwell, 1848.
5. Ibid.
6. L&P, Vol 19(i).
7. Grafton, 1809.
8. L&P, Vol 19(i).
9. Ibid.
10. Guy, 2013.
11. Halliwell, 1848.
12. Guy, 2013.
13. Skidmore, 2009.
14. Halliwell, 1848.
15. Mackie, 1916.
16. Grafton, 1809.
17. Ibid.
18. Ibid.
19. Smith, 1971.
20. CSP Spain, Vol 8.
21. Ibid.
22. Foxe, 1836.
23. Ibid.
24. Ibid.
25. Starkey, 2003.
26. Foxe, 1836.
27. Ibid.
28. Ibid.
29. Skidmore, 2009.
30. Loach, 1999.
31. Ibid.
32. Halliwell, 1848.
33. Ibid.
34. Skidmore, 2009.
35. Foxe, 1881.
36. Skidmore, 2009.
37. Nichols, 1857.

Chapter 5
1. Halliwell, 1848.
2. Ibid.
3. L&P, Vol 21(i).
4. Halliwell, 1848.
5. CSP, Spain, Vol 8.
6. Potter, 2011.
7. Grafton, 1809.

8. Wriothesley, 1875.
9. Grafton, 1809.
10. Foxe, 1836.
11. Wriothesley, 1875.
12. Sessions, 2003.
13. Nichols, 1857.
14. Halliwell, 1848.
15. Ibid.
16. Ibid.
17. Sessions, 2003:380-381
18. Ives, 2004.
19. Smith, 1971.
20. Ibid.
21. Sessions, 2003.
22. Ibid.
23. L&P, Vol 21(ii).
24. Sessions, 2003.
25. Skidmore, 2009.
26. Grafton, 1809.
27. L&P, Vol 21(ii).
28. CSP, Spain, Vol 8.
29. Ibid.
30. L&P, Vol 21(ii).
31. Ibid.
32. Ibid.
33. Skidmore, 2009.
34. L&P, Vol 21 (ii).
35. Wriothesley, 1875.
36. Sessions, 2003.
37. Ibid.
38. Ibid.
39. Ibid.
40. Grafton, 1809.
41. Ibid.
42. Skidmore, 2009.
43. CSP, Spain, Vol 8.
44. CSP, Spain, Vol 9.
45. Foxe, 1836.
46. Grafton, 1809.

Chapter 6
1. Skidmore, 2009.
2. Nichols, 1857.
3. CSP, Spain, Vol 9.
4. L&P, Vol 21(ii).
5. It would explain why Edward wrote letters to his stepmother and elder sister about Henry VIII's death, but did not send one to Elizabeth.
6. Journal of Edward VI.
7. CSP, Spain, Vol 9.
8. Wriothesley, 1875.
9. Nichols, 1857.

10. Ibid.
11. Muller, 1933.
12. Wriothesley, 1875.
13. Nichols, 1857.
14. Ibid.
15. Wriothesley, 1875.
16. CSP, Spain, Vol 9.
17. Halliwell, 1848.
18. Ibid.
19. Nichols, 1857.
20. Skidmore, 2009.
21. The Stone of the Scone was returned to Scotland in 1996, but they promised to lend it back whenever a new coronation occurred.
22. Cox, 1846.
23. Wriothesley, 1875.

Chapter 7
1. Skidmore, 2009.
2. CSP, Spain, Vol 9.
3. Skidmore, 2009.
4. Halliwell, 1848.
5. CSP, Spain, Vol 9.
6. Ibid.
7. Turner, 1829.
8. Skidmore, 2009.
9. Hoak, 1976.
10. CSP, Spain, Vol 9.
11. Loades, 1996.
12. Wriothesley, 1875.
13. CSP, Spain, Vol 9.
14. Halliwell, 1848.
15. Grafton, 1809.
16. James, 2008.
17. Halliwell, 1848.

Chapter 8
1. Ibid.
2. CSP, Spain, Vol 9.
3. Ibid.
4. Ibid.
5. Ibid.
6. Grafton, 1809.
7. MacCulloch, 2001.
8. MacCulloch, 2001.
9. Thornbury, 1878.
10. Turner, 1829.
11. Skidmore, 2009.
12. Thornbury, 1878.
13. Ibid.
14. Skidmore, 2009.
15. Ibid.

16. Tanner, 1930.
17. CSP, Spain, Vol 9.
18. Ibid.
19. James, 2008.
20. CSP, Spain, Vol 9.
21. Skidmore, 2009.
22. Nichols, 1857.
23. Skidmore, 2009.
24. CSP, Spain, Vol 9.
25. Ibid.
26. Ibid.
27. Ibid.
28. Skidmore, 2009.
29. Ibid.
30. Foxe, 1836.

Chapter 9
1. Plowden, 2011.
2. Skidmore, 2009.
3. Ibid.
4. Skidmore, 2009.
5. Nichols, 1857.
6. Blunt, 1882.
7. Ibid.
8. Skidmore, 2009.
9. Ibid.
10. Ibid.
11. CSP, Spain, Vol 9.
12. Skidmore, 2009.
13. Burnet, 1848.
14. Nichols, 1857.
15. For his services in slaughtering his fellow Englishmen, Baron Russell would be made the 1st Earl of Bedford in 1550, and created the Lord Lieutenant of Devon in 1552.
16. CSP, Spain, Vol 9.
17. CSP, Spain, Vol 9.
18. Skidmore, 2009.
19. Tytler, 1839.
20. Ibid.
21. Halliwell, 1848.
22. Nichols, 1857.
23. CSP, Spain, Vol 9.
24. Nichols, 1857.
25. Ibid.
26. Ibid.
27. Skidmore, 2009.
28. Ibid.

Chapter 10
1. CSP, Spain, Vol 9.
2. Crewdson, 2000.
3. Ives, 2009.

4. CSP Spain, Vol 10.
5. CSP, Vienna, Vol 5.
6. Ibid.
7. Ibid.
8. Ibid.
9. Ibid.
10. Skidmore, 2009.
11. Vermigli, 1865.
12. Ibid.
13. Skidmore, 2009.
14. Haynes, 1740.
15. Halliwell, 1848.
16. Edward's Journal.
17. Skidmore, 2009.
18. CSP Spain, Vol 10.
19. Ibid.
20. Ibid.
21. Ibid.
22. Ibid.
23. Ibid.
24. CSP Spain, Vol 10.
25. Ibid.
26. Ibid.
27. Ives, 2009.
28. Ibid.
29. Skidmore, 2009.
30. Ives, 2009.
31. CSP Spain, Vol 10.
32. Ibid.
33. Ibid.
34. Markham, 1907.
35. Ibid.
36. Nichols, 1857.
37. CSP Spain, Vol 10.
38. Ibid.
39. Ibid.
40. Ibid.
41. Ibid.
42. Knighton and Loades, 2013.
43. Oppenheim, 1896.
44. Ibid.
45. Skidmore, 2009.
46. Edward's Journal, 1884.
47. CSP Spain, Vol 10.
48. Ibid.
49. Ibid.

Chapter 11
1. Skidmore, 2009.
2. Foxe, 1836.
3. Nichols, 1857.
4. Skidmore, 2009.

5. Aston, 1993.
6. CSP Spain, Vol 10.
7. Ibid.
8. Ibid.
9. Duffy, 2005.
10. Ibid.
11. CSP Spain, Vol 10.
12. Ibid.
13. Edward's Journal, 1884.
14. CSP Spain, Vol 10.
15. Grafton, 1809.
16. Ibid.
17. Ibid.
18. Markham, 1907.
19. Ibid.
20. Ibid.
21. CSP Spain, Vol 10.
22. Ibid.
23. Skidmore, 2009.
24. CSP Spain, Vol 10.
25. Loach, 1999.
26. CSP Spain, Vol 10.
27. Ibid.
28. Loach, 199.
29. Skidmore, 2009.
30. CSP Spain, Vol 10.
31. Ibid.
32. Ibid.
33. Skidmore, 2009.
34. Nichols, 1857.
35. Skidmore, 2009.
36. Ibid.
37. CSP Spain, Vol 10.
38. Ibid.
39. Ibid.
40. Skidmore, 2009.
41. Ibid.
42. CSP Spain, Vol 10.
43. Ibid.
44. Pollnitz, 2015.

Chapter 12
1. Burnet, 1843.
2. Edward VI, 1884.
3. Ibid.
4. Porter, 1995.
5. Burnet, 1843.
6. Ibid.
7. Ibid.
8. Skidmore, 2009.
9. Ibid.
10. Ibid.

11. CSP Spain, Vol 10.
12. Skidmore, 2009.
13. Edward's Journal, 1884.
14. Ibid.
15. CSP Spain, Vol 10.
16. Skidmore, 2009.
17. Edward's Journal, 1884.
18. CSP Spain, Vol 10.
19. CSP Spain, Vol 10.
20. Nichols, 1857.
21. Ibid.
22. Grafton, 1809.
23. CSP Spain, Vol 10.
24. CSP Spain, Vol 10.
25. Nichols, 1857.
26. Ibid.
27. Ives, 2012.
28. CSP Spain, Vol 10.
29. Skidmore, 2009.
30. Skidmore, 2009.
31. CSP Spain, Vol 10.

Chapter 13

1. CSP Spain, Vol 10.
2. Ibid.
3. Nichols, 1857.
4. Halliwell, 1848.
5. Ibid.
6. Ibid.
7. CSP Spain, Vol 10.
8. Halliwell, 1848.
9. CSP Spain, Vol 10.
10. CSP Spain, Vol 10.
11. *Hieronymus Cardanus* in Latin.
12. Skidmore, 2009.
13. Ibid.
14. Ibid.
15. Ibid.
16. Nichols, 1857.
17. Skidmore, 2009.
18. Nichols, 1857.
19. Ibid.
20. Ibid.
21. CSP Spain, Vol 10.
22. Ibid.
23. Skidmore, 2009.
24. Ibid.
25. Skidmore, 2009.
26. Nichols, 1857.
27. Ibid.
28. Ibid.

Chapter 14

1. Grafton, 1809.
2. Ibid.
3. Ibid.
4. Nichols, 1857.
5. Nichols, 1857.
6. Turner, 1829.
7. Skidmore, 2009.
8. CSP Spain, Vol 11.
9. Ibid.
10. Nichols, 1857.
11. Ibid.
12. Nichols, 1857.
13. CSP Spain, Vol 11.
14. Nichols, 1857.
15. Ives, 2012.
16. Ibid.
17. CSP Spain, Vol 11.
18. Ibid.
19. Ives, 2012.
20. Skidmore, 2009.
21. CSP Spain, Vol 11.
22. CSP Spain, Vol 11.
23. Ibid.
24. Turner, 1829.
25. Nichols, 1857.
26. CSP Spain, Vol 11.
27. Turner, 1829.
28. Robinson, 1846.
29. CSP Spain, Vol 11.
30. Skidmore, 2009.
31. Ibid.
32. CSP Spain, Vol 11.
33. Ibid.
34. A maternal descendant of King Edward IV and the second cousin of King Edward VI.
35. Ibid.
36. Ibid.
37. Ibid.
38. Ibid.
39. Ives, 2012.
40. Skidmore, 2009.
41. Ibid.
42. Ives, 2012.
43. Ives, 2012.
44. Ibid.
45. Ibid.
46. Despite being a devout Protestant, Justice Sir James Hales would not sign due to some of his reservations about the legality of the will.

47. Nichols, 1857.
48. CSP Spain, Vol 11.
49. Ibid.
50. Ibid.
51. Ibid.
52. Skidmore, 2009.

Chapter 15
1. Lodge, 1791.
2. Loach, 2014.
3. Skidmore, 2009.
4. Ibid.
5. CSP Spain, Vol 11.
6. Loach, 2014.
7. Murphy, 2011.
8. Skidmore, 2009.
9. Holmes, et al, 2001.
10. Murphy, 2011.
11. CSP Spain, Vol 5(ii).
12. CSP Spain, Vol 11.
13. Guy, 2013.
14. Tremlett, 2010.
15. Whitelock, 2010.
16. Penn, 2011.
17. Ricks, 2009; Wallis, 2010.
18. Starkey, 2003.
19. Wallis, 2010.
20. Smith, 1855.
21. Gunter, 2012.
22. Childe-Pemberton, 1913.
23. Childs, 2007.
24. Penn, 2013.
25. Gelardi, 2008.
26. Penn, 2013.
27. Tremlett, 2010.
28. This gene is necessary to create a protein that functions as a channel across the membrane of cells that produce mucus, sweat, saliva, tears, and digestive enzymes. The transport of chloride ions is necessary for the production of the thin, freely flowing fluid that lubricates the lining of organ systems, and is particularly important to the pulmonary, digestive, and reproductive systems. The CFTR protein also regulates the function of the cell membrane channels that transport positively charged sodium ions, which is necessary for the normal function of organs such as the lungs and pancreas.
29. Groman et al., 2002.
30. Keating et al., 2010.
31. Boyle, 2003.
32. Boeck et al., 2006.
33. Nick and Rodman, 2005.
34. Ibid.
35. Keating et al., 2010.
36. Moskowitz et al., 2008.
37. Metersky, 2012.
38. Moskowitz et al., 2008.
39. Fick, 1992.
40. Fletcher and Martin, 1982
41. Eickmeier et al., 2010.
42. Verratti et al., 2007.
43. Greenstadt, 2013.
44. Okerlund, 2009:169.
45. Starkey, 2003:86-87.
46. Starkey, 2003:76.
47. Fraser, 1992:162.
48. Bernard, 2005:21.
49. Lindsey, 1995:79.
50. Bernard, 2005:22.
51. Temlett, 2010:10-11.
52. Tremlett, 2010:89.
53. Tremlett, 2010:91.
54. Schram et al., 2012.
55. Groman et al., 2002.
56. Ibid.
57. Ibid.
58. Schram, 2012.
59. Sayre, 2009.
60. Whitley and Kramer, 2010.
61. Purohit et al., 1992.
62. Anstee, 2010.
63. Ibid.
64. Shah et al., 2013.
65. Stuppia et al., 2005.

Chapter 16
1. CSP Spain, Vol 5(ii).
2. Loach, 1999.
3. Nichols, 1857.
4. Foxe, 1836.
5. Robinson, 1846.
6. Foxe, 1836.
7. Nichols, 1857.
8. Turner, 1829.

Bibliography

Andrews K. M., Brouillette D. B., and Brouillette R. T., eds. (2008). *Encyclopedia of Infant and Early Childhood Development*. Elsevier.

Anstee, David J. (2010). 'The Relationship between Blood Groups and Disease'. *Blood* 115 (23): 4635–43. doi:10.1182/blood-2010-01-261859.

Anonymous. (1836). 'Cominge into Englande of the Lorde Grautehuse'. *Archaeologia*, volume 26: 265-286.

Aston, Margaret. (1993). *The King's Bedpost: Reformation and Iconography in a Tudor Group Portrait*. Cambridge. Cambridge University Press.

Avent, Neil D. (2009). 'Large-Scale Blood Group Genotyping – Clinical Implications'. *British Journal of Haematology* 144 (1): 3–13. doi:10.1111/j.1365-2141.2008.07285.x.

Bates, Calton M., Michel Baum, and Raymond Quigley. (1996). 'Cystic Fibrosis Presenting with Hypokalemia and Metabolic Alkalosis in a Previously Healthy Adolescent'. *Journal of American Society of Nephrology*, American Renal Training Centers, 352–55.

Bernard, G. W. (2005). *The King's Reformation: Henry VIII and the Remaking of the English Church*. Yale University Press.

Blunt, John Henry. (1882). *The Reformation of the Church of England: Its History, Principles, and Results*. London. Rivingtons.

Boeck, K De, M Wilschanski, C Castellani, C Taylor, H Cuppens, J Dodge, and M Sinaasappel. (2006). *Thorax* 61: 627–35.

Boyle, Micheal P. (2003). 'Nonclassic Cystic Fibrosis and CFTR-Related Diseases: Current Opinion in Pulmonary Medicine'. *Current Opinion in Pulmonary Medicine* 9 (6). http://journals.lww.com/co-pulmonarymedicine/Fulltext/2003/11000/Nonclassic_cystic_fibrosis_and_CFTR_related.9.aspx.

Breverton, Terry. (2016). *Henry VII: The Maligned Tudor King*. Amberley Publishing.

Burnet, Gilbert. (1843). *The History of the Reformation of the Church of England*. NY. D. Appleton & Company.

Castellani, C., C. Quinzii, S. Altieri, G. Mastella, and B. M. Assael. (2001). 'A Pilot Survey of Cystic Fibrosis Clinical Manifestations in CFTR Mutation Heterozygotes'. *Genetic Testing* 5 (3): 249–54. doi:10.1089/10906570152742317.

Calendar of State Papers and Manuscripts in the Archives and Collections of Milan 1385-1618. (1912). Allen B. Hinds. (ed). London: His Majesty's Stationery Office.

Calendar of State Papers, Spain, Volume 1, 1485-1509. (1862). G. A. Bergenroth. (ed). London: Her Majesty's Stationery Office

Calendar of State Papers, Spain, Volume 5 Part 2, 1536-1538. (1888). Pascual de Gayangos. (ed). London: Her Majesty's Stationery Office,

Calendar of State Papers, Spain, Volume 8, 1547-1549. (1904). Martin A. S. Hume. (ed). London: His Majesty's Stationery Office,

Calendar of State Papers, Spain, Volume 9, 1545-1546. (1912). Martin A. S. Hume and Royall Tyler. (eds). London: His Majesty's Stationery Office.

Calendar of State Papers, Spain, Volume 10, 1550-1552. (1914). Royall Tyler. (ed). London. His Majesty's Stationery Office.

Calendar of State Papers, Spain, Volume 11, 1553. (1916). Royall Tyler. (ed). London: His Majesty's Stationery Office.

Calendar of State Papers Relating To English Affairs in the Archives of Venice, Volume 5, 1534-1554. (1873).. Rawdon Brown. (ed). London: Her Majesty's Stationery Office.

CFTR - Cystic Fibrosis Transmembrane Conductance Regulator (ATP-Binding Cassette Sub-Family C, Member 7). (2015). *Genetics Home Reference.* March 30. http://ghr.nlm. nih.gov/gene/CFTR.

Challis, Christopher Edgar. (1978). *The Tudor Coinage.* Manchester University Press.

Chawla et al., (2010). 'When to suspect atypical cystic fibrosis'. *Journal of Family Practice.* September; 59(9):509-513.

Childe-Pemberton, William S. (1913). *Elizabeth Blount and Henry VIII.* London.

Childs, Jessie. (2007). *Henry VIII's Last Victim: The Life and Times of Henry Howard, Earl of Surrey.* Macmillan.

Clifford, Arthur. (ed). (1809). *The State Papers and Letters of Sir Ralph Sadler.* Edinburgh, Scotland: Archibald Constable and Co.

Clifford, Henry. (1887). *The Life of Jane Dormer Duchess of Feria.* London. Burns and Oates.

Cox, John E. (1846). *The Works of Thomas Cranmer.* Cambridge. The University Press.

Crabtree, Pamela. (2013). *Medieval Archaeology - Crabtree.* Routledge.

Cressy, David. (1997). *Birth, Marriage & Death: Ritual, Religion, and the Life-Cycle in Tudor and Stuart England.* Oxford University Press.

Crewson, Richard. (2000). *Apollo's Swan and Lyre: Five Hundred Years of the Musicians' Company.* Woodbridge, Massachusetts. The Boydell Press.

Cunningham, Sean. (2013). *Prince Arthur: The Tudor King Who Never Was.* Amberley Publishing.

Das, D. et al. (2018). 'Complex interactions between malaria and malnutrition: a systematic literature review'. *BMC Medicine.* Vol 16.

Dixon, William Hepworth. (1873). *History of Two Queens: 1. Catherine of Aragon; II. Anne Boleyn. Vol 2.* Leipzig, Berhard, Tauchnitz Publishers.

Duffy, Eamon. (2005). *The Stripping of the Altars: Traditional Religion in England, c. 1400 – c. 1580* (2nd ed.) New Haven and London. Yale University Press.

Edward VI. (1884). *The Journal of King Edward's Reign, Written with His Own Hand.* Privately printed for the Clarendon Historical Society.

Eickmeier, Olaf, Marisa Huebner, Eva Herrmann, Ulrich Zissler, Martin Rosewich, Patrick C. Baer, Roland Buhl, Sabina Schmitt-Grohé, Stefan Zielen, and Ralf Schubert. (2010). 'Sputum Biomarker Profiles in Cystic Fibrosis (CF) and Chronic Obstructive Pulmonary Disease (COPD) and Association between Pulmonary Function'. *Cytokine* 50 (2): 152–57. doi:10.1016/j.cyto.2010.02.004.

Ferdell, Elizabeth L. (2001). *The Royal Doctors 1485-1714: Medical Personnel at the Tudor and Stuart Courts.* New York. University of Rochester Press.

Fick et al., (1992). 'Emergence and persistence of Pseudomonas aeruginosa in the cystic fibrosis airway'. *Seminars in Respiratory Infections,* Sep; 7(3):168-78.

Fletcher, E. C., and R. J. Martin. (1982). 'Sexual Dysfunction and Erectile Impotence in Chronic Obstructive Pulmonary Disease'. *Chest* 81 (4): 413–21.

Foxe, John. (1836). *The Acts and Monuments of John Foxe: A New and Complete Edition.* Cattley, Stephen Reed, (eds). London. R.B Seeley and W. Burnside, Publishers.

Foxe, John. (1881). *Fox's Book of Martyrs.* Philadelphia. E. Claxton & Company.

Gairdner, James. (1904). 'Arthur (1486-1502)' in *Dictionary of National Biography,* Vol 2. London. Smithe, Elder, & Co.

Gairdner, James. (ed). (1880). 'Historical Memoranda of John Stowe: The baptism of Prince Arthur, son of Henry VII', in *Three Fifteenth-Century Chronicles with Historical Memoranda by John Stowe.* London.

Gelardi, Julia P. (2009). *In Triumph's Wake: Royal Mothers, Tragic Daughters, and the Price They Paid for Glory.* Macmillan.

Gilljam, Marita, Lynda Ellis, Mary Corey, Julian Zielenski, Peter Durie, and D. Elizabeth Tullis. 2004. 'Clinical Manifestations of Cystic Fibrosis among Patients with Diagnosis in Adulthood*'. *Chest* 126 (4): 1215–24. doi:10.1378/chest.126.4.1215.

Grafton, Richard. (1809). *A Chronicle at Large, 1569*, vol. 2. London.

Greenstadt, Dr Amy. (2013). *Rape and the Rise of the Author: Gendering Intention in Early Modern England.* Ashgate Publishing, Ltd.

Groman, Joshua D., Timothy W. Hefferon, Teresa Casals, Lluís Bassas, Xavier Estivill, Marie Des Georges, Caroline Guittard, et al. (2004). 'Variation in a Repeat Sequence Determines Whether a Common Variant of the Cystic Fibrosis Transmembrane Conductance Regulator Gene Is Pathogenic or Benign'. *The American Journal of Human Genetics* 74 (1): 176–79. doi:10.1086/381001.

Groman, Joshua D., Barbara Karczeski, Molly Sheridan, Terry E. Robinson, M. Daniele Fallin, and Garry R. Cutting. (2005). 'Phenotypic and Genetic Characterization of Patients with Features of 'nonclassic' Forms of Cystic Fibrosis'. *The Journal of Pediatrics* 146 (5): 675–80. doi:10.1016/j.jpeds.2004.12.020.

Groman, Joshua D., Michelle E. Meyer, Robert W. Wilmott, Pamela L. Zeitlin, and Garry R. Cutting. (2002). 'Variant Cystic Fibrosis Phenotypes in the Absence of CFTR Mutations'. *New England Journal of Medicine* 347 (6): 401–7. doi:10.1056/NEJMoa011899.

Gunn, Steven J. and Monckton, Linda. (2009). *Arthur Tudor, Prince of Wales: Life, Death & Commemoration.* Boydell Press.

Gunter, Jen. (2012). 'Cancer v. the Constitution.' *Dr. Jen Gunter.* https://drjengunter. wordpress.com/2012/03/28/cancer-v-the-constitution/.

Guy, John. (2013). *The Children of Henry VIII.* Oxford. Oxford University Press.

Harris, A. (1990). 'DNA Markers near the Cystic Fibrosis Locus: Further Analysis of the British Population'. *Journal of Medical Genetics* 27 (1): 39–41.

Halliwell, James Orchard. (1848). *Letters of the Kings of England.* London. Henry Colburn Publishers.

Haynes, Samuel. (1740). *A Collection of State Papers Relating to Affairs in the Reigns of King Henry VIII, King Edward VI, Queen Mary, and Queen Elizabeth.* William Bowyer. London.

Hoak, D. E. 1976. *The King's Council in the Reign of Edward VI.* Cambridge. Cambridge University Press.

Hodson, Margaret, Andrew Bush, and Duncan Geddes. (2012). *Cystic Fibrosis, Third Edition.* CRC Press.

Holmes, Grace, Frederick Holmes, and Julia McMorrough. (2001). 'The Death of Young King Edward VI'. *New England Journal of Medicine* 345 (1): 60–62. doi:10.1056/ NEJM200107053450111.

Hoskins, W. G. (1964). 'Harvest Fluctuations and English Economic History: 1440-1619'. *The Agricultural History Review.* Vol. 12. No. 1. pp. 28-46

'How Chromosome Mutations Occur.' (2015). *About.com Education.* Accessed April 11. http://biology.about.com/od/genetics/ss/chromosome-mutation.htm.

Hughes, Jonathan. (2005). 'Politics and the Occult at the Court of Edward IV'. In *Princes and Princely Culture* 1450 -1650 Vol. 2. Eds. Vanderjagt, A.J. et al. Leiden, The Netherlands. Koninklijke Brill NV.

Hunt, Alice. (2009). 'The Monarchical Republic of Mary I'. *The Historical Journal,* 52, 3, p. 557-572.

Hutchinson, Robert. (2011). *The Last Days of Henry VIII: Conspiracy, Treason, and Hearsay at the Court of the Dying Tyrant.* London. Weidenfeld & Nicolson.

Ives, Eric William. (2004). *The Life and Death of Anne Boleyn:'The Most Happy'.* London. Wiley-Blackwell.

Ives, Eric William. (2009). *Lady Jane Grey: A Tudor Mystery.* London. Wiley-Blackwell.

James, Susan. (2008). *Catherine Parr: Henry VIII's Last Love.* Gloucestershire. The History Press.

Jones, Clay. (2013). 'Separating Fact from Fiction in Pediatric Medicine: Infant Teething.' In *Science-Based Medicine*. 8 November 2013.

Joshi, Deepak, Anil Dhawan, Alistair J. Baker, and Michael A. Heneghan. (2008). 'An Atypical Presentation of Cystic Fibrosis: A Case Report'. *Journal of Medical Case Reports* 2 (1): 201. doi:10.1186/1752-1947-2-201.

Jr, Robert B. Fick. (1992). *Pseudomonas Aeruginosa the Opportunist*. CRC Press.

Kahar, Manoj A., and Rajnikant. D. Patel. (2014). 'Phenotype Frequencies of Blood Group Systems (Rh, Kell, Kidd, Duffy, MNS, P, Lewis, and Lutheran) in Blood Donors of South Gujarat, India'. *Asian Journal of Transfusion Science* 8 (1): 51–55. doi:10.4103/0973-6247.126693.

Keating, Claire L., Xinhua Liu, and Emily A. DiMango. (2010). 'CLassic Respiratory Disease but Atypical Diagnostic Testing Distinguishes Adult Presentation of Cystic Fibrosis'. *Chest* 137 (5): 1157–63. doi:10.1378/chest.09-1352.

Keohane, Elaine, Larry Smith, and Jeanine Walenga. (2015). *Rodak's Hematology: Clinical Principles and Applications*. Elsevier Health Sciences.

Knighton, Dr. C. S. and Loades, David. (2013). *The Navy of Edward VI and Mary I*. Ashgate Publishing, Ltd.

Köseoğlu, N., H. Köseoğlu, E. Ceylan, H. A. Çimrin, S. Özalevli, and A. Esen. (2005). 'Erectile dysfunction prevalence and sexual dysfunction status in patients with chronic obstructive pulmonary disease'. *The Journal of Urology* 174 (1): 249–52. doi:10.1097/01. ju.0000163259.33846.74.

Kramer, Kyra. (2012). *Blood Will Tell: A Medical Explanation of the Tyranny of Henry VIII*.

Lao, Oscar, Aida M. Andrés, Eva Mateu, Jaume Bertranpetit, and Francesc Calafell. (2003). 'Spatial Patterns of Cystic Fibrosis Mutation Spectra in European Populations'. *European Journal of Human Genetics* 11 (5): 385–94. doi:10.1038/sj.ejhg.5200970.

Letters and Papers, Foreign and Domestic, Henry VIII, Volume 12 Part 2, June-December 1537. (1891). James Gairdner. (ed). London: Her Majesty's Stationery Office, *British History Online*.

Letters and Papers, Foreign and Domestic, Henry VIII, Volume 13 Part 1, June-December 1537. (1891). James Gairdner. (ed). London: Her Majesty's Stationery Office, *British History Online*.

Letters and Papers, Foreign and Domestic, Henry VIII, Volume 14 Part 2, June-December 1537, (1891). James Gairdner. (ed). London: Her Majesty's Stationery Office, British History Online.

Letters and Papers, Foreign and Domestic, Henry VIII, Volume 16, 1540-1541. (1898). James Gairdner and R. H. Brodie. (eds). London: Her Majesty's Stationery Office, *British History Online*.

Letters and Papers, Foreign and Domestic, Henry VIII, Volume 18 Parts 1 and 2, January-December 1543. (1901). James Gairdner and R. H. Brodie. (eds). London: Her Majesty's Stationery Office, *British History Online*.

Letters and Papers, Foreign and Domestic, Henry VIII, Volume 19 Part 1 and 2, January-July 1544. (1903). James Gairdner and R. H. Brodie. (eds). London: Her Majesty's Stationery Office, *British History Online*.

Letters and Papers, Foreign and Domestic Henry VIII, Volume 21 Part 1 and 2, January-August 1546, (1908). James Gairdner and R. H. Brodie. (eds). London: Her Majesty's Stationery Office, *British History Online*.

Leland, John. (1774). *Antiquarii De Rebus Britannicis Collectanea*. Vol 4. Thomas Hearne. (ed). Oxford.

Licence, Amy. (2012). *In Bed With the Tudors: The Sex Lives of a Dynasty from Elizabeth of York to Elizabeth I*. Amberley Publishing.

Licence, Amy. (2013). *Elizabeth of York: The Forgotten Tudor Queen*. Amberley Publishing.

Licence, Amy. (2014). *The Six Wives & Many Mistresses of Henry VIII: The Women's Stories*. Amberley Publishing.

Lisle, Leanda de. (2009). *The Sisters Who Would Be Queen: Mary, Katherine, and Lady Jane Grey: A Tudor Tragedy*. Random House.

Loach, Jennifer. (1999). *Edward VI*. Yale University Press.

Loades, David. (1996). *John Dudley, Duke of Northumberland: 1504-1553*. Oxford. Clarendon Press.

Lodge, Edmund. (1791). *Illustrations of British History, Biography, and Manners: In the Reigns of Henry VIII, Edward VI, Mary, Elizabeth, and James I, Exhibited in a Series of Original Papers*. Sold by G. Nicol.

MacCulloch, Diarmaid. (2001). *The Boy King: Edward VI and the Protestant Reformation*. University of California Press.

Mackie, Robert Laird. (1916). *Scotland: An Account of Her Triumphs and Defeats, Her Manners, Institutions and Achievements in Art and Literature from Earliest Times to the Death of Scott*. United Kingdom. George G. Harrap & Company.

Magner, Lois N. (1992). *A History of Medicine*. CRC Press.

Markham, Sir Clements R. (1907). *King Edward VI: His Life and Character*. London. Smith, Elder, & Co.

Martiniano, Stacey L., Jordana E. Hoppe, Scott D. Sagel, and Edith T. Zemanick. (2014). 'Advances in the Diagnosis and Treatment of Cystic Fibrosis'. *Advances in Pediatrics* 61 (1): 225–43. doi:10.1016/j.yapd.2014.03.002.

McConkie-Rosell, A., Y. T. Chen, D. Harris, M. C. Speer, M. A. Pericak-Vance, J. H. Ding, W. E. Highsmith, M. Knowles, and S. G. Kahler. (1989). 'Mild Cystic Fibrosis Linked to Chromosome 7q22 Markers with an Uncommon Haplotype'. *Annals of Internal Medicine* 111 (10): 797–801.

Metersky, Mark L. (2012). *Bronchiectasis, an Issue of Clinics in Chest Medicine*. Elsevier Health Sciences.

Metzler, Irina. (2006). *Disability in Medieval Europe: Thinking about Physical Impairment During the High Middle Ages, c. 1100-1400*. London and New York. Routledge.

Moskowitz, Samuel M., James F. Chmiel, Darci L. Sternen, Edith Cheng, Ronald L. Gibson, Susan G. Marshall, and Garry R. Cutting. (2008). 'Clinical Practice and Genetic Counseling for Cystic Fibrosis and CFTR-Related Disorders'. *Genetics in Medicine* 10 (12): 851–68. doi:10.1097/GIM.0b013e31818e55a2.

Mueller, Janel. (2011). *Katherine Parr: Complete Works and Correspondence*. University of Chicago Press.

Muller, James A. (1933). *The Letters of Stephen Gardiner*. Cambridge. University Press.

Murphy, Beverley. (2011). *Bastard Prince: Henry VIII's Lost Son*. The History Press.

Mussaffi, H., D. Prais, M. Mei-Zahav, and H. Blau. (2006). 'Cystic Fibrosis Mutations with Widely Variable Phenotype: The D1152H Example'. *Pediatric Pulmonology* 41 (3): 250–54. doi:10.1002/ppul.20343.

Naderi, Neda, Soheil Peiman, Azam Alamdari, Taraneh Dormohammadi Toosi, and Foad Taghdiri. (2014). 'A Salty Cause of Cough in a 24-Year-Old Man'. *Oxford Medical Case Reports* 2014 (4): 71–73. doi:10.1093/omcr/omu029.

Network, From CDC National Prevention Information. (2001). 'The Death of Young King Edward VI'. *TheBody.com*. July 6. http://www.thebody.com/content/art20580.html.

New World Encyclopedia. (2013). 'Book of Common Prayer'. http://www.newworld encyclopedia.org/entry/Book_of_Common_Prayer

Nichols, Francis. (1721). *The British Compendium*. London. Bettesworth.

Nichols, John Gough. (1848). *The Diary of Henry Machyn Citizen and Merchant-Taylor of London (1550-1563)*. London.

Nichols, John Gough. (1857). *Literary Remains of King Edward the Sixth: Edited from His Autograph Manuscripts, with Historical Notes and a Biographical Memoir*. London. B. Franklin.

Nick, Jerry A., and David M. Rodman. (2005). 'Manifestations of Cystic Fibrosis Diagnosed in Adulthood'. *Current Opinion in Pulmonary Medicine* 11 (6): 513–18.

Norton, Elizabeth. (2011). *Jane Seymour: Henry VIII's True Love*. Amberley Publishing Limited.

Norton, Elizabeth. (2012). *Bessie Blount: Mistress to Henry VIII*. Amberley Publishing Limited.

Oppenheim, Michael. (1896). *A History of the Administration of the Royal Navy and of Merchant Shipping in Relation to the Navy: From MDIX to MDCLX, with an Introduction Treating of the Preceding Period*. London. J. Lane Publishers.

Paranjape, Shruti M., and Pamela L. Zeitlin. (2008). 'Atypical Cystic Fibrosis and CFTR-Related Diseases'. *Clinical Reviews in Allergy & Immunology* 35 (3): 116–23. doi:10.1007/s12016-008-8083-0.

Peckham, D., S. P. Conway, A. Morton, A. Jones, and K. Webb. (2006). 'Delayed Diagnosis of Cystic Fibrosis Associated with R117H on a Background of 7T Polythymidine Tract at Intron 8'. *Journal of Cystic Fibrosis: Official Journal of the European Cystic Fibrosis Society* 5 (1): 63–65. doi:10.1016/j.jcf.2005.09.009.

Penn, Thomas. (2011). *Winter King: Henry VII and the Dawn of Tudor England*. Simon and Schuster.

Perlman, Nicola C. and Carusi, Daniela A. (2019). 'Retained placenta after vaginal delivery: risk factors and management'. *International Journal of Womens' Health*, 11:527-534.

Plowden, Alison. (2011). *The Young Elizabeth*. London. History Press Limited.

Pointon, Marcia. (2009). *Brilliant Effects: a Cultural History of Gem Stones and Jewelry*. New York and London. Yale University Press.

Pollnitz, Aysha. (2015). *Princely Education in Early Modern Britain*. Cambridge University Press.

Poos, R.L. (1986). 'Life Expectancy and Age of First Appearance in Medieval Manorial Court Rolls'. Local Population Studies. Vol. 37: 45-52.

Porter, Linda. (2010). *Katherine the Queen: The Remarkable Life of Katherine Parr*. Macmillan.

Porter, Roy. (1995). *Disease, Medicine and Society in England, 1550-1860*. Cambridge University Press.

Potter, David L. (2011). *Henry VIII and Francis I: The Final Conflict, 1540 - 1547*. Leiden and Boston. Brill.

Punchard, George. (1865). *History of Congregationalism*.

Purohit, K. R., J. L. Weber, L. J. Ward, and B. J. Keats. (1992). 'The Kell Blood Group Locus Is close to the Cystic Fibrosis Locus on Chromosome 7'. *Human Genetics* 89 (4): 457–58.

Ricks, Delthia. (2009). *100 Questions & Answers About Influenza*. Jones & Bartlett Learning.

Ridgway, Claire. (2014). *Sweating Sickness in a Nutshell*. MadeGlobal.

Robinson, Hastings. (1846). *Original Letters Relative to The English Reformation*. Cambridge. Cambridge University Press.

Ross, David. (2005). *Wales: History of a Nation*. Geddes & Grosset.

Sayre, Carolyn. (2009). 'Cystic Fibrosis, Complicated and Variable'. *The New York Times*, April 24, sec. Health / Health Guide. http://www.nytimes.com/ref/health/healthguide/esn-cystic-fibrosis-expert.html.

Scarisbrick, J.J. (1997). *Henry VIII*. New Haven and London. Yale University Press.

Schram, Carrie A. (2012). 'Atypical Cystic Fibrosis Identification in the Primary Care Setting'. *Canadian Family Physician* 58(12):1341-1345

Schwarz, Ernst R. (2013). *Erectile Dysfunction*. Oxford University Press.

Semple, P. D., G. H. Beastall, T. M. Brown, K. W. Stirling, R. J. Mills, and W. S. Watson. (1984). 'Sex Hormone Suppression and Sexual Impotence in Hypoxic Pulmonary Fibrosis'. *Thorax* 39 (1): 46–51.

Sermet-Gaudelus, Isabelle, Emanuelle Girodon, Dorota Sands, Nathalie Stremmler, Vera Vavrova, Eric Deneuville, Philippe Reix, et al. (2010). 'Clinical Phenotype and Genotype of Children with Borderline Sweat Test and Abnormal Nasal Epithelial

Chloride Transport'. *American Journal of Respiratory and Critical Care Medicine* 182 (7): 929–36. doi:10.1164/rccm.201003-0382OC.

Sessions, William A. (2003). *Henry Howard, the Poet Earl of Surrey: A Life*. Oxford University Press.

Shah, FaisalYounis, FaizanYounis Shah, and Mohd Younus Shah. (2013). 'Incidence of Kell Blood Group in Kashmiri Population Attending Blood Bank SKIMS as Donors'. *Annals of Tropical Medicine and Public Health* 6 (2): 183. doi:10.4103/1755-6783.116508.

Shaz, Beth H., Christopher D. Hillyer, Charles S. Abrams, and Mikhail Roshal. (2013). *Transfusion Medicine and Hemostasis: Clinical and Laboratory Aspects*. Newnes.

Skidmore, Chris. (2009). *Edward VI: The Lost King of England*. Macmillan.

Smith, Lacey Baldwin. (1971). *Henry VIII*. Gloucestershire. Amberley Publishing.

Smith, William Tyler. (1855). *The Pathology and Treatment of Leucorrhœa*. Blanchard & Lea.

Starkey, David. (2003). *Six Wives: The Queens of Henry VIII*. Harper Collins.

Stern, Robert C. et al. (1977). 'Cystic Fibrosis Diagnosed after Age 13 in Twenty-Five Teenage and Adult Patients Including Three Asymptomatic Men'. *Annals of Internal Medicine* 87 (2): 188–91.

Stewart, Alan. (2000). *Philip Sidney: A Double Life*. London. Chatto & Windus.

Strickland, Agnes. (1853). *Queens of Henry VIII, and His Mother, Elizabeth of York: Complete in One Volume*. Philadelphia. Blanchard and Lea.

Strickland, Agnes. (1861). *Lives of the Batchelor Kings of England*. London. Simpkin, Marshal, and Co.

Stuppia, L., Antonucci, I., Binni, F. et al. (2005). Screening of mutations in the CFTR gene in 1195 couples entering assisted reproduction technique programs. Eur J Hum Genet 13, 959–964.

Tanner, J. R. (1930). *Tudor Constitution Documents A.D 1485 - 1603 With an Historical Commentary*. Cambridge University Press.

'The Death of Prince Arthur, Prince Of Wales, 1502'. (2015). *English History*. http://englishhistory.net/tudor/the-death-of-prince-arthur/.

Thornbury, Walter. (1878). 'St Paul's: To the Great Fire' in *Old and New London: Volume 1*. London. Cassell, Petter & Galpin.

Tiemersma, Edine W., Marieke J. van der Werf, Martien W. Borgdorff, Brian G. Williams, and Nico J. D. Nagelkerke. (2011). 'Natural History of Tuberculosis: Duration and Fatality of Untreated Pulmonary Tuberculosis in HIV Negative Patients: A Systematic Review'. *PLoS ONE* 6 (4). doi:10.1371/journal.pone.0017601.

Tremlett, Giles. (2010). *Catherine of Aragon: Henry's Spanish Queen*. Faber & Faber.

Turner, Sharon. (1829). *The History of the Reigns of Edward the Sixth, Mary, and Elizabeth*. London. Longman et al.

Tytler, Patrick Fraser. (1839). *England Under the Reigns of Edward VI. and Mary: With the Contemporary History of Europe*. London. R. Bentley.

Vermigli, Pietro Martire. (1865). *Historical Narration of Certain Events that Took Place in the Kingdom of Great Britain in the Month of July, in the Year of Our Lord 1553*. London. Bell and Daldy.

Verratti, V., C. Di Giulio, F. Berardinelli, M. Pelliciotta, S. Di Francesco, R. Iantorno, M. Nicolai, S. Gidaro, and R. Tenaglia. (2007). 'The Role of Hypoxia in Erectile Dysfunction Mechanisms'. *International Journal of Impotence Research* 19 (5): 496–500. doi:10.1038/sj.ijir.3901560.

Wailoo, Keith. (2011). *How Cancer Crossed the Color Line*. Oxford University Press.

Wallis, Faith. (2010). *Medieval Medicine: A Reader*. University of Toronto Press.

Weiss-Amer, Melitta. (1993). 'Medieval Woman's Guides to Food During Pregnancy: Origins, Texts, and Traditions'. *Canadian Bulletin of Medical History*. Vol. 10; p. 5-23.

'When to Suspect Atypical Cystic Fibrosis : The Journal of Family Practice.' (2015). Accessed April 1. http://www.jfponline.com/index.php?id=22143&tx_ttnews[tt_news]=175330.

Whitelock, Anna. (2007). 'Princess Mary's Household and the Succession Crisis'. *The Historical Journal*, 50, 2, p. 265-287.

Whitelock, Anna. (2010). *Mary Tudor: Princess, Bastard, Queen*. Random House Publishing Group.

Whitley, Catrina Banks, and Kyra Kramer. (2010). 'A New Explanation for the Reproductive Woes and Midlife Decline of Henry VIII.' *The Historical Journal* 53 (04): 827–48.

Woolgar, C.M. (1999). *The Great Households in Late Medieval England*. New Haven and London. Yale University Press.

Wriothesley, Charles. (1875). *A Chronicle of England During the Reigns of the Tudors, from AD 1485 to 1559*. William D. Hamilton. (ed). Westminster. J.B Nichols and Sons.

Zelinski, T., G. Coghlan, Y. Myal, R. P. Shiu, S. Philipps, L. White, and M. Lewis. (1991). 'Genetic Linkage between the Kell Blood Group System and Prolactin-Inducible Protein Loci: Provisional Assignment of KEL to Chromosome 7'. *Annals of Human Genetics* 55 (Pt 2): 137–40.